PIERRE FOURNIER

To the memory of my parents

Pierre Fournier

Cellist in a landscape with figures

Angela Hughes

Ashgate

Aldershot • Brookfield USA • Singapore • Sydney

Published by
Ashgate Publishing Limited
Gower House
Croft Road
Aldershot
Hants GU11 3HR
England

Ashgate Publishing Company
Old Post Road
Brookfield
Vermont 05036–9704
USA

British Library Cataloguing-in-Publication data

Hughes, Angela
  Pierre Fournier
  1. Fournier, Pierre 2. Violoncellists – France – Biography
  I. Title
  787.4'092

Library of Congress Cataloging-in-Publication data

Hughes, Angela.
  Pierre Fournier / Angela Hughes.
  Includes bibliographical references, discography
and indexes.
    ISBN 1–85928–422–1
    1. Fournier, Pierre. 2. Violoncellists—Biography.
  I. Title
ML 418.F814H84   1998
787.4'092—dc21   97–33080
                      CIP
                      MN

ISBN 1 85928 422 1

Printed on acid-free paper

Typeset in Sabon by Bournemouth Colour Press and printed in Great Britain at The University Press, Cambridge

Errata

Text
p.xiv, l.15: for 'Furtwänger' read 'Furtwängler'
p.4, l.6: for 'Françoise' read 'François'
p.4, l.34 : for 'Seine at Marne' read 'Seine-et-Marne'
p.9, l.16: for '50 and 80 per cent' read '50 to 80 per cent'
p.44, note 1: for 'J.-A. Azéma' read 'J.-P. Azéma'
p.53, l.15: for 'the father' read 'his father'
p.96, note 21: for 'Pierre-Françoise Touzé' read 'Pierre-François Touzé'
p.138, l.17: 'H' incorrectly inserted after Mehta
p.158, ll.24-26: should read '...rounded life was to bring the last figure, at an age when relinquishment is more common than discovery.' Bottom line 'Tagushi' should read 'Taguchi'.

Discography
p.174, 1st entry: for J. Fournier vlc/ read J. Fournier vln/
p.174, 2nd entry: for 'vlo' read 'vlc'
p.181, 1st column: 'Studio 3 ... Davidson' should be raised 3 lines
p.184, 2nd line up: for 'Cassado' read 'Cassadó'
p.185, 5th line up: for 'hebraïques' read 'hébraïques'
p.187, 1st column, 3rd entry: '25.2.61' should read '25-26.2.61'
p.188, 2nd column, 1st entry: 'Disque 1962...Tokyo' should be raised one line
p.190, 1st column, 1st entry, l.2: for 'Christ' read 'Christus'
p.193, 2nd column, 5 lines up: 'BWV 622' should be indented
p.196, 2nd column, 2nd entry: for 'Perre' read 'Pierre', and for 'Martinu' read 'Martinů'
p.199, 2nd column, 3rd entry: for 'Trio on B' read 'Trio in B'
p.207, 2nd column, 2nd entry: bracket should be aligned with 'Beethoven Sonatas', ending at 'Hubeau'
p.207, 2nd column, 4th entry: '1943' should be aligned with 'Stravinsky'
p.208, 2nd column, mid-page: for 'Grandos' read 'Granados', and for 'Sonate No 6' read 'Sonata No 6'
p.217, 2nd column, '[Junko née] Tagushi' should read 'Taguchi'

Bibliography
p.209, 2 lines up: for 'Willet' read 'Willett'

Index
p.214, 2nd column, l.13: for 'Françoise' read 'François'
p.219, 2nd column, l.13: for 'Hopital' read 'Hôpital'
p.221, 2nd column, mid-page: for 'Mauriac, Françoise' read 'Mauriac, François'
p.222, 1st column, mid-page: should read 'Moore, Gerald 129n'

Abbreviations

ORTF	Office de la Radio-Télévision Française. Former name of French Radio now Radio France
OSCC	Orchestre de la Société des Concerts du Conservatoire. Dissolved in 1967 and replaced by the Orchestre de Paris.
OSR	Orchestre de la Suisse Romande
RSR	Radio Suisse Romande
VSM	Voix de son Maître (HMV France)
PF	Pierre Fournier
JFF	Jean Fonda Fournier (Jean Pierre)

Note

Pierre Fournier's letters to Peta Fisher are reproduced exactly as they were written, in English. Translations from French are by the author unless otherwise specified.

List of Plates

Every effort has been made to obtain the necessary permissions regarding copyright photographs. If any sources remain unacknowledged the author and publishers extend their apologies for the omission which will be remedied in future editions.

Acknowledgements are owing to the following:

Foto-Blau Bruder of Bonn for the Beethovenhaus photograph; Foto Ilse Buhs (Pierre Fournier and Sir Malcolm Sargent); Peter Hastings of Cleveland (Pierre Fournier and George Szell); Nigel Luckhurst (Pierre Fournier and Lamar Crowson); Werner Neumeister of Munich for the jacket photograph and the portrait on page 102.

For other photographs I have to thank Mrs Peta Fisher, Jean Fonda Fournier, Mme Jeanine Krettly-Pérès, Mme Jacqueline Peltier and Mme Cécile Niklaus.

Foreword
by Felix Aprahamian

After the Liberation of Paris in 1944, French musicians soon returned to London musical life, where a series of *Concerts de musique française* thrived at the Wigmore Hall. Begun in 1942 under the auspices of the (Free) French Embassy, it provided a wartime audience for French music, and continued its important role when the war ended. Having encouraged newcomers, both young and old, to enhance their repertoire with French music, it also came to provide a valuable London platform for the returning French. Among the new names were Ginette Neveu and Gérard Souzay; others included familiar pre-war visitors, also some who had made a pre-war bow in London but were yet to become popular here. One such person was Pierre Fournier. Those immediate post-war years brought a plethora of fine cellists to London, but none more remarkable than Fournier. He had long known Tony Mayer, the *Chargé de Mission* at the French Embassy, at whose instigation the French concerts had been subsidized, so, as the LPO Concert Director responsible for organizing them, I also came to know Pierre as a friend.

Long before he recorded the Elgar Cello Concerto, I remember how baffled I was by his essentially Elgarian interpretation when he sight-read it with me at home. He pointed out that he was only observing Elgar's printed markings exactly. But Fournier's absolute respect for a composer's indicated nuances was typical of the fastidious musicianship that had made him the dedicatee of works I was anxious to hear him play. One was the Concertino inscribed to him by Albert Roussel, which Fournier played in the Wigmore Hall series. Another was the Cello Sonata Francis Poulenc wrote for him, and of which they gave the first performance together at the Jordans Music Club. On another memorable evening, after dinner with Tony and Thérèse Mayer in Chester Square, we took Pierre back to his hotel to play some unaccompanied Bach. At the entrance, we came across another famous visiting musician. Happy to meet Fournier for the first time, Victor de Sabata asked if he could join us. That midnight, the empty ballroom of the Hyde Park Hotel provided the setting for an unforgettable private recital.

Preface

In a conversation with his son towards the end of his life, Pierre Fournier broached the idea of writing his memoirs. Jean Pierre volunteered to put some notes together and his father was touched. 'You would do that for me?' he asked, almost surprised. But the tours continued and the project remained just that.

At the end of 1987, browsing among music shelves, I found profiles of virtuosos and studies of performers, some not even having reached maturity; of Pierre Fournier there was barely more than a passing reference in someone else's biography. Through his recordings much of the artist could survive, but the man had closed his cello case and vanished in January 1986. How long would he be remembered?

This book is the result of that conversation between father and son, and of my own concern that a unique artist should continue to inspire not only cellists of the future but musicians of all disciplines.

*　　*　　*

To contend with childhood polio and then become one of the finest instrumentalists of the century cannot be less than a triumph, but it is doubtful that Fournier ever saw his life in such a light. For him the artist's fate was the perpetual pursuit of the unattainable, his objective ever receding, like a mirage.

It was Fournier's cello which saved him from melancholy as a boy; as an adult it was the talisman which brought him renown and took him many times across the world.

Besides the reminder of his disability, two things were instantly clear to his audience: the exceptional beauty of his cello 'voice' and his supreme artistry. Among writers and others who were subjugated were René Clair, Charlie Chaplin, André Gide, Hermann Hesse and Colette whose inscription in a copy of *La Naissance du jour* is part of musical history: '*A Pierre Fournier qui chante mieux que tout ce qui chante*' ('To Pierre Fournier who sings better than anything that sings'). His elegance and bearing were also remembered, and it was said of his concerts that he played as though for his own guests. Less obvious, and something I have attempted to address, were the influences which fashioned him as an artist in a climate totally different from ours today. The young Fournier grew up in a less driven and now vanished musical world led by musicians.

My aim was not a single, isolated portrait, but rather the artist in a landscape with figures. The background plays a part, from the secure Belle Epoque childhood into the musical core of Twenties Paris and the congenial summers among Gabriel Fauré's friends at Annecy-le-Vieux, to the sudden explosion into the cellist's life of the brilliant and sophisticated Lyda Piatigorsky. Together with her musical insight she brought an aura saved from the desolation of 1919 St Petersburg as well as a deep nostalgia for the Berlin she had come to know before the deluge of 1933. Through Lyda, the old allegiances would affect Fournier and influence their life together.

Lyda rapidly drew her husband into international circles where he met Furtwängler, Joseph Szigeti, Pierre Monteux and members of the Russian diaspora: Heifetz, Milstein, Nikita Magaloff and Serge Lifar. She gave him a son, Jean Pierre, who as the pianist Jean Fonda became his father's concert partner on many tours. Through good times and bad, and right up to her death in 1978, Lyda's musical opinion was constantly sought; in my view this alone warrants a close examination of her own background. If the reader is put out by the break I have made at Chapter 7 to examine Lyda's early years, then so be it: to have ignored this aspect of Fournier's life would have been to close one's eyes to the truth.

The two personalities could not have been more different, Fournier being a very private man and full of contradictions. Beneath the composure and the initial *vieille France* formality, was a mass of conflicting elements, much of which he confided in letters to friends, but chiefly and very regularly, to his son. Yet for all that he had a sly sense of humour and a robust fondness for all the good things in life.

The chamber music training of his youth affected his entire approach to music-making. The least self-serving of performers, he shunned facile publicity and abhorred platform antics. In our media-driven era this would go some way to explain why up to now so little has been written about him. Even for many of his friends, the life of this secret and elegant man remained a patchily-covered canvas. With the study which follows I hope to have filled some of those waiting spaces.

AH

Acknowledgements

My first thanks must go to Pierre Fournier's son and concert partner, Jean Fonda Fournier, without whose enthusiastic co-operation from the outset and generous loan of private papers this book could not have been written. His patient and meticulous response to all my queries, and his unfailing good humour, eased my work over its long gestation. Regarding Fournier's last years, I am greatly indebted to Mme Junko Fournier for her personal kindness and help.

Mme Cécile Niklaus, the younger of Fournier's two sisters and with whom I corresponded over several years, encouraged me from the beginning and to her I owe my affectionate thanks. She was my chief source of information about their childhood and Pierre's early career. Their younger brother, M. Jean Fournier, was also very helpful and guided me to Mme Jeanine Krettly-Pérès, sister of Pierre's first cello teacher, Odette Krettly. To Mme Krettly-Pérès I owe the details of the events on the Barneville holiday in 1915 of which she was a witness, as well as much of the family background.

I am most grateful to Pierre Fournier's nieces and nephews for their kind hospitality and advice as well as their admirable patience: Comtesse Hélène Zamoyska, Mme Jacqueline Peltier, Mme Denise Peltier; M. Philippe Fournier and M. Michel Fournier.

Sadly, since this book was in the making many musicians who knew Pierre Fournier have left us, a number of whom made their own contributions to this book: Henri Sauguet, Nathan Milstein, Rudolf Firkušny, Sir Charles Groves, Mme Etiennette Tombeck-Correa, Joan Dickson. Of all the musicians the closest to Fournier was without doubt Nikita Magaloff, to whom I am indebted for memories of Lyda Fournier even before she became Mme Piatigorsky, as well as much about Fournier's life and career. To his widow Irène (née Szigeti) I extend my thanks for her warm hospitality and the loan of letters to her husband.

My affectionate gratitude goes to Tony Mayer, with fond memories of Thérèse, who gave me not only hospitality on many occasions during the research, but also the loan of letters and the benefit of Tony's acute and critical eye during the writing.

The late Peter Heyworth kindly sent me an unpublished extract from the second volume of his biography of Otto Klemperer while it was under way.

For the kind loan of Fournier letters I must particularly thank Amaryllis Fleming, Mme Néry Martinon and Peta Fisher.

Dr Geoffrey Spencer of the Lane-Fox Respiratory Unit at St Thomas's Hospital kindly found the time to explain to me in detail the workings and effects of the polio virus.

I have benefited from the unstinting and unhurried co-operation of many people active within the musical profession or associated with it, as well as other specialists, a few in writing but the majority in person:

Claudio Abbado, Chanoine Georges Athanasiades, M. Jean-Pierre Azéma, Mme Anik Baehr, Artur Balsam, Lady Barbirolli, Dr Sue Bawden, Mr and Mrs Douglas Blyth, Mme Marie-Françoise Bouillon, Madeleine Bourreil, Lamar Crowson, Sylvia Darley, Sir Colin Davis, John Denison, Felix Dietrich-Kienberger, Prof. Wolfgang Drechsler, David Drew, Gabriel Dussurget, Tony Fell, Emma Ferrand, Dr A M Finch, Eric Forder, Marie-Thérèse Fourneau, Prof. M R D Foot, Mme Kiki Fouré, A E Frost, Frau Elisabeth Furtwänger, Prince Yuri Galitzine, Mavis Gallant, Mme Victoire Gavoty, M. Philippe Gentil, Jacques Genty, Josef Gingold, Paul Griffiths, Jonathan Groves, Mme Huguette Guthmann, Elizabeth Harrison, Mme Margaret Hartog, Dr E T Hughes, S P Hughes, Sir Ian Hunter, Mrs László Igloi, Agnes Járfás, Rebecca John, Alfred Kaine, Jo Kendall, M. Camille Kiesgen, Ralph Kirshbaum, Mme Elisabeth Köhler, Prof. Philip Kolb, Hans Kramer, Elbie and Norman Lebrecht, Daniel Lesur, Julian Lloyd Webber, Mark Lubotsky, Rachel Lynch, Dr Michael Minden, M. Philippe Muller, Kathy Murrell, M. Pierre Naudin, M. Jean-Michel Nectoux, Patrick O'Connor, John Owen, M. Alain Pâris, M. Vlado Perlemuter, M. Pierre-Petit, Robert Ponsonby, Pastor Eckhardt von Rabenau, Maria Sabina Reitinger, Dr Ritchie Robertson, Dr Ruth Rosenberg, Jonathan Ruffer, Elizabeth Russell, Pauline Samuelson, Dominic Scott, Dr J J Scott, Derek Simpson, Mrs Gwen Solomon, János Starker, David Strange, Wolfgang Stresemann, Prof. Jean-Yves Tadié, Mrs Catherine Temerson, M. Philippe Thibaud, André Tubeuf, M. Pierre Vidoudez, Jacob de Vries, Eleanor Warren, Alla Weaver, Olivier Wieviorka, John Willett, Jonathan Williams. To them all I extend my grateful thanks. If any name has briefly escaped my memory I ask its owner's indulgence.

I am particularly indebted to the London-based Oppenheim John Downes Memorial Trust, a late-discovered spring in a financial desert, for the award of a grant to help me finish the research.

I want also to acknowledge the help received from the following during the research: The Wellcome Institute Library, the British Library Science and Information Service, the British Library Document Supply Centre at Wetherby, Cambridge University Library, the National Library of Scotland, the British Polio Fellowship, the Royal College of Music Library, the Westminster Music Library, Bury St Edmunds Public Library; Dr Peter James, Warden, Royal Academy of Music; Michael Gough-Matthews, former Director, Royal College of Music; Deutsche Grammophon Gesellschaft, Alfred Kaine and Dr John Stopford; Radio Suisse Romande; the Archives of Paris and the Municipal Archives of the cities of

Rheims, Laon and Nîmes; in Paris the Bibliothèque Musicale Gustav Mahler; the Music Department of the Bibliothèque Nationale and Mme Colette Chabaud; the Archives Nationales, Mme Chantal Bonazzi and Mme Paule-Renée Bazin; Institut d'Histoire du Temps Présent and Prof. François Bédarida; Secrétariat d'Etât aux Anciens Combattants and Mme Christina Jakobs; the Mairie at Vincennes; the Musée de l'Opéra and Mme Martine Kahane; the Museum of the Paris Conservatoire National Supérieur de Musique and Mme Bran-Ricci, and the Music Library of Radio France where the staff combined in a miracle of efficiency when time was short, a métro strike having half-paralysed Paris.

I am also grateful for information from the South Bank Centre, Boosey & Hawkes Music Publishers Ltd, the Performing Right Society, the Mechanical Copyright Protection Society, SACEM in Paris, and especially M. Bruno Peluso of SUISA in Zürich.

I am particularly indebted to Felix Aprahamian for applying his formidable knowledge and experience not only to reading the manuscript but also contributing the Foreword, and to Derek Simpson for having the kindness to check a relevant chapter for any cellistic impertinence.

I am especially grateful to Pat Nicholson for her kindness and hospitality, allowing me on several occasions to work at her house untrammelled; and to my own family on both sides of the Channel for help, hospitality and encouragement throughout.

For permission to quote from letters to Pierre Fournier, I am indebted to a number of copyright holders. First, I am glad to thank Mme Rosine Seringe for kindly allowing me to reproduce eight unpublished letters from her uncle, Francis Poulenc. I wish to thank Maître Laurent Kasper-Ansermet for a letter from Ernest Ansermet, M. René Verges for a letter from Louis Beydts, Mme Bronia Clair for one from her husband René Clair, Frau Elisabeth Furtwängler for two letters from her husband to Lyda Fournier; Mme Victoire Gavoty for a letter from her husband Bernard Gavoty; M. Camille Kiesgen for his own letter to Jean Fonda Fournier; Mme Maria Martin for two letters from her husband, Frank Martin; the Bohuslav Martinů Foundation in Prague for two letters from the composer; Lamar Crowson and André Raynaud for letters to myself, and Lady Walton for kindly allowing me to publish a letter from her husband to Fournier with the indications for the Cello Concerto reproduced in Appendix 3.

The authors and publishers would like to thank all the writers, publishers and literary representatives who have given permission for quoted material from books and newspapers. In some cases it has been difficult to trace copyright owners and the publishers would be glad to make good the omission in future editions. I have had the kind permission of the following for extracts from concert reviews or articles: *Nazional Zeitung Basel*, *The Daily Telegraph*, *Le Figaro* © 9731370, *The Guardian* (*Manchester Guardian*), *Journal de Genève*, *Journal La Lanterne*, *The Musical Times*, *The New Statesman* (*New Statesman and Nation*), the New York Times Co © 1948, 62 (*New York Times*); the New York Times Syndicate (*New York Herald Tribune*); *The Strad*, Times Newspapers Ltd (*The Times*).

I have also had the kind permission of Radio France, France Inter and M. Jacques Santamaria to quote from Jacques Chancel's programme *Radioscopie*; and of Radio Suisse Romande and M. Jacques Donzel for René Bofford's *Entrée en question*.

A number of writers and publishers have kindly given permission to quote from copyright material: Bärenreiter for an extract from *J S Bach Dokumente*; Editions Buchet-Chastel for two extracts from Bernard Gavoty's *Anicroches*; John Calder for Franz Kafka's letter for Oskar Pollak in *Letters to Friends, Family and Editors* translated by R. and C. Winston; Cambridge University Press and Editions de la Maison des Sciences de l'Homme for quotations *passim* from the *Cambridge History of Modern France* originally published by Editions du Seuil, Paris; Flammarion for extracts from two letters from Gabriel Fauré in the composer's *Correspondance* edited by Jean-Michel Nectoux; Victor Gollancz for material from *Francis Poulenc 'Echo and Source' Selected Correspondence 1915–1963*, translated and edited by Sidney Buckland; Librairie Hachette for the extract from André Maurois' *Lélia ou la Vie de George Sand*; John Heath-Stubbs and Carcanet for an extract from the *Collected Poems*; Michael Joseph Ltd for a quotation from George Melly's introduction to Daniel Farson's *Soho in the Fifties*; Oxford University Press for the lines from Hermann Hesse's *Die Morgenlandfahrt* cited in Gordon A Craig's *Germany 1866–1945*; M. Alain Pâris for an extract from *Universalia*, annual supplement to *Encyclopaedia universalis*; Random House Inc for the quotation from Joseph Szigeti's *With Strings Attached* published by Alfred A Knopf; Sidgwick and Jackson for a letter from *Selected Letters of Virgil Thomson* edited by T Page and V Weeks Page and published by Summit Books; and André Tubeuf for a quotation from his article in Deutsche Grammophon's *Pierre Fournier In Memoriam*.

PART I
(1906–1944)

1   A Bridge and Two Families

For Parisians the spring of 1900 meant more than the turn of a century. It brought a shift of attention towards the future, a jolt which enabled them at last to bury some unhappy memories. Under all the froth of the nineties, older citizens had been conscious of the bitter residue left by the defeat at Prussian hands and the times when 'their dishonoured capital still smelled of blood and smoke'.[1] France had, as a result, lost Alsace and Lorraine and as if that were not enough, political scandals had disturbed the national sense of propriety.

The new spirit of adventure arrived punctually in the shape of an engineer from Strasbourg, Alfred Picard. Organizer of the 1889 Exhibition, he persuaded the government to mount another, even more splendid than its predecessors. One of the many inauguration ceremonies on 14 April was the opening by the President of the Republic of a new bridge linking the Petit Palais on the right bank with the Esplanade des Invalides. This feat of engineering fulfilled Napoleon's old dream: a single-span bridge of low profile to set off the perspective of the splendid Hôtel des Invalides. With a diplomatic nod to the Franco-Russian entente, it was named the Pont Alexandre III after the late Tsar; above the arch and visible from the water's edge its elegant decoration symbolizes the rivers Seine and Neva.

Among the spectators as President Loubet disembarked from the river steamer was a sculptor from the southern town of Nîmes, Léopold Morice, then at the height of his career. His contribution to this composite work was two bronzes which future generations of ever-hurrying Parisians would vaguely remember as angels; they are instead two plump and pagan water-spirits, with the traditional dolphin and conchshell, frolicking separately at the north end of the bridge.

Three weeks after the opening ceremony, on 7 May 1900, Léopold Morice married his eldest daughter Gabrielle to a promising young infantry lieutenant, Gaston Fournier. The couple's fourth child was to grow up to be the cellist Pierre Fournier.

Léopold Morice was born in Nîmes on 9 July 1843, the eldest of the three children of a cabinet-maker, François Morice, and his wife née Désirée Boutin, a dressmaker. The couple started their married life at 2 rue Caguensol, to the east of the famous Roman Maison Carrée, a street inhabited by workers in the 400-

year-old textile industry, shearmen and dyers who needed the local stream for their trade.

By the time that the youngest Morice child was born in 1848 the family had moved to 1 place de la Salamandre near the town hall, indicating an improvement in their condition. Perhaps it was simply professional pride which induced Françoise to enter 'couturière' beside his wife's name on the birth register, or she may have been obliged to work throughout her childbearing years to help support her growing family, for when the second child Désirée was born François' profession was given as bank clerk and when Charles followed in 1848 he was listed as merchant. Poor or not, the Morice family had expectations: Léopold went to Paris to study with the *dijonnais* sculptor and Prix de Rome winner François Jouffroy (1806–1882), exhibiting his first bust at the Salon on 1866 and going on to win a number of medals; Charles became an architect.

Léopold Morice had a successful career and a street in Nîmes is named after him. Twenty-six of his works can be traced today, including in Colombia a monument to Christopher Columbus. His most famous commission was won jointly by the two brothers from a field of eight competitors: the monument to the Republic in Paris at the former place du Château d'eau, now the place de la République, a column crowned with a female figure, its base surrounded with bas-reliefs of scenes from the Revolution.

Léopold married Geneviève Mollex of Lyon on 4 May 1871 when their address was given as rue de Moulin-Raspail in Nîmes. It was a world of craftspeople. Geneviève's father was a carpenter; her uncle, a witness at the wedding, a shoemaker; the other witnesses all lived locally: a building contractor, a fabric finisher and a tailor. François Morice had reason to be proud: his two sons 'went up' to Paris and to success and fortune. Some years after his mother's death, Léopold moved his entire family to Paris and the comfortable quarter of Auteuil where he brought a house with a large garden.

Léopold and Geneviève Morice had four children: Charles, Désirée Gabrielle (the cellist's mother) and the twins Lucie and Berthe. If art entered Pierre Fournier's ancestry with Léopold, a great deal of craftsmanship and hard work already existed in the genes on both the Morice and Fournier sides.

The cellist's paternal grandfather, Paul Fournier, was born in 1840, the son of Joseph-Napoléon Fournier, pharmacist at Meaux (Seine at Marne). He went into the hardware business in Paris and married a girl from Rheims, Marie-Julie Delécluse, born in 1848, who came from a long line of master clothiers, guild members and cloth merchants originally from Rouen. Paul Fournier died at the early age of 38, leaving three children. At his death Gaston, the youngest, was only five years old and therefore barely remembered him.

The eldest of the three, Georges, born in 1867, did very well at naval college, joined the service and at seventeen saw action aboard the Vipère in the Franco-Chinese war over Indo-China. At 33 he resigned from the navy to take up a Jesuit novitiate. Ordained in 1907, he became a missionary in China four years later at his own request; he was never to return. Leaving behind a mission in China which at least until recent times bore his name, he died in Shanghai in 1919 of typhoid fever caught from a dying man to whom he had administered the last sacraments.

Lucie, the second child, born in 1869, entered the Order of Nazareth and, like her father, died young. Gaston-Émile, the youngest and father of the cellist, was the survivor, born in Paris on 21 November 1873.

At the start of a career in which he was to display intelligence, leadership and nerve, Gaston Fournier entered the military academy of Saint-Cyr in 1894. He was commissioned in 1896. In 1903, already married and with two daughters, he attended Staff College for two years, emerging second out of 86 students. By the time war was declared he was a captain and had spent five years seconded to Army Staff Headquarters.

Gaston's wife Gabrielle Morice was intense, romantic-minded and musical. Her parents had disapproved of her entering the Paris Conservatoire, considered by many people as an undesirable place for young ladies, so she attended a local music school where she won diplomas in solfège and harmony. Gabrielle was independent-minded. Although (and perhaps because) both Léopold and Geneviève Morice were atheists she became a devout Catholic before her marriage. This was in tune with the reaction among certain of her generation against the frivolity of the Belle Epoque, and with a return to an idealism of discipline, sacrifice and loyalty to the Church.

Notes

1. Daniel Halévy *The End of the Notables*, Middleton, Conn: Wesleyan University Press 1974. Cited in J.-M. Mayeur and M. Rebérioux *The Third Republic from its Origins to the Great War 1871–1914*. *Cambridge History of Modern France*, Editions de la Maison des Sciences de l'Homme and Cambridge University Press 1984, vol. 4, p. 5.

2   A Boy in Auteuil

Gabrielle and Gaston Fournier had five children. The two eldest, Geneviève and Cécile, born in 1901 and 1902, were followed in 1904 by a boy, Paul. Pierre Léon Marie, the future cellist, was born at six in the morning on 24 June 1906 at 145 avenue de Suffren, near the Ecole Militaire. The last child Jean, arrived in 1911, after the family had moved across the Seine to 66 avenue de Versailles.

Pierre Fournier was born into a world which was both secure and forward-looking; proud, too, of its social reforms and its ability to handle new ideas. The year of his birth saw the right to a weekly holiday, the *repos hebdomadaire*, become law. The separation of church and state had been ratified and church property was being confiscated. 2500 church schools were closed, famous orders like the Carthusians expelled. A sequestrated convent in the rue de Vaugirard provided the sculptor Auguste Rodin with a studio. The Dreyfus affair which had dragged on for twelve years and split France in two ended this year with the captain declared innocent. Meanwhile Marie Curie began to teach at the Sorbonne, the writer Colette was appearing as a dancing faun at the Théâtre des Mathurins; André Gide was mocking the Catholic poet Francis Jammes, and the visitors to the Salon d'automne the paintings of Paul Gauguin. The composer Gabriel Fauré was appointed Director of the Conservatoire and Claude Debussy's first set of *Images* for piano received its première. In November the Brazilian engineer and aviator Alberto Santos-Dumont flew his plane 220 metres in the Bois de Boulogne. For the bourgeoisie it was a prosperous and confident world, suddenly to be overtaken by the horrors of the First World War which in France would leave barely a family intact.

France had much to lose. A stable regime, wealth, job security and a low level of taxation all contributed to the material wellbeing of the thriving middle classes. 'The Fairy Electricity' had brought the telephone, the electric lift, central heating and the proliferating cinema; Paris led the way in public transport (as she still does today) with the opening of the first métro line, Neuilly-Vincennes. Most families had a domestic servant (Gabrielle Fournier employed a Bretonne maid). Propriety and thrift were important. Women were expected to stay at home: working elsewhere caused raised eyebrows. Clothes were kept in repair, money was saved and much attention given to the children's health and education.

Tradition, prosperity and progress had combined to create this convenient state of affairs reinforced by a close family life.

The Fourniers lived comfortably. The sixth-floor apartment at 66 avenue de Versailles overlooked the Seine at the southern boundary of that most desirable of neighbourhoods for parents and children, Auteuil. Less glamorous than Passy, less patrician than the historic seventh arrondissement, Auteuil was and is serviceable, a haven for families in which to breathe an unvitiated air of respectability.

A photograph of 1909 shows Pierre in the time-honoured sailor suit, an engaging three-year-old with wide-apart dark eyes, arabesques of curls and a cautious expression; in another, two years later, the schoolboy of rue Boileau, his hair boyishly shorter, is at ease now with the camera: he leans stylishly on one leg, hands in pockets like the bigger boys, posing with aplomb in front of a giant aspidistra. He wears a double-breasted cossack shirt and corduroy shorts, a cummerbund elegantly masking waistband mechanics and a fine pair of boots.

Pierre's childhood was set to follow the traditional pattern. A sensitive, tractable child, he did well both at his primary school and at the Jesuit college Saint-Louis de Gonzague. The thread of music was to run through it all, for Gabrielle was quick to detect musical talent in her children. Pierre was seated at the piano and she gave him regular lessons herself. He showed an aptitude which gave her much hope for the future. In his turn, Jean would study the violin.[1]

But outside the family circle the world was changing. When, on 28 June 1914, Franz Josef's heir the archduke Franz Ferdinand was shot in Sarajevo, the average Frenchman was less concerned with a new Balkan crisis (the Emperor had already lost three of his family in violent deaths) than he was worried with the imminent arrival of income tax. Over the next six weeks, however, the mood changed quickly. On 1 August the notices for general mobilization were pasted up; two days later Germany declared war on France. Some were alarmed; others saw the war as a glorious new adventure. In the suburb of Neuilly the Governor of Paris had ordered the trees to be cut down and laid across the avenue. Fences were set up as barricades against the German cavalry. Although some Parisians fled the capital, the general public displayed a surge of patriotism. Many artists joined the army: the poet Guillaume Apollinaire, the painters Georges Braque and André Derain. Raoul Dufy drove an army postal van, and Jean Cocteau in his Paul Poiret suit became an ambulanceman. Behind all this was the immense courage of the ordinary soldier, the *poilu*.

Captain Gaston Fournier, among the first to be called, left for the front in the 49th Battalion of light infantry. Two months later he was mentioned in dispatches. The citation dated 2 October 1914 reads:

> [He] showed self-control and initiative while carrying out aerial reconnaissance up to 150 kilometres inside enemy territory. Although frequently engaged in combat and his plane hit by enemy fire, he was not deflected from his mission.

For the rest of the Fournier family life and lessons continued much as before. In the spring of 1915 Georgette Krettly, mother of the violinist Robert Krettly, invited Gabrielle Fournier to dinner at 15 rue de Bruxelles. Plans were laid for Robert's sisters Odette and Jeanine to join the Fourniers in Normandy for the summer holidays.

Barneville-sur-mer in 1915 was an undistinguished family resort with sand dunes and safe bathing on the west coast of the Cotentin peninsula. Gabrielle took a third-class carriage with Odette and Jeanine, her own five children, the young Bretonne maid and an overflowing picnic hamper for the slow journey to the sea. The prophetically named Villa Gavotte overlooked an almost deserted beach and the only close neighbours were friends from Paris, a Mme Glasgow and her daughters, and a family called Suquet, relations of an engineer who had worked on the first Paris métro. The children swam and paddled, played croquet and made cakes on wet afternoons. One day Jean, the youngest, frightened them all by disappearing; he was found an hour later, wandering on his own at the end of the beach. The girls took turns to accompany Gabrielle to the market on Thursdays. There was a piano in the tiny sitting-room, and often music after dinner. Odette had left her cello behind in Paris but Gabrielle sang a little and Jeanine accompanied her in emotional renderings of Massenet's *Werther*. A favourite was *Va, laisse couler mes larmes*.

One evening Pierre was listless. Unusually for him he had eaten no dinner and, complaining of a headache, he pleaded to go to bed. This brief malaise might have gone unrecorded but for what followed a few days later when he was on the beach. Gabrielle was shaking out the bathing towels and called to Pierre who was on all fours, playing at a distance. There was no response: unusually, for he was an obedient child. She tried again, urging him to get up. 'I can't', he called. His legs had collapsed under him. Before Gabrielle had time to realize her predicament an elderly American left his deck-chair to speak to her. He was alarmingly frank. He believed he recognized the boy's trouble: it could be infantile paralysis – there was a lot where he came from, he said.[2] She must put her son at once in a bath of hot salt water. Gabrielle did as she was told; the bath was soothing.

Then one night the whole household awoke to Pierre's screams; he had a high fever. Gabrielle took him into her bed, putting Jean into Pierre's in the little room overlooking the sea, unaware of the risks she was taking.

The following day, instead of the usual expedition to the market there was a frantic search for a doctor. They were all at the front. Gabrielle telephoned a family friend in Paris, the paediatrician Dr Jules-Joseph Milhit of the Bretonneau hospital, and an unorthodox consultation followed. The symptoms were confirmed to be those of infantile paralysis and Pierre was to be isolated at once. Nothing could be done at this stage beyond complete rest, and later a type of electrotherapy called faradism, an unpleasant electric shock treatment 'with a machine', Cécile recalled, 'which was unobtainable'. There was no point in cutting short the holiday; the fatigue of a transfer to hospital or a return to Paris would only make matters worse.

In 1915 medical knowledge had little answer to infantile paralysis, as poliomyelitis was then called, and it continued to be treated with purges, bleeding and blistering. Pierre was spared these procedures but he underwent the faradism, a treatment which was to remain in use until the 1950s. Research had been accelerating since the discovery of the virus in 1908 by Karl Landsteiner, a Viennese pathologist and Nobel prizewinner whose team went on to produce numerous papers on the subject. The Rockefeller Institute published an important study in 1912,[3] still highly praised in 1955.[4] But epidemics continued and more than 40 years were to pass before a safe vaccine would provide immunity. Protection can lead us to forget the devastation caused by this disease in the first half of the century: fiercely contagious, it could strike down the entire staff of a hospital. Since it is not degenerative we have been able to witness outstanding cases (President Roosevelt and the violinist Itzhak Perlman among them) achieving long and successful careers, proving to the world that victims they are not. Their very success can blind us to the extreme severity of the onset in many instances, although in 50 and 80 per cent of cases the patient does not develop paralysis. Pierre Fournier was unlucky. Initially all his limbs were affected; in time he was left with a withered right leg.

Gaston Fournier, meanwhile, was more than occupied at the front. Since May, while at Ypres the British were contending with the first poison gas and flamethrowers, the French were on the attack in Artois, hoping for a breakthrough; in the course of the single year of 1915 they were to count 400 000 dead or taken prisoner.[5] When Pierre's fever dropped he wrote to his father 'Cher Papa, I didn't vomit today.'

The captain joined his family on 48 hours' compassionate leave. The Glasgow girls were keen to present him with a bouquet at the station – a patriotic mixture of cornflower, marguerites and poppies – but Odette and Jeanine had misgivings; in the event the enterprise was not a success. 'What are those flowers?' asked the captain, embarrassed to be treated as a hero.

Urged by their mother to return to Paris, Odette and Jeanine left Barneville reluctantly; when Gabrielle and her brood arrived in Paris at the end of August, the two girls were waiting at the station.

In Paris there were attempts at treatment. Massage was tried, and electric shocks. The diminutive Jean observed the dreaded big black box which dispensed them, standing in the middle of the room. Memory is selective. In later life Pierre confided that he remembered little of the onset of polio, but for the others in the household at the time, the events at Barneville in 1915 were unforgettable. Seventy years later Jeanine Krettly recalled 'I can still hear those screams.'[6]

Notes

1.   The distinguished violinist and teacher Jean Fournier entered the Paris Conservatoire in 1923 as a pupil of Albert Born, having first studied with Germaine Pouant and

Robert Krettly. He obtained a first prize in 1931 in M. Brun's class.

2.   The following year the US was to have 'the most extensive epidemic the American nation had ever seen'. (John R. Paul *A History of Poliomyelitis*, New Haven: Yale University Press 1971, p. 338.)

3.   Peabody, Draper and Dochez *A Clinical Study of Poliomyelitis*, New York: Rockefeller Institute Medical Research Monograph 1912.

4.   Paul, Debré, Thieffry and Russell *Poliomyelitis*, Geneva: WHO Monograph Series, no. 26, 1955, p. 110.

5.   Philippe Bernard and Henri Dubief *The Decline of the Third Republic 1914–1938*. *Cambridge History of Modern France*, Editions de la Maison des Sciences de l'Homme and Cambridge University Press, vol. 5, 1985, p. 14.

6.   Jeanine Krettly-Pérès in conservation with the author. Professor Robert Debré described the pains of the onset of polio as 'agonizing and excruciating' (see note 4).

3 The End of a Holiday

Before his illness Pierre had left the primary school in the rue de Boileau for the Jesuit college, Saint-Louis de Gonzague. From now on a teacher would bring work to be done at home under his mother's supervision. The enjoyable sensation of an unexpected holiday soon gave way to boredom and loneliness. No classmates or enemies, no tumbles, feuds, nudging or giggles: he was left with only his isolation to explore.

The piano lessons came to an end because he could no longer work the pedals, but for Gabrielle Fournier salvation could come only from music. She consulted a friend, Mme Massart, a professor of solfège at the Conservatoire, who suggested that Pierre take up the cello since it could be played sitting down; she also recommended the young Odette Krettly to teach him.[1]

Anxiety, resentment and depression now threatened Pierre, but if he had been fortunate in his consultant, he was doubly so in his mother. It is unlikely that Gabrielle would have spent afternoons consulting a manual on the psychological sequelae of paralysis even if such a thing had been available; she relied instead on two simple things, her instinct and her love of music. Somehow she managed to steer a safe and confident course, avoiding the common pitfalls of unrelenting severity and excessive indulgence, or a dangerous lurching between the two. Following Mme Massart's suggestion about the cello was an interesting prospect. The instrument would give Pierre a means of physical exertion, teach him useful lessons in discipline and self-control, provide an outlet for self-expression and, for a while, answer his emotional needs; above all, he would probably enjoy it.

On Thursday, therefore, the weekly school holiday, Odette came to lunch at avenue de Versailles to the delight of the Fournier children who saw her as barely older than themselves. Pierre's lesson followed, and as the weeks and months passed, 'what had been a pastime turned into a passion'.[2]

The Krettly connection played an important part in Pierre Fournier's early life. They were an outstandingly musical family and Odette was a very strong influence on his approach to the instrument. She was born in Paris in 1897 and had two elder brothers, Robert, born in 1891, who became a well-known violinist and leader of the Krettly Quartet, and Pierre, two years younger, who started the flute belatedly and ended by going into business. Her sister Jeanine, born in 1899, was to become a fine pianist and on occasion Pierre Fournier's duo partner. The Krettly parents, Eugène who worked for the Huiles Lesieur and his wife Georgette, a seamstress before her marriage, were not musical, although Georgette had artistic leanings and wrote verse. Eugène was understandably taken aback when faced with his small son Robert holding a violin borrowed from his grandfather and insisting upon learning to play it. Robert entered the Conservatoire in 1903 and three times a week his mother accompanied him to the Faubourg Poissonnière, making part of the journey by river steamer from the rue du Point du jour to Concorde. All Conservatoire pupils were expected to reach a high standard in solfège (rewarded with a medal) and it was in this class that Robert Krettly came to know the young son of a Béziers shoemaker, later the distinguished pianist and teacher Yves Nat.[3] Robert frequently brought Yves and his other friends home and there was music-making. In time Odette and Jeanine followed Robert's example. After qualifying in solfège under Mme Chéné, Odette won a first prize in 1912 at the age of fifteen as a pupil of Cros Saint-Ange, cellist of the Capet Quartet; Jeanine, in Isidor Philipp's class, won the same award in 1918.

When Odette Krettly took up the offer to teach Pierre Fournier, the pupil was nine, the teacher eighteen. In this intense, deeply religious girl who shied away from parties with the excuse that she 'didn't know the people',[4] Pierre found the second important figure in his musical life: a teacher of insight, imagination and drive. He was to recall the debt he owed her: 'Through her unique personality I learned patience with technique and the control of intonation and phrasing; she also taught me about the colour of sounds.'[5] There must have been a rare and subtle chemistry at work, and something of Odette's inwardness also left its mark.

On 11 November 1918 the composer Maurice Ravel who was at Saint-Cloud heard the fanfares of the armistice. On the Opéra balcony the soprano Marthe Chénal sang the *Marseillaise*.[6] But when the euphoria had simmered down it was followed by a great weariness. France had lost more than 10 per cent of her active male population (double the British losses) and was left with over a million disabled or severely wounded. In the occupied provinces there had been much suffering: bombardment, curfew, forced labour, the pillage of livestock and the requisitioning of property. Some areas had been irreversibly devastated, towns had been levelled and the transport systems rendered unusable. The land of cornucopia was driven to import her food. The value of shares had plummeted and savings had vanished while commodities were short and prices high. Many families, now without a breadwinner, faced hopeless poverty. The middle classes were badly hit, particularly the small *rentier* who had previously been living on a well-husbanded unearned income. Many people found their lives turned upside down.

But not Gaston Fournier. A captain at the outbreak of war, he was a lieutenant colonel by the time it ended, having served at Verdun and in the Ardennes and escaping death when a bullet went through his greatcoat.[7] Neither wounded, severely impoverished nor out of work, this survivor became a member of the Interallied Armistice Commission and in April 1920 was appointed head of the Deuxième Bureau (military intelligence). He had shown financial flair in selling his Russian bonds before the revolution and was now in a position to buy property. He settled for an apartment house a few hundred yards along the street at 11 avenue de Versailles, this at a time when most people were content to rent flats rather than buy houses. In 1923 he moved his family to the new address and for decades this house was to provide a home for them and later an income for Gabrielle.

On 17 May 1917, Pierre made his first communion in the school chapel of Saint-Louis de Gonzague. A year later a mildly reluctant and incredulous Pierre was ready for the entry competition at the Conservatoire where he was admitted to the new preparatory class under Paul Bazelaire. There were twelve vacancies but only six candidates.[8] Pierre was exempt from the solfège course having reached the necessary standard at home. It was in the middle of his first term at the Conservatoire that war ended.

Pierre's new cello teacher was to prove 'a total inspiration in his enthusiasm and love of music'.[9] Born in 1886, the composer and cellist Paul Bazelaire taught at the Conservatoire from 1918, the year of Pierre's entry, until 1956. (The preparatory class which he founded was to continue after his death in 1958, until 1970.) He was by all accounts a warm and genial man, a former infant prodigy who had won a first prize for cello at the age of eleven and had followed this up with prizes in harmony, counterpoint and fugue. He had studied organ with Vierne and accompanied his cello pupils on the piano.

Pierre took ensemble with Camille Chevillard, son-in-law and successor of the conductor Charles Lamoureux (founder of the concerts which bore his name), and chamber music with Lucien Capet whose quartet were famous exponents of Beethoven.[10]

Conservatoire life made new demands. Gabrielle accompanied her son in the métro, carrying his cello. Although the station was not far, Pierre had a caliper over his right boot and walking was difficult. One day he was offered a seat; he was furious. His mother tried to humour him: 'It's meant kindly.' Another day a small boy, a *titi parisien*, noticing the awkward trio of mother, son and cello, called out *'Ben alors, t'aurais pu lui apprendre la flûte!'* ('Crikey, you could have taught him the flute!')

Sundays were spent either with *l'oncle* Charles the architect, or with the Morice grandparents. Léopold Morice had sold his original house and half the garden once his children had grown up. He kept the other half (including his studio) and enough garden space to build a smaller house. It was here that the family gathered for Sunday lunch. Gabrielle and four of the children came on foot; Pierre followed on his new acquisition, a tricycle. Cécile remembered:

> I adored my grandparents and for us five children it was a joy to visit them. I always remembered a particular menu, Italian-style lamb with beans. For pudding in winter the *gâteau de marrons* and in summer the *gâteau aux quatre fruits rouges*. These were legendary.[11]

Sometimes the children gave a concert. Geneviève sang, Cécile and Paul recited poems and Pierre played his cello. They performed Sully Prud'homme's poem *Le Cygne* ('*Sans bruit, sous le miroir des lacs profonds et calmes/le cygne chasse l'onde ...*') to Pierre's accompaniment in the Saint-Saëns piece.

His Conservatoire career was not a spectacular affair, but rather the first stage of a steady growth in musicianship to be enriched later by years of chamber music and quartet playing. The second-class medal of his first year in the preparatory class (no first-class medals were awarded that year) was followed by a first on 28 June 1920 and promotion to André Hekking's class at the age of fourteen. Hekking (1866–1925), who had joined the Conservatoire the previous year, came from a Dutch family of cellists and had been trained by his father Robert. Hekking also taught at the Ecole Normale de Musique and at the American Conservatory at Fontainebleau. His brother Anton and cousin Gérard were also cellists.[12]

On 21 June 1922 Pierre's account of the finale of Saint-Saëns' A minor Concerto brought him the disappointment of a second prize. But the following year on 26 June, with the Sarabande from Bach's E flat Suite and the finale of Lalo's Concerto, his name headed the list of first prizes.

Initially Gaston Fournier had been sceptical about his son's choice of career and at this stage Pierre still had no ambition to become a soloist. Like all the sons of professional people he was expected to pass his baccalauréat examinations, which he did, in the classics section. Gradually, however, the father was won over, and when Pierre emerged from the Conservatoire at seventeen, his career began immediately. He had been working at the steady, unforced pace which he would later recommend to his own pupils in a markedly different, impatient and fiercely competitive musical world.

His illness was a thing of the past, or so he believed. The physical legacy he would contend with, showing energy and a lack of self-pity, helped by a robust physique; it was psychologically that it left its greatest mark. The isolation from other children which he had experienced from the age of nine had sharpened his sensitivity. To use his own words, he believed that it gave him a degree of fatalism in his approach to life, and by driving him into himself possibly hastened his development as an artist.[12]

Notes

1. Jeanine Krettly-Pérès in conversation with the author.
2. Pierre Fournier, Archive.
3. Yves Nat (1890–1956), pupil of Louis Diémer, protégé of Debussy and duo partner of Ysaÿe, Thibaud and Enescu, specialized in Beethoven and Schumann. He once declared that the harpsichord gave him a rash (Yves Nat *Carnets*, cited by Elise Yves-Nat in *Les Yeux fermés*, Paris 1983).
4. See note 1.
5. See note 2.

6. Marcel Marnat *Maurice Ravel*, Paris: Fayard 1986, p. 426.
7. This coat was later donated by the general's grandson, Colonel Bernard Peltier, to the Verdun museum.
8. Jean Fournier in conversation with the author.
9. See note 2.
10. This quartet's viola player was known to have recorded in his log-book 1,069 performances of one Beethoven quartet between 1918 and 1928.
11. Cécile Niklaus to the author, 15 February 1988.
12. It was on Gérard Hekking's insistance that Paul Paray, conductor of the Lamoureux Orchestra, gave a first Paris hearing to the eleven-year-old Yehudi Menuhin in 1927.
13. Pierre Fournier, Radio Suisse Romande, *Entrée en question*, 7 April 1975.

4 'My Career Started in the Greatest Obscurity'

For Pierre music and life were now inseparable. Free time was spent playing chamber music with friends, and Gabrielle took him to concerts. He heard Fritz Kreisler, an experience which marked him profoundly.

This was a very different life from his childhood since he now had an abundance of musical friends: among them the Baur family in the rue de Rivoli overlooking the Tuileries gardens, a pianist neighbour in the avenue de Versailles, a Mlle Robinet, and on the other side of Paris the Tombecks.

Daniel Tombeck, remembered as something of a martinet, was secretary to the Science Faculty and later professor of physics and chemistry at the Sorbonne. The family occupied an official apartment in the rue Cuvier next to the Jardin des Plantes in the Panthéon district, where Marie Curie was a frequent visitor. Daniel Tombeck's daughter Etiennette was a violinist and Pierre's fellow student. She was always chaperoned by her elder sister, especially to the Conservatoire.

When a cellist was needed at a friend's house in Neuilly, Etiennette was asked if she had any ideas. She suggested a boy in her class, saying he was young but 'better than the others'. His mother, she added, came with him.[1] Gabrielle Fournier duly set off for the fashionable suburb of Neuilly with Pierre, his cello and her knitting.

Louis Mayer, personal adviser and close friend of Prince Albert of Monaco, lived in a large private house with a garden at 32 rue Charles Laffitte. All four Mayer boys played an instrument; the eldest, Armand, was the pianist, Max played the cello, Charles the violin and the youngest, Tony, the violin and later the viola. From that moment Tony became a lifelong friend to Pierre, orderly, patient and supportive, uncomplaining when asked to forward Pierre's forgotten spare cane or a stray overcoat.[2]

Making music was a serious matter and at rue Charles Laffitte every repeat was meticulously observed. With the impatience of youth Pierre often found that the session had lasted long enough. What spurred him on was his equally youthful appetite, for in the Mayers' house music was always followed by a delicious dinner.

There was much coming and going between Neuilly and the Jardin des Plantes, avenue de Versailles and the Tuileries gardens. In his turn the youngest Fournier, Jean, played his violin on Mme Tombeck's 'day'. There were few cars an the young musicians travelled by bus or métro and addressed each other with the formal *vous*.

The Mayer and Tombeck families had been 'friends for generations'. Nevertheless Etiennette's parents had reservations about her associating so freely with the Mayer boys. 'They are so much better off that they belong to a different world' they told her. Whatever the Tombecks' prejudices, anti-Semitic or otherwise, Etiennette took no notice and the friends continued in tireless music-making, barely stopping for meals; long sessions of trios and quartets, pent-up spirits exploding in horseplay, with Mme Fournier, 'her hair drawn back from her forehead', turning a blind eye to the battles at table with the *petits-suisses*. 'He must get rid of his energy' she would say of Pierre's high spirits.[3]

At a Tombeck wedding in the cathedral of Saint-Brieuc Etiennette and Pierre played Fauré's *Dolly* as a duo for violin and cello. An excellent string player, first prizewinner in the same year as Pierre (1923), Etiennette also accompanied him for fun on the piano. There was a fair number of wrong notes. 'Never mind', Pierre soothed, 'it will be a useful experience for when I have to play with bad provincial orchestras.'[4]

Once, after he had played at a party given by her parents, not wishing to give him money, Etiennette presented him with a pair of fur-lined gloves which pleased him greatly. Some time later, when she was living at Sèvres, Pierre played an old cello of hers and a buzz revealed a crack. He spent a large part of the afternoon repairing the instrument with seccotine. It was to remain in her possession until her death.

She lent him a dog-eared score of Rachmaninov's *Vocalise* (Op. 34/14). Years later she often heard the cello arrangement on the radio and wondered if it had been made from her tattered copy.[5]

*   *   *

Following his prize in 1923, Pierre's first engagement outside Paris was at Royan Casino. Of this episode his sister Cécile wrote:

> Maman thought we should go together.... We left by train, Pierre and I, with his tricycle and his cello and our lunch in a bag. I can't remember who helped us or how we found lodgings. What I do know is that we had a large room with two beds behind a curtain. Outside in the yard was a little gas stove to cook on. We were with a kind elderly couple who thought we were man and wife: when we wanted to turn in there was only one bed made up! On the first evening we went directly to the casino, Pierre on his tricycle and I on foot carrying his cello. Happily it wasn't very far. During a silent film he played in the orchestra pit with two or three other musicians, but for the gala evening he came on to the stage to play his competition piece which won him a lot of

applause. On his days off we went for walks, he always with his tricycle. We took photographs. He was very proud of his camera and would set it up to take a picture of us both.[6]

One of Pierre Fournier's first Paris concerts was a recital with Jeanine Krettly in February 1924 at the Salle Erard, 13 rue de Mail, in a programme including Schumann pieces and Beethoven's A major sonata, Op. 69. The hall was full.

The young cellist took every job which came his way: orchestras, bandstands, spas and the cinema. The last was a formidable training in versatility and quick response which, to his regret, was to disappear before he could recommend it to his own students. In a small band at the Lyon-Palace, a Paris 'picture-house', he accompanied silent films from a desk laden with sheet music, eyes darting from score to screen and back to conductor, extracting the last drop of pathos from the epic blinking and juddering above his head. He enjoyed it as he did anything which was physically demanding and with which he could dominate his disability. Like a fellow cellist Emanuel Feuermann he became a lifelong film addict.

The theatre also brought him work and opened a new world. Jacques Copeau was an innovator. Actor, stage director and literary critic, he had been co-founder with André Gide and Gaston Gallimard of the influential *Nouvelle Revue Française*. In 1913, with the help of Gide and Gallimard, he founded the Vieux Colombier theatre where he could put his theories into practice. His company became renowned and was sometimes compared to Stanislavsky's Moscow Art Theatre.

At the Vieux Colombier Fournier was part of a small band – flute, harp, violin, cello and percussion – playing the incidental music to Prosper Mérimée's *Le Carrosse du Saint Sacrement* or Gide's *Le Roi Saül*. In the company were Valentine Tessier, Lucien Nat and Louis Jouvet; on percussion was the young composer Arthur Honegger who appeared in one production as a troubadour playing a drum. Fournier whiled away spare moments playing billiards with Nat and Honegger.

The Vieux Colombier was also a busy centre for new music. The singer Jane Bathori organized regular concerts there, promoting works by the composers known since 1920 as 'Les Six' and consisting of Georges Auric, Louis Durey, Germaine Tailleferre, Arthur Honegger, Darius Milhaud and Francis Poulenc. Their nickname was the invention of the *Comoedia* critic Henri Collet, in allusion to the Russian 'Five'. It was a heterogeneous group, individual in their styles and in their tastes but who were friends and shared concerts.[7] They also had the common goal of renewing French music. Together with Bathori, one of the most frequent performers at these concerts was the pianist Andrée Vaurabourg, later to marry Arthur Honegger.

When Jacques Copeau moved with his young company to Burgundy, Fournier lost his employment at the Vieux Colombier since he needed to stay in Paris, but for a time he kept his links with the theatre. In this little world where all the artists knew each other and their word was law, Louis Jouvet stepped in to engage him at the Comédie des Champs Elysées when musicians were needed.

Notes

1. Pierre Fournier quoted on *Entrée en question*, Radio Suisse Romande, 7 April 1975.
2. Armand Mayer later graduated from the Ecole Polytechnique, seedbed of industrialists, financiers and senior civil servants; Max was killed in the First World War; Charles, a doctor, was deported to Germany in 1943, but survived. Tony became a stockbroker, escaped from Vichy France to London and, appointed director of De Gaulle's issuing bank, founded the prestigious series of French concerts at London's Wigmore Hall, which continued until 1966.
3. The late Etiennette Tombeck-Correa in conversation with the author.
4. Id.
5. Id.
6. Cécile Niklaus to the author, 15 February 1988.
7. Darius Milhaud *Notes sans musique*, Paris: Julliard 1949, p. 97.

5 Listening to the Others

It was at Louis Mayer's house that Fournier's career took a crucial turn. The violinist Robert Krettly (Odette's elder brother) heard the young cellist and lost no time in inviting him to join his string quartet.

Robert Krettly had won a first prize at the Conservatoire in 1909. While leader of the Colonne Orchestra under Pierre Monteux he spent his summers in Dieppe, taking part in casino concerts with, among others, Yves Nat and the flautist Gaston Blanquart. Military service interrupted his career in 1912 and he remained in the army until after the war when he founded the Krettly Quartet. The ensemble made a name for itself in modern French music, championing Darius Milhaud, Arthur Honegger and Charles Koechlin. In 1928 it was to record Gabriel Fauré's last completed work, the String Quartet (Op. 121). The critic Emile Vuillermoz described the Krettly Quartet as 'courageous exponents of modern chamber music'[1] and declared that composers owed them a great deal.

And not only composers: five years of intensive quartet playing and the study of a wide repertoire not only broadened Fournier's outlook and provided him with a living but also taught him two great principles: following the composer's wishes and listening to the other players. He would later refer to Robert Krettly as his 'companion and guide'.

Through Robert the thread of Fournier's career stretched back to Odette and forward to another figure: a musical patron. The banker Fernand Maillot and his wife Louise were ardent music-lovers and friends of Gabriel Fauré. They helped many young musicians recommended by the composer, entertaining them in Paris at 4 rue Talleyrand near Les Invalides, and in summer at a house they rented at Annecy-le-Vieux in the Haute Savoie. The Maillots also owned a group of houses, the Cité Maillot, at Menthon Saint-Bernard. Although originally intended as an investment, the houses were often lent in summer to musicians.[2]

Their friend Gabriel Fauré had suffered since 1903 from an unpleasant and distorting form of deafness which diminished intervals in the high and low registers, and muted any sounds in the middle. This cruel affliction which increased with the years caused him to resign, in 1919, from his post as Director of the Paris Conservatoire, delicately nudged out by the Ministry of Fine Arts. While retirement was something of a deliverance and freedom from administrative chores a relief since it gave him time for his own music, he found himself in financial difficulties. Fernand Maillot came to the rescue in several ways. He organized a tribute to the composer in the Sorbonne amphitheatre, attended by the President of the Republic, Alexandre Millerand. The festival was a triumph, one concert ending after midnight. Afterwards the audience turned spontaneously towards the composer who, sadly, could hear neither the music nor the applause.[3] Maillot also arranged a performance of Fauré's *Messe basse* in the little church of Saint-Laurent at Annecy-le-Vieux.[4]

Some patrons might have stopped there, but for Maillot nothing was too much trouble when it concerned his musicians, and he provided the ailing Fauré with a summer refuge in the last years of his life. This was a house called Les Charmilles above Annecy, at Annecy-le-Vieux. The composer had seen it first:

> ...a house large enough to hold us all. It must be about five hundred metres up, and being at a distance from the lake we would enjoy very good air, without the damp, right through the season. What do you think of this [he wrote to Louise Maillot], assuming we could secure it, a matter I shall investigate with M. Gentil who is a friend of the owner ... ?[5][6]

Fauré had waited a lifetime to compose a string quartet, inhibited, like so many before and after him, by the monumental achievement of Beethoven. When he started work in the summer of 1923 he wrote to his favourite pupil, Jean Roger-Ducasse, of 'that devil of a quartet', adding 'How I find this work *difficultueux*!'[7] The Quartet was finished at Annecy-le-Vieux in September 1924 but, always diffident about his work and now in failing health, Fauré wanted the approval of his peers before publication. He instructed the pianist Marguerite Hasselmans that it was to be tried out before a small group of trusted friends who were in the habit of hearing any new work of his and to whom he gave the responsibility of deciding whether the Quartet was to be published or destroyed. Accordingly the friends gathered at Marguerite's house at 123 avenue de Wagram: the composers Roger-Ducasse, Paul Dukas and Pierre de Bréville, Arthur Honegger and Philippe Gaubert, and the pianist Robert Lortat who had taken Fauré's works to London ten years earlier. Playing in this first private performance of the String Quartet (Op. 121) were Jacques Thibaud, Robert Krettly, the viola player Maurice Vieux and Fournier's teacher André Hekking. A second private performance followed at the Maillots' house in rue Talleyrand; this time ill-health obliged Hekking to cancel and his place was taken by Fournier. The Quartet was Fauré's farewell: he died on 4 November 1924. The public première took place at the Société Nationale on 12 June 1925.

Not yet twenty, Pierre Fournier was at the core of French musical life, fortunate in the calibre of the musicians around him who recognized his unique talent. Besides Yves Nat, Arthur Honegger and Fauré's friends, he began to encounter other members of 'Les Six', Darius Milhaud, Francis Poulenc, Germaine Tailleferre and Georges Auric. At Le Havre in 1925 he gave a performance of Honegger's Cello Sonata with the composer's wife, Andrée Vaurabourg, at the piano. Because the work was new to the audience it was given twice, once at the beginning and again at the end of the programme. A listener approached Fournier in the artists' room afterwards. 'I liked the last work you played', he said, 'but what on earth was the one at the beginning?'

Most of Fournier's engagements were coming to him through his contact with musicians who had heard him or played with him. His concerto début came about by accident: he was again asked to replace the ailing Hekking, this time with the Colonne Orchestra in a performance of the *Rapsodie sur des thèmes ariégeois* (*Rhapsody on themes from the Ariège*) by the young composer Marc Delmas. On 24 February 1925 he shared the bill with the pianist Jeanne-Marie Darré and the Krettly Quartet in a programme which included a *Prelude and Fugue in the Russian Style* by Nicolas Karjinsky, also a cellist and a pupil of Hugo Becker. At his own pace he was heading towards a career as a soloist.

But chamber music still beckoned and Les Charmilles would continue to cast its spell on other musicians after Fauré's death. While working with the Krettly Quartet Fournier formed a trio with the violinist Gabriel Bouillon[8] and the pianist Vlado Perlemuter, a pupil of Ravel. From 1925 for three summers at Annecy-le-Vieux, the trio lived as guests of Fernand and Louise, building up their repertoire for concerts, sponsored by the couple, in the historic Great Hall of the Conservatoire. Vlado Perlemuter remembered Fournier sixty years later:

> He was not yet the great international figure he was later to become, but he was already a magnificent artist and he brought an element of great joy to my youth. We performed the entire repertoire for cello and piano, Brahms, Fauré and all the rest...[9]

At Annecy-le-Vieux, besides playing in the trio, Fournier joined a quartet, also subsidized by the Maillots, with the violinists Van Hoorebeck and Jo Bouillon, and the viola player Despiau. Bouillon and Van Hoorebeck put up at a small hotel in the square; Despiau lodged with the curé. Louise Maillot carefully gave Fournier a room apart, in a turret opposite the main house and overlooking the lake.

Saved now from the pot-boiling tedium of cinemas and orchestra pits, free from material worries, Pierre was able to mature as a musician in conditions any artist would dream of. He was the favourite of his benefactress and if this experience was not strictly an initiation it was, to say the least, an education of the most classic nature with an elegant and wholly sympathetic woman of an older generation. To crown it all, Louise and her husband took the young man to hear Wagner at Bayreuth.

Despite all the serious music-making the inhabitants of Les Charmilles still found time for lighter moments. A photograph has survived of the entire household in fancy dress, with Gabriel Fauré costumed as the local mayor, complete with sash of office and false beard. Pierre played bridge with his brother Jean and the Maillots' daughter Louise (Loulou). Jean, aged fifteen, was present at a grand candlelit dinner with a bar supplied by Maxim's after which Honegger and Gaubert sprawled, blissfully drunk, at the feet of their hostess. Mme Gaubert pleaded with her husband 'Voyons, Philippe, I beg you, don't drink! Have you forgotten? Tomorrow you are conducting the *Ninth*!' 'The Ninth can go to hell..!' was the reply.[10]

* * *

In April 1926 Maurice Ravel finished his *Chansons madécasses*, a cycle for voice and chamber ensemble. The work had been commissioned by his neighbour Elizabeth Sprague Coolidge (1864–1953) who in 1925 had established a foundation to subsidize festivals, concert halls, composers and performers.

Ravel was a bibliophile and when he settled at Montfort l'Amaury outside Paris he bought the complete works of the eighteenth-century aristocrat and erotic poet Evariste de Forges, vicomte de Parny. Born at La Réunion in 1753, Parny lost his fortune in the Revolution and died in 1814, pensioned off by Napoleon; his *Chansons madécasses* date from 1787. For Ravel's work the gestation went smoothly but the birth in the concert hall was postponed by politics: the Rif War in Morocco against French and Spanish domination was not yet over and there was a fear that heightened sensibilities might be offended by the anti-white slant of the second song in particular, the bellicose *Aoua*! with its exhortation to be wary of the white people. Replacing Hekking again, Fournier took part in a private performance of the work at Montfort l'Amaury, probably at the house of Elizabeth Sprague Coolidge. With him were the soprano Madeleine Grey, the flautist Louis Fleury and the composer himself at the piano. The public performance finally took place at the Salle Erard on 13 June 1926.[11]

Among Fournier's other notable concerts during this period was a programme as soloist with the Krettly Quartet in the Hall of the Conservatoire on 9 February 1927, his place in the ensemble being taken for the evening by his first teacher Odette, now thirty years old. Another was a Fauré programme at the Salle Erard on 27 February 1928 when he was paired with Marguerite Hasselmans, Fauré's *compagne* in his last years; one could hardly be closer to the composer than that.[12] At the Conservatoire again, he appeared with Vlado Perlemuter and the OSCC in Vivaldi and Lalo under Philippe Gaubert, and in November of the same year in a recital at the Salle Gaveau. The break with the Krettly Quartet came naturally at that time, his solo career having begun in earnest. One of the early orchestral performances was Bloch's *Schelomo* in the Hall of the Conservatoire.

There was another break in 1928, this time within the family when the eldest boy Paul left France for the Far East. Paul Fournier worked first for the Compagnie des Caoutchoucs in Cambodia, later setting up his own business and building an airstrip for it. He married the Siberian-born Anna Pisarevska from Shanghai, and liked to say that he had three children: Philippe, Thérèse and his work.

From 1926 Gaston Fournier was in Morocco as Resident High Commissioner. In 1929 he was appointed Governor-General of Corsica, a post he was to hold until the Second World War.

Notes

1.   Emile Vuillermoz, *Excelsior*, 4 January 1926.

2.   Philippe Gentil in conversation with the author.

3.   Robert Orledge's study of Fauré (London: Eulenburg 1979, pp. 20–21) gives both the composer's own description of his deafness and a leading otologist's opinion.

4.   The Messe basse consists of a *Kyrie, Agnus Dei, Sanctus* and *Benedictus*, and was drawn from Fauré's contribution to the *Messe de l'Association des Pêcheurs de Villerville* (1881) written jointly with André Messager. The *Benedictus*, not in the original work, was an adaptation of the *Qui tollis* from the unpublished Gloria.

5.   The violinist Victor Gentil owned a house at neighbouring Menthon-Saint-Bernard.

6.   Gabriel Fauré to Mme Fernand Maillot, 17 March 1919. *Gabriel Fauré Correspondance*, ed. Jean-Michel Nectoux, Paris: Flammarion 1980, p. 300.

7.   Gabriel Fauré to Jean Roger-Ducasse, 6 September 1924. Gabriel Fauré, op. cit, p. 336.

8.   The Bouillons were a family of violinists. Gabriel (1898–1984) studied in Montpellier with his father Jean Bouillon (1871–1950), later obtaining a first prize at the Paris Conservatoire as a pupil of Lucien Capet (see p. 13) whom he later succeeded. He also worked with Ysaÿe and his own pupils included Ginette Neveu and Henryk Szeryng. He turned to conducting in about 1974. His brother Jo gave his name to a highly successful orchestra and was married to Josephine Baker. The eldest brother Georges was leader of the Orchestre National and of the Orchestre Pasdeloup.

9.   Vlado Perlemuter in conversation with the author. This artist, whose interpretations of Ravel were guided by the composer, has that rare quality: simplicity. Whereas today's latest virtuoso is protected by an unlisted telephone number and a regiment of musical administrators, this august musician's name can be found in the Paris telephone directory. Describing Perlemuter, Sir William Glock's words, 'His aim was to reveal, not to astonish' (*Notes in Advance*, Oxford 1991, p. 65), reflect those of Alain Pâris on Fournier (See p. 103 of the present work), underlining the humility of the two musicians' approach to their art and their mutual understanding.

10. Jean Fournier in conversation with the author.

11. The song *Aoua*! presented an additional problem – an entry 'cold' on a high G. Roger Nichols (*Ravel Remembered*, London: Faber 1987) relates how Ravel solved this for his soprano by giving her the note while pretending to flick dust off the keyboard, a trick which Madeleine Grey recalled that he repeated every time they performed together.

12. Marguerite Hasselmans (1876–1947) was the pianist daughter of the harpist Alphonse Hasselmans to whom Fauré dedicated an Impromptu for harp (Op. 86). According to the Fauré specialist Jean-Michel Nectoux, she was the depository of the composer's musical intentions to a far greater degree than her rival, the long-lived establishment figure, Marguerite Long (J.-M. Nectoux, op. cit., p. 266).

6 First Tours

On 19 February 1929, Tony Mayer married Thérèse Raynal and Fournier played at the ceremony in the synagogue of rue de la Victoire. At about this time he visited London for the first time. As first cello in a Paris orchestra at the Queen's Hall he played 'the' tune in Lalo's Overture to *Le Roi d'Ys*.

By 1932, the year his father reached the rank of major-general, Pierre had already made his first solo tours in France and abroad: The Hague, Amsterdam, Antwerp, Monte Carlo, Spain and Berlin. On 18 November 1933 he applied to l'Expansion artistique (an early version of Action artistique), run by Louis Joxe and designed to present French artists abroad, in the hope that the organization would finance a British tour, but the board turned him down, blaming a lack of funds for the year 1934.

The reviews for these early tours of 1932–1933 show that Fournier's particular characteristics were already clearly discernible: a brilliant technique (leading him on occasion to hurry the tempo), the beauty of his tone, the Latin polish (much appreciated by Berlin critics), his sense of style in a wide variety of works, and already his remarkable bowing; but above all his sensitivity and adherence to the composers' wishes which made his technical prowess subservient to the music. 'An incredibly sure technique', 'the individuality of his tone', and 'he has immediately placed himself in the front rank, with the masters.'[1]

Before the visit to Berlin in March 1933, General Fournier wrote to the ambassador, André François-Poncet, asking him if he would hear Pierre at the embassy before his Beethovensaal début with the pianist Michael Raucheisen.[2] The request was partly granted: a pre-début was arranged at the residence of the military attaché, General Renaudeau. After the concert François-Poncet congratulated the two artists and explained his initial reticence: he had given up inviting French musicians to play at the embassy after the succession of mediocrities inflicted upon him by the Quai d'Orsay. 'But *you* will always be welcome!' he added quickly. Later he was to appoint Furtwängler's secretary, Berta Geissmar, as musical adviser, so we can safely assume that standards in general improved.

From a balcony the following day, François-Poncet and Fournier watched a

Panzer parade, with goose-stepping troops and aircraft in formation overhead. The ambassador turned to the cellist: 'My dear Fournier, I constantly write to the Quai, but nobody believes me when I tell them what is going on here.'

In Marseilles Fournier played Darius Milhaud's First Concerto under the composer's baton. During rehearsal he plucked up enough courage to ask Milhaud if certain orchestral passages could be lightened on account of what Fournier was to describe later as 'packets of chords', with doubled and tripled notes submerging the cello. The composer was adamant: once a work was completed he never made any alterations. Poulenc told Fournier that Milhaud 'had been like that all his life'. Undeterred, Fournier bought the miniature score and studied it carefully. From then on, with other conductors, these heavy chords were redistributed, alternating wind and strings. 'It provided contrast while being much lighter.'[3] This was a rare departure from Fournier's strict principles of loyalty to a score.

If polio had devastated Pierre's childhood, it had far less power over his youth. For one thing he was now surrounded with friends; he also joyfully discarded his virginity with the sister of Gabrielle's *femme de chambre*. Nevertheless, his father the general, his solicitude heightened by those long absences from home, suspected that Pierre was feeling stifled by family life. His remedy was to advance the rent of a bachelor flat, a *garçonnière*. Here Pierre celebrated his emancipation by installing Marguerite, a dressmaker whose favours he then shared with a well-known figure in Marcel Pagnol's films, the actor Charpin. Marguerite was every filmgoer's idea of the typical *parisienne*: slight, dark, chic; *piquante* was the word which came to mind for those who knew her.

While Pierre was on his first European tour, at home his parents' marriage was in trouble. Puerperal fever after the birth of Jean, her youngest child, had brought Gabrielle close to death (she received the last sacraments), and the doctors advised against a further pregnancy. Temperamental incompatibility had been compounded by wartime separation; then followed the hideous pattern of strained relations, coldness and finally verbal cruelty; Gabrielle, distressed, would later confide her unhappiness to a daughter-in-law. In January 1935 the ailing marriage ended with divorce.

Six months later Gaston Fournier married Antoinette Marcelle Mattei, a native of Bastia. His declared intention had been to wait until all his children were wed; he almost succeeded.

Pierre was very fond of his stepmother who is generally remembered as gentle, unassuming and devoted to her husband. He had an easy relationship with his father who had a sense of humour (Cécile recalled saying silly things on purpose just for the pleasure of hearing him laugh) and whose letters to Pierre often began '*Cher fils et grand artiste…*'

In later years the general followed up his grandchildren's careers with interest. When his granddaughter Jacqueline Peltier (Geneviève's second daughter) translated Marguerite Liberaki's *Trois étés*, he sent her Emile Henriot's review. He was proud also of his soldier grandson Bernard Peltier (Geneviève's son), to whom he gave his sabre.[4]

On his retirement the couple settled in Nice, where General Fournier died on 27 January 1960, in his 87th year.

In Pierre Fournier poliomyelitis had, as often happens, latched on to a physique which was fundamentally robust. Unmistakably Latin in appearance, he had a broad forehead and thick wavy hair which was to grey early, making him look slightly older than his age. He had expressive, slightly prominent brown eyes and sensitive features, with a wide forehead, dominant nose and narrow jaw. People accustomed to seeing him in evening clothes would rightly associate him with urban elegance: he looked like a continental ambassador with the manners and, with strangers, the formality to match: his voice and bearing were unequivocally patrician. He had not the slightest talent for dissembling, and his expression registered anger, irritation, pleasure or anxiety with the candour of a child. He laughed easily, but if wounded he would stare into the distance as if flinging the hurt beyond any unwelcome scrutiny.

In Paris the young friends' music-making continued until the outbreak of the Second World War, although the demands of Pierre's developing career took him increasingly away. He was in Paris, however, when Etiennette Tombeck passed her driving test and the clan gathered to celebrate at a corner café in the avenue Montaigne. She gave a lift to Gregor Piatigorsky (introduced to her by Pierre) and played at scaring him as they lurched, all fits and starts, to the Ecole Normale de Musique. Pierre was recovering from the latest in a series of operations on his bad leg. There was also a new factor in his life, as Etiennette discovered, but true to his nature he had been keeping it to himself. This factor was Lyda Piatigorsky.

Notes

1. *Berlin Deutschewochenschau*, 18 March 1933. *Gazette de Voss*, 11 March 1933. *De Residentiebode*, The Hague, 23 November 1933.
2. Michael Raucheisen, the distinguished accompanist of many great singers, was the second husband of Maria Ivogün, the Hungarian-born soprano whose pupils included Elisabeth Schwarzkopf and Rita Streich.
3. PF, *L'Ame et la corde*. No. 5, November 1983.
4. Jacqueline Peltier in conversation with the author.

7 Lyda in St Petersburg and Berlin

Elle était la musique-même (She was music itself)[1]

Born in Moscow on 22 October 1902, Lyda Antik spent her childhood in St Petersburg. Her father, Efim Antik, a distinguished lawyer and legal adviser to the Nobel brothers, divided his time between a large estate at Baku in Azerbaijan and a St Petersburg flat in an apartment house favoured by diplomats and senior civil servants. Although of Jewish blood, he was by religion an Orthodox Christian and therefore allowed to practise law. Lyda's mother, born Marie von Sillermann, came from a prosperous merchant family. A talented pianist, Marie had been a pupil of Vladimir Vilschau at the St Petersburg Conservatoire. Forbidden by her father to take up a professional career ('I would rather see my daughter dead than on a concert platform'), Marie had continued to practise, and her children Anatol and Lyda grew up with an Ibach and a Blüthner in the drawing-room, in constant use.

Lyda's talent was more intellectual than that of her mother; musical rather than pianistic. Turning her back on the Czerny and Moscheles studies, she worked eagerly at Bach, Brahms and Debussy, the last at the time still rarely played in Russia. At the St Petersburg Conservatoire, where as a newcomer she was expected to curtsey to the uniformed seniors (including Sergei Prokofiev), she studied with Irena Miklachewskaya.[2]

Lyda was lazy, and if she played badly she was punished with Mendelssohn whose music Miklachewskaya detested. Instead of the traditional repertoire of Chopin and Liszt 'to open the hands', she was put on to Bach and Brahms. Marie, who had been trained in another tradition, probably disapproved, for she sent Lyda to her own teacher, Vilschau. 'Bring me Chopin's First Impromptu in a fortnight' Lyda was told, but her laboured account of the work disappointed the master after her mother's brilliance and depth; he had thought it would go 'like a flowing stream'.[3]

Lyda's creative side, on the other hand, came to light at an examination when before the Conservatoire board (including Alexander Glazunov and Nicolas Tcherepnin) she was able to improvise a fugue after the regulation five minutes' reflection.

Conditions in post-revolution St Petersburg were atrocious: whole families were dying for want of food and medication; people were tearing down fences to heat their flats. Over the city lay an 'awful oppressive silence broken only by occasional shots'.[4] Efim Antik decided to emigrate and finally obtained permission to leave, through the simple device of lowering the children's ages on the passports. Lyda's birthdate, like that of her brother Anatol, was altered by four years; hers was given as 1906, a doubly convenient fiction which she would have been the last to contradict.

The night before the departure Glazunov called, bearing a signed photograph: 'To Lydotchka Antik, in the hope that her outstanding talent for composition will develop as it should, and with faith in her future since she has so much to give. A. Glazunov.'

Leaving Russia via Riga in 1919, Efim Antik and his family travelled to Berlin. After defeat the German capital was undergoing an astonishing rebirth. Materially the country had collapsed but Berlin was breathing the oxygen of discovery. There was hunger everywhere, for bread and for novelty. The poet and novelist Hermann Hesse described the prolific years of the Weimar Republic, which started in ruin and ended in Nazism, as 'dismal, desperate and yet so fruitful'.[5]

The arrival of the Antik family in Berlin coincided with the flowering of this 'strange time'. Now within reach of the impressionable Lyda was a feast for the imagination, and this, coupled with the lasting human bonds she formed there – friends, lovers and her first husband – were to mark the rest of her life, and through her, have an incalculable effect on Fournier's.

To understand this it is worth remembering the riches on offer. Artists were converging upon Berlin: Bertolt Brecht from Bavaria, Arnold Schönberg and Artur Schnabel from Vienna. At the cosmopolitan Bauhaus, first in Weimar, then in Dessau, its founder the architect Walter Gropius worked with the Swiss Johannes Itten and the Hungarian Moholy-Nagy, with Paul Klee, Wassily Kandinsky, Mies van der Rohe and Eric Mendelsohn. The avant-garde, absorbing the music of Stravinsky and Les Six, were discovering the ideas of Le Corbusier in the French magazine *L'Esprit nouveau*. The golden twenties, *die goldenen zwanziger Jahre*, scorned by the Nazis as pollution, opened new roads in design, painting and architecture and left, besides the writings of Thomas Mann, Rilke and Kafka, and Alban Berg's opera *Wozzeck*, the stage productions of Brecht, Reinhardt and Piscator and the films of Pabst and Fritz Lang.

Berlin's Russian colony was large enough to justify three daily newspapers, five weeklies, several publishing houses and two football teams. The Russians had brought their language and skills, but above all their artistic talents: actors, fresh from the Moscow theatre with the theories of Stanislavsky; outstanding figures such as the painter Kandinsky, the writers, Maiakovsky, Gorki, Ehrenburg, and in music Feodor Chaliapin, Vladimir Horowitz and Nathan Milstein. The young Vladimir Nabokov translated *Alice in Wonderland* into Russian, gave English and tennis lessons and enjoyed 'tea, intrigue and interminable poetry readings'.[6] The pianist Artur Schnabel was to recall those years as the most stimulating and perhaps the happiest of his life.[7]

Berlin was the musical capital of the world; a soloist could make a living there without leaving the country. Supporting three major opera houses, the legendary Philharmonic and two prestigious music schools, the city also had a healthy appetite for new works. The conductors Otto Klemperer, George Szell, Leo Blech, Erich Kleiber and Bruno Walter shared the field of opera; at the Prussian Academy of Arts Anton Webern and Alban Berg were Schönberg's pupils, while Paul Hindemith, Carl Flesch, Emanuel Feuermann and Egon Petri taught at the Hochschule für Musik. The Philharmonic, with Wilhelm Furtwängler at its head, had a policy of engaging composers to perform their own works, thus Berliners had the chance to hear definitive interpretations by Strauss, Stravinsky and Bartók. New works appeared by Busoni, Hans Pfitzner, Franz Schreker and Prokofiev, and Ernst Krenek produced his boxing opera *Jonny spielt auf*. Duke Ellington's revue *Chocolate Kiddies* won devotees to jazz, among them the young Kurt Weill. The pianist Rudolf Serkin played the occasional violin sonata with Albert Einstein who had no vibrato but enjoyed playing. There was an abundance of other talented pianists: Claudio Arrau, Edwin Fischer, Wilhelm Backhaus, Joseph Hofmann; their undisputed leader was Schnabel. Profoundly serious (he was in his forties before he felt ready to undertake the complete Beethoven sonatas), he was not a virtuoso, regarding himself as the servant of the music and not of the listener, thereby attracting Rachmaninov's sneer 'the great Adagio player'.

Presiding over the rivalries was Luise Wolff. Widow of the impresario Hermann Wolff who had brought Hans von Bülow to Berlin as the Philharmonic's first conductor, Luise continued to manage the family firm for more than 30 years after her husband's death. Menuhin described her as the high priestess of music in Berlin; Franz Werfel called her 'Queen Luise'.[8]

Manners and morals had broken their bonds: women cut their hair, adopting the *bubikopf* and *herrenschnitt* styles; George Grosz's adipose noctambulists snorted cocaine while the transvestites paraded past the café tables; small wonder that the Berliner viewed his fellow German as a stodgy provincial.[9] There was hunger and cold but the lifts worked, Ehrenburg noticed. Berlin was orderly and pleasant; even the vice was well-ordered. 'Everything was colossal, prices, abuse, despair', in the 'city of hideous monuments and anxious eyes'.[10]

On the edge of this cauldron and longing to throw herself in was the beautiful and susceptible Lyda. Not yet seventeen, she lost her heart to a handsome adventurer called Otto Krohn and, using forged papers stating that he was an university graduate, the couple eloped and married. But after only a few weeks a tearful Lyda was brought home by her father; legal resourcefulness then brought down a quick curtain on the episode.

As a foreign lawyer, Efim Antik was banned from practising independently in Germany, but through a Berlin colleague he found a situation with a law firm. Marie obtained work as a rehearsal pianist at the Berlin Opera.[11]

Armed with Miklachewskaya's recommendation, Lyda entered the Hochschule für Musik as a pupil of Leonid Kreutzer. Her playing gained in warmth and fluency but Kreutzer complained of her laziness and lack of professional ambition. There were plenty of distractions, old friends from St Petersburg for example. Jascha Heifetz reappeared. In 1923 Lyda and he became engaged and the same year she crossed the Atlantic to meet his parents. On the beach at Long Island she heard Russian spoken a few yards away and discovered the eleven-year-old Nikita Magaloff with his mother. In the Magaloff apartment Nikita played Lyda a scherzo of his own composition; some years later, returning to New York she sat at the piano and played Nikita's little piece back to him from memory.

Lyda was in New York to meet her future in-laws, or so she thought, but already her heart's desire had turned his attentions elsewhere. She countered by directing hers towards the idol of the western world, the Italian-born film star Rudolf Valentino, then at the height of his fame. However, by the time they met again in Berlin, yet another star had risen in Lyda's firmament.

At the Russian club she met Ilya Ehrenburg and Marc Chagall, sent by the first Soviet commissar for the arts, Anatol Lunacharsky, to immerse themselves in western culture. (The commissar himself also full enjoyed the amenities.) Then, at a recital given by the pianist Ossip Gabrilovich, the conductor Efrem Kurtz introduced Lyda to Gregor Piatigorsky.

After a successful Russian career, Piatigorsky had been rescued from poverty in Berlin by the Hungarian Géza de Kresz, violinist of the Pozniak Trio which he invited Piatigorsky to join, thus sparking off the cellist's second career. He took part in the première of Schönberg's *Pierrot Lunaire* and became leading cello of the Berlin Philharmonic under Furtwängler; he joined one trio with Leonid Kreutzer and the latter's Hochschule colleague Josef Wolfsthal, and another trio with Schnabel and Carl Flesch whose rehearsals were attended by Aldous Huxley and James Joyce.

Married to Piatigorsky, Lyda focused all her ambition on her husband's career. Through him she met Furtwängler who was later to declare that she was the most musically competent woman he had ever met. It is said that once, while rehearsing Brahms' First Symphony with the orchestra, with Lyda in attendance like a true *Orchesterfrau*, Rachmaninov arrived to go through his D minor Concerto. Too impatient for the music to end, he thumped Furtwängler on the back shouting 'Ich bin da!' ('I'm here!'). A witness, Paul Kletzki, who was studying in Berlin at the time, commented that the real triumph of the evening turned out to be the symphony.

The Piatigorsky flat in the Sudwest Corseaux was a famous partying place for musicians: Huberman, Heifetz (whom Lyda watched giving her husband a lesson in staccato), Horowitz and Joseph Szigeti also, who became another close friend. At her suggestion Szigeti and Piatigorsky toured together, giving solo pieces between duos by Ravel and Kodály. She also arranged for Rachmaninov's Sonata to be performed by Piatigorsky and the Polish pianist Karol Szreter at a private party given by Luise Wolff. At the end Rachmaninov complained of the cuts they had made.

Another visitor to the Piatigorsky flat was Friedrich Holländer who came to try out some sketches for a new film score he was working on. He praised its young star: 'You'll see, she'll have a great future...' She did. The film was *Blue Angel* and the young star was Marlene Dietrich.

In 1932, when Berlin was changing fast as Nazi supremacy approached, the Piatigorskys left for Paris and the Résidence Majestic near the avenue Kléber, a focus for musicians, especially of the displaced Russian constellation. Nicolas Nabokov introduced them to the well-known salons and they were soon adopted by Misia Sert, the friend of Diaghilev, Jean Cocteau and Chanel.[12]

But there were strains on the marriage and Lyda's brief affair with the conductor Massimo Freccia finally drove Piatigorsky to seek 'a peaceful divorce' after nine childless years.[13]

Echoes of the turbulent Berlin days had followed Lyda to Paris. Witty, outspoken and provocative, there lingered about her, even when she was over fifty, an alluring aura of scandal. Many people who thought they knew her – among them the shocked, the titillated or the merely gossip-hungry – were unaware that this was more an afterglow of her Berlin twenties than Parisian incandescence in later years. She was, besides, never fully at ease with the French. But like fame or great wealth, talent can be a powerful aphrodisiac; it was often so with Lyda.

Notes

1. Mme Victoire Gavoty and the late Etiennette Tombeck-Correa, independently, in conversation with the author.
2. A pianist of enormous power and virtuosity, Irena Miklachewskaya tackled difficult works, devoted whole recitals to Bach and gave *Liederabend* at home, wearing a scarlet-tailed tailcoat over a black skirt and accompanying herself in songs by Hugo Wolf and Richard Strauss. Her technique is remembered as heavy rather than mercurial but with a fine legato. Her red hair, green eyes and lovers of both sexes provided musical society with a steady supply of gossip.
3. Nikita Magaloff recalled Lyda as a very talented pianist 'with a beautiful legato' (Nikita Magaloff in conversation with the author).
4. Emma Goldman *My Disillusionment with Russia*, London 1925.
5. Herman Hesse *Die Morgenlandfahrt*, Berlin 1932. Cited in Gordon A Craig *Germany 1866–1945*, Oxford University Press 1978, p. 469. "Unsere merk würdige Zeit: die trübe, verzweifelte und doch so fruchtbare Zeit nach dem grossen Krieg."
6. Susanne Everett *Lost Berlin*, London: Hamlyn 1979, p. 142.
7. Cesar Saerchinger *Artur Schnabel*, London: Cassell 1957, pp. 130–131.
8. Both Luise Wolff and her partner Emil Sachs were to disappear in the Holocaust. The agency did not survive.

9. Otto Friedrich *Before the Deluge*, London: Michael Joseph 1972, p. 6.

10. Ilya Ehrenburg *Men, Years, Life*, Vol. III, *Truce 1921–33*, London: Macgibbon and Kee, pp. 10–16.

11. In later years Marie Antik was rehearsal pianist at the Studio Wacker in Paris, accompanying Yvette Chauviré, Serge Lifar and others.

12. In time Misia Sert's place in Paris society was taken by the 'three Maries', sharing French culture between them: Marie-Louis Bousquet (fashion), Marie-Blanche de Polignac (music) and, looking like a cross between George Sand and Louis XIV, Marie-Laure de Noailles (literature and painting). An invitation from one of the Maries could open many doors to a young artist.

13. Gregor Piatigorsky *Cellist*, New York: Doubleday 1965. Da Capo Press 1976, p. 123.

8 Pierre and Lyda

It was another Russian cellist, the composer and gallery-owner Nicolas Karjinsky, who in 1935 introduced the rising young star Pierre Fournier to Lyda, ex-Madame Gregor Piatigorsky, in the interval of a Cortot–Thibaud–Casals concert at the Salle Pleyel. Lyda was living at 11 rue Saint-Didier, her own little star shining merrily in a musical galaxy.

That particular evening Fournier was not looking his best: he was recovering from chickenpox and his face was blue, swabbed with *bleu-de-méthylène* and dotted all over with little dressings. Mercifully another opportunity presented itself, this time an evening at Karjinsky's flat which may well have ended at 11 rue Saint-Didier, for it was certainly this occasion which sealed their future. Their musical première came later, again at Karjinsky's, when Fournier played Rimsky-Korsakov's *Hymn to the Sun* from *The Golden Cockerel*. Lyda was sitting next to the violinist Danya Karpilovsky. Taken aback by the sound, they turned to each other. 'C'est... *vaginal*' said Karpilovsky.

Late one evening the telephone rang at avenue de Versailles. Lyda's former lover François Lang, the pianist son of a textile magnate, fancied a little chamber music. Would Pierre like to come over? Unwilling to disturb his mother at that late hour (that, at least, is what he said), Pierre declined. Lyda registered this.

Lyda had remained on good terms with her ex-husband who had the use of her key and whose cello, mail and clothes she continued to house. When she was out one day, Grisha (as he was known to his friends) returned unannounced to find a telegram addressed to PIATIGORSKY 11 RUE SAINT DIDIER PARIS. Assuming this was for him, he opened it and read

BARCELONA PLAYING WITH CASALS AND HIS ORCHESTRA THINKING OF YOU PIERRE

When Lyda returned she found Grisha waving the telegram and shouting 'Isn't one career on this damned instrument enough for you without starting all over again?'

Pierre and Lyda were married at the Mairie of the 16th arrondissement on 16 July 1936. They spent part of the honeymoon at Eze in the house lent to them by the Yugoslav violinist Zladko Balakovic and his wife Joy.[1] Keen to take his wife to Monte Carlo in style for the hospital charity event, the *Bal des Petits lits blancs*, Pierre hired a splendid car. It only disadvantage was its horn, a colossal rubber affair; Lyda was mortified. François Lang was at Le Sporting the same evening. Lyda danced with him once, and Pierre exploded in a jealous scene.

In Paris the couple settled in a flat at 11 avenue de Versailles, the Fournier family house. 'And we tried *all* the beds' Fournier reminisced to his son in old age.

Lyda was indeed starting all over again, channelling her energy and connections into furthering a second cellist's career. She introduced Pierre to all her musical friends, the Serts, the Baronne de Marvitz (later godmother to their son), Nathan Milstein, Furtwängler, Pierre Monteux and Serge Lifar. She also drew him out of the family nest. Her niece Denise Peltier recalled two images from childhood visits to Lyda: an impressive row of shoes, and the photograph of Piatigorsky. Grisha remained a fine romantic musical figure, but a close friend to whom Lyda opened her heart stressed that her great love was Pierre. She confided 'I have known many men, and the most handsome in the world, but for me the real thing is Pierre.'[2]

Musicians came to the house, among them the gifted young cellist Maurice Gendron. Although fourteen years younger and possessed of classic good looks, Gendron never took any trouble to hide his hostility to Fournier which was to take several forms over the years. In the early days he tended to call on Lyda at avenue de Versailles rather too often for her husband's taste. That he was not discouraged by Lyda may well have been caused by the marks of affection which Fournier continued to show the pianist Monique Haas, an earlier flame. It has been said that Gendron's visits were nothing more than a public relations exercise suggested by Lyda's musical connections; they were certainly no threat to the marriage. Whatever the truth of it, Fournier was irritated enough one day to show his cellist colleague the door. Gendron once asked Lyda 'Don't you think that Pierre has something of the bank clerk about him?' 'If he looks like a bank clerk' Lyda retorted, 'you look like a lady's hairdresser.'

The composer Albert Roussel finished what was to be his last orchestral work, the Concertino Op. 57 for cello and orchestra, in Nice in 1936. In March, Fournier was the soloist at is first performance in the Salle Pleyel with Charles Munch and the OSCC. Munch had many friends among composers: Tibor Harsányi (a pupil of Kodály), Arthur Honegger and the Czech musician Bohuslav Martinů, who had studied with Roussel. Fournier's long friendship with Martinů dated from this occasion and was to bring about two dedications, the First Cello Sonata and the First Concerto in its second version.

When Alfred Cortot invited Fournier to join the staff at the Ecole Normale de Musique, and take over the chamber music classes of Diran Alexanian who was leaving for the USA, the extra salary was welcome, for Lyda was expecting a child.

Artur Rodzinski came to Paris on a European tour to recruit players for the Cleveland Orchestra. Lyda accompanied Pierre in the Schumann Concerto for his audition.[3] Rodzinski was looking for a leading cellist; he had, he said, a sixteen-year-old (Leonard Rose) at the first desk. Fournier was slightly nettled; besides, he had no desire to leave Europe. With Piatigorsky, Feuermann and Cassadó *in situ* were there not already enough established soloists? Rodzinski offered him the post of leading cellist, a teaching job at the Cleveland Institute and guaranteed solo appearances. Lyda urged him to accept, but without success: he treasured his independence, and in spite of everything that followed he never regretted this decision. Rodzinski bore him no grudge for the refusal: later they planned joint recordings but the conductor's ill-health prevented them taking place.

In February 1937 Lyda accompanied Pierre for a recital in Nancy, to gratifying reviews for both of them. Pierre repeatedly asked Lyda to continue as his concert partner, but she refused. With all her talent she never hankered after a professional career; she had neither the ambition nor the self-discipline, nor, while appreciating its advantages, a consuming desire for money. With her looks, personality and temperament she had had ample opportunity to net a rich second husband instead of a young soloist who, however outstanding a player, had as yet only an embryonic international reputation. But Lyda possessed an unshakeable belief in the validity of her own judgments, both in music and in life; in music she was usually right. Pierre had a gentle reserve born of intelligence and sensitivity, and an initial if brief diffidence with strangers. Lyda was an extrovert, an excellent linguist, sophisticated, flirtatious and with strong opinions. Generous in her admiration, she was also very outspoken and could wound, but even her enemies conceded that her musical role was immeasurable. She praised, criticized, cajoled, admonished and infuriated. In the early days, while Pierre's tone and phrasing were outstanding, he needed to break through a certain caution in his playing, to let himself go. He drew back one day at the start of a crescendo. 'Go *on*!' Lyda shouted from the next room. 'Right through to the end of it...like Grisha!'

On 12 December 1937 Lyda gave birth to a boy at the Belvedere Clinic in Boulogne, just outside Paris. He was christened Jean Pierre after his father and the younger of his uncles, Jean, who was also his godfather. The son of doting parents, Jean Pierre had by his own account the happiest of childhoods in a lively household which always seemed to be full of friends.

Furtwängler had heard Fournier's second Berlin recital in 1935. Lyda wrote to Furtwängler but the season was already fully booked; he would arrange a later date (he was to keep his promise). Meanwhile Fournier was invited to appear at the Berlin Philharmonic with Paul Paray in the Haydn D major Concerto. With tours of Italy and Yugoslavia this was one of his last important concerts before the outbreak of war.

Bohuslav Martinů's First Cello Concerto had received its première in Berlin in 1931 with Gaspar Cassadó as soloist. Never satisfied with his work, Martinů revised and extended it, dedicating this new version to Fournier who performed it in 1939 with Charles Munch and the Société Philharmonique. During the first winter of the war Martinů worked in France at the First Cello Sonata and dedicated this work also to Fournier. Reflecting much of the composer's anger and fears after the annexation of his country by the Nazis, it was first heard in the hall of the Archives de la Danse in Paris, at a concert of the Society for Contemporary Music (an off-shoot of the Triton concerts founded in 1932 by Pierre-Octave Ferroud). At the piano was Rudolf Firkušny; it was 19 May 1940 and it happened to be the last concert in Paris before the German occupation.[4] The Sonata was well received and a merry party of friends accompanied the composer back to his roof top flat in the rue des Marronniers in Auteuil. Three weeks later he left Paris for a long absence; blacklisted by the Nazis, he had fled, abandoning his manuscripts and other possessions.

For the summer of 1939 Gabrielle Fournier took a house at Andrésy near Saint-Germain-en-Laye. Geneviève Peltier brought her three children and they were soon joined by Lyda and Jean Pierre. The family stayed on at this convenient refuge after war was declared.

The French National Radio moved immediately to Rennes where Fournier was offered a soloist's contract at 4500 francs a month. He found a pleasant flat in the town where in November his family was able to join him, and for the months of the phoney war, the *drôle de guerre*, he worked in a congenial atmosphere with many good musicians: Vlado Perlemuter, Marcelle Meyer, Jean Doyen and others.

On 10 May 1940 Hitler's elite divisions began their lightning advance; six weeks later, insufficiently equipped and sold out by her leaders, France fell apart.

Notes

1. This house was later to become the Chèvre d'Or restaurant.
2. Gabriel Dussurget in conversation with the author.
3. Auditioning in the neighbouring Salle Pleyel were the young violinist Ginette Neveu and the flautist Louis Cortet.
4. The late Rudolf Firkušny to the author, 2 January 1989. Firkušny had met Martinů in 1933 and had made a piano arrangement of a scene from the composer's opera *Julietta*. In 1941, as refugees carrying the barest necessities, the two musicians left by the same boat for the USA. The composer worked on his *Fantaisie* for Firkušny as they waited.

9   Occupation

'A wind of madness was blowing over France.'[1] So Henri Amouroux described the panic which swept the country as the Germans advanced. By 20 June 1940, well over six million people had taken to the roads, at least two million of them Parisians abandoning their homes. Some had known previous occupation, many feared bombing or brutality; all hoped for safety beyond the quasi-mystical boundary of the Loire. As they fled there was looting, even extortion; hostages were massacred and one whole family, at Bousselange, preferred collective suicide to capture. The country was suffering from atavistic terror.

For the next four years the rigours of the Occupation were felt in varying degrees at different times, according to the region or social class. To be a Jew meant deportation and probable death; to be young and male, exile to Germany under the STO or compulsory work service. Deportation could be avoided by taking to the *maquis* and the Resistance or joining a Vichy-run youth movement. There were also the nameless men and women who hid fugitives and committed other unsung acts of bravery at the risk of their lives, but between the active Resistant and the blatant pro-Nazi, between Pierre Brossolette and Marcel Déat, the divisions were often blurred.[2]

The shutters were closed and the streets deserted as Paris became the conquerors' playground amid fluttering swastikas, slogans and verdigris uniforms. The ordinary citizen who had no relations with a farm or smallholding in the countryside suffered from hunger and cold. Many of the rich continued to amuse themselves, entertaining in their unheated houses to provide distraction from the endless search for food and fuel. Comfort depended on bargaining with the occupier or recourse to the black market.

Although deportation was a constant threat, many people, artists among them, managed to close their eyes and ears to alarming incidents. Often this was impossible, as when the poet Max Jacob, after heartrending appeals to his friends, was arrested and the order for his release arrived too late to save him.[3]

As in all societies, there were contradictions. The Spanish painter Jose Maria Sert was an arch-Fascist; his wife Misia (who had a Jewish grandmother) a self-proclaimed believer in the Resistance while depending on the comfort which through his German friends Sert had little difficulty in providing. Yet Sert is said to have saved Maurice Goudeket, the writer Colette's Jewish husband, from being sent to Germany.[4] Many people accused later of collaboration used their questionable connections to save fellow countrymen or colleagues under arrest.

The French Radio was now divided into two sections, Radio Paris in the capital, now under German control but still staffed by the French, and Radio Libre at Marseilles in the Free Zone. The orders which reached Fournier were symptomatic of the general confusion: two letters confirming his appointment at Rennes, followed by a third cancelling everything and summoning him back to Paris. He wanted to move his family to the Free Zone where Radio Libre was under the directorship of Ernest Leguillard who intended to engage him. In the event there were no vacancies left and Fournier was told that he would better serve French musical life if he returned to the capital. He accepted.

Fournier was also signed up by VSM (His Master's Voice) through its director, Jean Bérard. A man of many talents, Bérard was not only a gifted painter but also a fine pianist, and Jacques Thibaud's son Philippe recalls being taken to lunch with him by his father, and hearing their host give a 'beautiful and unforgettable' account of Beethoven's entire C sharp minor ('Moonlight') Sonata.[5]

It was under Bérard's aegis, and on the very day of the German offensive, 10 May 1940, that the now historic recording of Fauré's Second Piano Quartet (Op. 45) was made; the artists were Thibaud, Maurice Vieux, Fournier and the pianist Marguerite Long who left an account of what she called 'that tragic morning'. Bombs had fallen all night, and early that day the radio had announced Hitler's invasion of the Netherlands. Long was to pick up Thibaud on the way to the Pathé Marconi studios, and she dreaded speaking to him, knowing his son Roger to be in the front line, but Thibaud had already heard the news when she arrived.

It was a memorable session. The extraordinary beauty of Thibaud's tone focused all the anxiety and empathy of the players and the quartet was recorded without a flaw on that single day; Emil Gilels was to speak of this disc as 'one of life's great moments'. In spite of his anguish, Thibaud's sense of humour never left him. After the Scherzo (in which the piano has the lead), and once the red light was off, he put his hand in his pocket and produced a ten-centime coin. Putting it down on the piano he said 'What you have done, ma chère Marguerite, is worth a lot of money.'[6] [7]

On 16 June 1940, Philippe Thibaud, Roger's younger brother, was taken prisoner. Months passed before there was any news of Roger. The truth emerged in August: he had been killed near Sedan on 14 May, four days after the Fauré recording.[8]

*   *   *

In Paris following the armistice the musical community had scattered. After the initial shock those left behind half enjoyed the novelty of provincial torpor. Bewildered composers compared notes. In the country and deprived of electricity for weeks, Francis Poulenc heard the wildest rumours: the Opéra on fire, the

Invalides destroyed. Writing later, Henri Sauguet complained of spending a fortune to eat next to nothing, as well as being unable to earn any money with the theatres and cinemas closed. He was upset that Darius Milhaud (who was Jewish) had left for the USA: he still thought that there was nothing to fear. Writing to Poulenc he wondered where they were heading, and hoped that the winter might see the return of the 'beautiful Sérénade concerts'.[9] [10]

Turning their minds away from the hardships, Parisians who could afford it were flocking to concerts, theatres and cinemas, art galleries and libraries, and not only to keep warm. Against a background of continuing intellectual life and literary production (Montherlant, Claudel, Sartre, Camus), there was a pullulation of society events. At the Orangerie a soirée was given in honour of the sculptor Arno Breker; Alfred Cortot and Wilhelm Kempff played on two pianos, jointly but rather severally it was reported, in a curious account of Chopin's F minor Study (Op. 25/2) in unison. At Chaillot Kempff had a triumph in a Beethoven concerto with Munch and the OSCC, the occasion of the first contact between the pianist and Fournier. They were introduced by Lyda whose own friendship with Kempff dated from Berlin in 1929 when he was Director of the Stuttgart Musikhochschule where Piatigorsky had appeared. Kempff once asked her about Furtwängler's own music: where did he draw his inspiration? Somewhere between Brahms and Strauss, she thought. 'Ach, ich verstehe', Kempff nodded gravely, '*Strahms*!' A Paris friend, the lawyer-photographer Roger Hauert, witnessed a rare event during a gathering at his apartment after a Kempff recital. Furtwängler sat down at the piano to demonstrate where he thought Kempff's reading of the Appassionata had not been totally convincing. Kempff was having none of it and told Furtwängler 'You stick to conducting and leave me the piano which I play better than you!'

Kempff had much success in Paris and in the audience at Chaillot for his Beethoven evenings with Hermann Abendroth (when he gave the five concertos) were Sacha Guitry, Henry de Montherlant, Jean Cocteau, Madeleine Renaud and Jean-Louis Barrault. Another discovery of the times was Herbert von Karajan, conducting *Fledermaus* and *Tristan* at the Opéra. The Fourniers were stunned by his talent but taken aback by his chilly personality.

Like a great many musicians, Fournier continued to earn his living. He shared the bill with Marguerite Long and Serge Lifar at the *Gala de la Valse*, an event which illustrates the giddy escapism which co-existed, at least for the better off, with the ordeals and fear. He appeared at Bolzano and Milan, and at the Salle Gaveau his recitals sold out with the audience spilling on to the platform. With two concerts at Geneva, giving the Saint-Saëns A minor Concerto, and the Brahms Double with François Capoulade, he made his début with the Suisse Romande Orchestra and its founder Ernest Ansermet. At the Champs Elysées Theatre he performed Haydn, Schumann and Dvořák with Charles Munch. More recordings for VSM followed, including Schubert's Arpeggione Sonata and some short pieces with the pianist Jean Hubeau; also his first disc of Tchaikovsky's Rococo Variations with the Lamoureux Orchestra and Eugène

Bigot – an ordeal in an unheated hall. With the same artists he recorded the Dvořák Concerto for the first time, but dissatisfied with the result he forbade release.

In 1941 the composer Claude Delvincourt became director of the Paris Conservatoire. Winner of the Prix de Rome in 1913, he had been badly wounded in the First World War; during the Second he helped his students to avoid deportation to Germany, and many joined the Maquis.[11] After the death of Louis Feuillard, Delvincourt invited Fournier to take over his class: Fournier chose the young Paul Tortelier as his assistant. On the first morning Fournier found two packages on the piano. One was from 'the grateful pupils of Louis Feuillard': it was a funeral wreath with a purple ribbon. The other bore a warning from another professor's widow about 'insatiable women students': 'Look what happened…' In the parcel was a very, very small courgette. Fournier knew the sender of both parcels was his friend Louis Beydts, composer and director of the Opéra-Comique.[12]

*   *   *

While Pablo Casals was in self-imposed exile in the French village of Prades, unwilling to return to Franco Spain, his Paris manager and former student Charles Kiesgen wrote begging him to come to the capital either as a soloist or with his trio partners, Alfred Cortot and Jacques Thibaud. A series of Beethoven trio concerts were planned at the Salle Pleyel. When Casals declined the invitation Fournier was engaged to take his place on 17, 22 and 24 June 1943. The trio appeared again in Beethoven's Triple Concerto with the Radio Paris Orchestra under Jean Fournet. Casals' biographers have referred to the older man's resentment towards Fournier, yet Charles Kiesgen's son Camille calls the suggestion that Casals bore a grudge against Fournier 'a flagrant inaccuracy'[13]: he elected on principle not to come to Paris and the Beethoven festival could not be postponed. According to one biographer the original trio had broken up in 1937 'due to minor irritations' and to Casals' feeling that 'his personal reputation was sustaining the success of the ensemble to an unnecessary degree.'[14] This antipathy was reinforced later when Thibaud played in occupied France and Spain; Cortot more grievously accepted a high-profile administrative post, albeit of a musical nature, under the Pétain-Laval government of Vichy.

The fact that Lyda had Jewish blood, which caused Fournier much anxiety, was not generally known. One would hardly have guessed it when at a gathering in Paris shortly before the war she expatiated on the marvels of Berlin musical life. Szigeti could bear it no longer and protested: 'Honestly Lyda! Just look at what is going on there now!'[15] Under the occupation she did nothing to hide her connections, as distinguished Germans, friends from her Berlin days, came to visit her in Paris. Among the pupils coming to avenue de Versailles there were German officers; gossip was rife, stimulated by Pierre's emergence as a top-ranking cellist. He drove his own car, a Simca 5: the permit was a concession to his infirmity as he was unable to walk long distances. The pianist Jacques Genty remembers touring northern France on deserted roads in this little car, Fournier begging him not to go over 60 km per hour: they might waste petrol or blow a gasket.

But above all Lyda was said to be the mistress of 'a high-ranking officer'; people often added 'of the Gestapo' but the truth was different. The so-called 'Gestapo officer' was in fact a civilian, Alex Spengler, a German industrialist[16] of the old school and a cousin of the writer Oswald Spengler, author of *The Decline of the West*. He had known Lyda in Berlin when she was Frau Piatigorsky; he was not a Nazi and refused to join his embassy's Franco-German Association. He had been married to the distinguished Australian-Jewish violinist Alma Moodie, whose chronic depression, exacerbated by her husband's infidelities, led her eventually to take her own life.[17]

When Spengler arrived in Paris he telephoned Lyda. He had a flat in Boulevard de Montmorency, furnished with his own possessions brought from Germany, including fine drawings and paintings. Would Lyda's husband care to come over on New Year's Eve to play the Schubert Quintet with the Loewenguth Quartet?

Alex Spengler had first set eyes on Lyda at a Berlin party in 1927 and had fallen instantly and incurably in love. So consuming indeed was his passion that in Paris he soon attempted to persuade Pierre to cede his wife: he, Spengler, would provide for Jean Pierre who would want for nothing, etc. The idea didn't appeal to Pierre who declined. As for Lyda, when she heard of this initiative she flew into a rage, rushed to Spengler's flat and slapped her tenacious suitor's face. Afterwards, very drunk, Spengler apologized to them both, begging them to remain his friends: 'You are the only *souls* I have in Paris!'[18]

As the war was nearing its end and he was about to return to Germany, Spengler called on the Fourniers with two violins, a Guarnerius and a Gagliano, and one request. The instruments were to be sold and the proceeds to be transferred to the Davos clinic where his son Georg was gravely ill with tuberculosis. This was done; Georg, however, did not survive.

Two years later Fournier saw Spengler again in Cologne. Destroying himself with drink, he was barely recognizable as the friend they had known in Paris.

*   *   *

Fournier had appeared in Berlin several times before the war; the last occasion was a performance of the Haydn D major Concerto with the Philharmonic under Paul Paray. Six years later, Furtwängler showed that he had not forgotten his pre-war promise: he invited Fournier to give the same concerto under his own baton. The cellist hesitated, but not for long. He asked if he might substitute the Schumann concerto and this was agreed. He was to accept a similar invitation to Munich the following year. After one of these concerts a group of French STO deportees went backstage to tell Fournier how moved they had been 'to hear a great French artist'.[19]

Furtwängler had refused to perform in Paris 'so long as a single jackboot remained there'.[20] Why did Fournier not show a corresponding restraint? He answered this many years later, when he admitted that his initial scruples had been swept away by 'a mixture of recklessness, vanity and the thirst for a unique musical experience, never yet having played with the giant Furtwängler'.[21] Loyal to a fellow musician, Henri Sauguet took an indulgent view: 'When Furtwängler invites you, you don't say no.'[22]

Furtwängler, Cortot and Fournier had more in common than great musical achievement and a certain political ineptitude. Many artists come from eccentric backgrounds; these three musicians had suffered an unusual degree of isolation in childhood. Cortot 'became a boy without having been a child'.[23] The seventh and last in a family of a middle-aged couple in an austere household, this lonely and solemn boy put into his work the energy most children put into their games. The young Furtwängler, quickly perceived to be exceptionally gifted, was removed from school and educated by private tutors; Fournier, also, was taught at home because of his illness, and was extremely lonely as a result. Did this deprivation feed a tendency to stand apart from things, to close the eyes to the crueller realities about them and focus simply on their art? Fournier often spoke of 'escape into music'. He shared with Furtwängler a deep devotion to the thought and music of Beethoven, an impatience with people he deemed unsympathetic and with the trivialities of social life; what mattered was the celebration of music. And Fournier was still waging his private battle against the diverse effects of polio and protecting himself with his talisman, the cello. It is certain that all three men placed their work and ambition above all other considerations and paid for it later to a greater or lesser degree. With the rest of the civilized world, Fournier was deeply shocked by the inescapable truth revealed at the opening of the death camps: material for painful and prolonged reflection. Thirty years later, asked to read a passage to round off a long and searching interview, he chose an astonishing extract from a letter of Kafka's:

> We are forsaken like children lost in the woods. When you stand before me and look at me, what do you know of my sufferings and what do I know of yours? And if I fell at your feet and cried and told you, would you know any more about me than you know about hell when they say it is hot and sets one shivering? Therefore we men should stand before each other with as much awe, thoughtfulness and love as before the gates of hell.[24]

It is difficult not to make the connection. Questioned about the war by another interviewer, Fournier answered simply 'The war was a black mark on my life.'[25]

Should musicians have ceased plying their trade? Occupied France would have been even more wretched a place. Some people believed that silence was the only proper choice; others that the need to earn a living for one's family justification enough, and it is a fact that noticeably few performing artists became involved in Resistance activities. It is also true that among non-collaborators professional envy sometimes lurked under virtuous restraint.

A small incident which occurred in 1943–44 was typical of the period. Late one night, when the family were all asleep at rue Lesueur, the doorbell rang. On the landing was a distinguished soprano with an urgent request. Could Pierre use his contacts to obtain her an 'aryanization certificate'? Pierre agreed and eventually the paper was safely delivered into her hands. Months later came the purges, and he was surprised to find out that one of his fiercest detractors had been this very singer. Still later, at the Menton Festival of 1953, dressed in the fashionable corsair breeches of the day, she was making her way backstage to congratulate the cellist. Finding her way blocked by an icily angry Lyda, she had to leave.

Notes

1. Cited in J.-A. Azéma *From Munich to the Liberation 1938–1944. Cambridge History of Modern France*, Vol. 6, Editions de la Maison des Sciences de l'Homme and C.U.P. p. 39.
2. The Resistant Pierre Brossolette, tortured, threw himself out of a window rather than betray his comrades. Marcel Déat, journalist politician and fanatical pro-Nazi, hid in an Italian convent at the Liberation and died in 1955.
3. Max Jacob died of pneumonia during his transfer to Drancy prison camp.
4. A. Gold and R. Fizdale *Misia, the Life of Misia Sert*, New York: Macmillan 1980, p. 240.
5. Philippe Thibaud in conversation with the author.
6. Marguerite Long *Au Piano avec Gabriel Fauré*, Paris: Julliard 1963, pp. 171–173.
7. Philippe Thibaud recalled that a Mozart sonata recording, made for Pathé Marconi by his father and Marguerite Long, vanished for about fifteen years. The reason emerged when it reappeared: Long had tried to have the discs suppressed because she disliked her own contribution.
8. As an observer in an artillery regiment Roger Thibaud had found himself isolated at Harancourt during the German bombing, hence the delay in the news of his death reaching headquarters. After the war, Colonel Philippe Thibaud, in charge of displaced persons in the Tyrol, organized concerts in which his father appeared several times.
9. Henri Sauguet to Francis Poulenc, 26 August 1940. *Francis Poulenc Correspondance 1915–1963*, ed. Hélène de Wendel, Paris: Editions du Seuil 1967, p. 121.
10. Le Triton, founded by Pierre-Octave Ferroud, and La Sérénade, run by Yvonne de Casa Fuerte, were two of the leading Paris music societies promoting the work of contemporary composers between the two wars. On the Triton committee, besides French musicians, were the Swiss Arthur Honegger, the Romanian Marcel Mihalovici and the Hungarian Tibor Harsányi. Le Triton disappeared after Ferroud's tragic death in 1936. La Sérénade included Darius Milhaud, Igor Markevitch, Francis Poulenc, Georges Auric, Nicolas Nabokov and Henri Sauguet. It was financed by a committee of leading society figures. Milhaud spoke of the 'charming snobbery which [allowed] La Sérénade to survive'. Nicolas Nabokov recalled the group's Salle Gaveau concerts as 'elegant society affairs with a touch of the same kind of snobbishness that surrounded Diaghilev's ballet season'. (Darius Milhaud *Notes sans musique*, Paris: Julliard 1949, pp. 234–236. Nicolas Nabokov *Old Friends and New Music*, London: Hamish Hamilton 1951, p. 111).
11. The pianist Jacques Genty, who partnered Fournier in Paris and on tour, recalls the extreme caution of young Resistance members which made it almost impossible to

communicate with them. In his case a recklessly heavy hint finally did the trick and he was asked 'Do you want to join us?'

12. Louis Beydts (1895–1953), musical director of the Opéra-comique 1950–1953. When Jean-Louis Barrault heard Beydts' score for Cervantes' *Numance*, he told the composer that his music was 'concave'. Unruffled, Beydts replied *'Je ne suis pas un homme qu'on vexe.'* ('I'm not someone you can vex.')
13. Camille Kiesgen to JFF, 20 January 1994.
14. H. L. Kirk *Pablo Casals*, London: Hutchinson 1974, p. 416.
15. The late Nikita Magaloff in conversation with the author.
16. Spengler's Frankfurt firm manufactured *gazogènes*, machines which converted wood or coal into combustible fuel, and which can be seen in contemporary newsreels as two clumsy parallel pipes fitted to car roofs.
17. Alma Moodie (1900–1943), pupil of Cesar Thomson and Carl Flesch, appeared as a child prodigy with Max Reger. She taught at the State Academy of Frankfurt and premièred the concertos of Krenek and Pfitzner. The latter concerto is dedicated to her.
18. JFF Archive.
19. *Service du travail obligatoire* or compulsory work service, under which 650 000 Frenchmen went or were sent to Germany, some in exchange for freed POWs. Suffering from malnutrition and solitude, 35 000 died in exile, many from tuberculosis, and some under Allied bombing.
20. Elisabeth Furtwängler in conversation with the author.
21. Pierre Fournier, Radio Suisse Romande, 7 April 1975.
22. The late Henri Sauguet in conversation with the author.
23. Bernard Gavoty *Alfred Cortot*, Paris: Buchet Chastel 1977, p. 24.
24. Franz Kafka to Oskar Pollak, 9 November 1903. Franz Kafka *Letters to Friends, Family and Editors*, tr. R. and C. Winston, London: John Calder 1978. Pierre Fournier, ORTF. 5 July 1976. I am indebted to the Kafka expert Dr Ritchie Robertson of St John's College, Oxford, for the source of this quotation. Since it is not very famous, he thought Fournier must have known his Kafka very well to come up with it (Dr Ritchie Robertson to the author, 10 August 1990). The following is the original of the Kafka quotation on page 43:

> *Verlassen sind wir doch wie verirrte Kinder im Walde. Wenn Du vor mir stehst und mich ansiehst, was weißt Du von den Schmerzen, die in mir sind und was weiß ich von den Deinen. Und wenn ich mich vor Dir niederwerfen würde und weinen und erzählen, was wüßtest Du von mir mehr als von der Hölle, wenn Dir jemand erzählt, sie ist heiß und fürchterlich. Schon darum sollten wir Menschen vor einander so ehrfürchtig, so nachdenklich, so liebend stehn wie vor dem Eingang zur Hölle.*

25. See note 21.

PART II
(1944–1956)

10   Aftermath

In June 1944, on orders from the Allies through the BBC, the Resistance was engaged in operations to distract the enemy. After De Gaulle's appeal for national mobilization weapons were dropped by parachute and there was such a large number of volunteers that guerilla activity had to be curbed by General Koenig, supreme head of the FFI (*Forces Françaises de l'Intérieur*) who feared that matters might get out of hand. Politically the Resistance was preparing to move into positions of power.

As the Liberation progressed the former underdogs became the justicers. Avenging Nazi and Vichy atrocities, old scores were settled with savagery, giving rein to the worst instincts of their castigators.

With the Nazis on the road to defeat and yet more suffering revealed, the Resistance had no judicial structure ready for the prosecution of collaborators. From June to September 1944 anarchy reigned: muddle, ferocity, errors, abuse, acts of private vengeance, crimes by 'volunteers of the eleventh hour' posing as Resistants, and summary justice without supporting evidence. Fearing that notorious collaborators might escape, the Resistance took the law into its own hands, in some instances even breaking into prisons or shooting released prisoners.[1] Things became so bad that on 31 August 1944 Pasteur Boegner wrote an article in *Le Figaro* headed 'Against Violence and Hatred'. In the same newspaper the following month François Mauriac begged for compassion, especially for the young and ignorant.

At the end of 1943 Pierre and Lyda left their flat in the family house at avenue de Versailles. They stayed at 5 rue du Docteur Blanche nearby until the following summer when they settled in the Passy flat at 15 rue Lesueur which would be their home for the next twelve years.

The rue Lesueur flat received a visit from the FFI in the shape of Sergeant M., an apprentice butcher in civilian life. By chance Fournier's former duo partner Jacques Genty, who was a member of the Resistance, was driving with his men through the neighbourhood. On an impulse he told the driver to stop and went up to the flat. He was met at the door by the sergeant pointing a revolver at him. Genty protested that he was 'one of them' and showed his armband and number to prove it. The sergeant went off to check Genty's credentials (telephones were kept working in occupied Paris), warning that he had come to make arrests. Genty told him that he would vouch for the family. The sergeant left, but not before he had removed pictures, ornaments and jewellery, 'to pay the lawyer's fees' he said.

The lawyer in question, Maître X., also called at rue Lesueur. Fournier explained that since he was on only half his salary he could not possibly afford the fees. Hanging on the wall and in the lawyer's line of vision were two Rembrandt sketches, a parting gift from Alex Spengler. Maître B. told Fournier not to worry: pointing at the sketches he said they would do very well, and left with them under his arm.[2]

The National Purge Committee for the performing arts came into being on 17 February 1945 by decree published the following day in the *Journal Officiel*. Events, however, had moved faster. At the Conservatoire in the autumn term of 1944 graffiti had appeared in the lavatories: 'Fournier à Berlin.' A musicians' purge committee sat on 16 October to examine his case; it was chaired by a colleague, the cellist Maurice Maréchal. In Fournier's file is a list of artists to appear before the committee. On the back of this is the additional mention of Fournier's two German visits with the words 'M. Maréchal will supply the details.'[3]

The formal charges against Fournier under the newly-defined offence of 'non-criminal collaboration' consisted of his 83 broadcasts from Radio Paris (under the control of the Germans), and the two visits to Germany, in 1943 to Berlin, and the following year to Munich. He was also accused of 'lack of patriotism, all the more grievous since he [was] professor at the Conservatoire and remunerated by the State'. The penalty called for was one year's suspension of professional activity as from 15 December 1944, the file to be forwarded to the Finance Ministry for consideration.

There is evidence of haste and improvisation in the compiling of the dossier. A handwritten and unsigned page, clumsily torn out of a child's exercise book, lists additional questions to be put to Fournier at his hearing, on the provenance of furniture, paintings and drawings at rue Lesueur, the relationship to Spengler, and the details of his income. Nowhere in the file is there any mention of the lawyer Maître X.

Fournier's hearing took place on the morning of 11 December 1944. He was not given a chair. He made the following statement:

> I accept the figure of 83 broadcasts from Radio Paris and the fees of 182 000 francs. These broadcasts, which took place between 1 January 1941 and July 1944, were purely musical (chamber music and orchestra).
> I played only under French conductors.
> I gave two concerts in Germany: in November 1943 in Berlin and in March 1944 in Munich, conducted by Furtwängler who was a friend of more than ten years' standing. I was paid 45 000 francs for the concert in Berlin and nothing for the concert in Munich: prevailing conditions prevented the transfer of the funds to me.
> I am prepared to give the following information about the details of my removal [to rue Lesueur]:

It was undertaken by the firm Pierre Crassier. I have at home no *objet d'art* owned by
M. Spengler. That gentleman had been a friend of my wife's since 1927. We were in
contact with him but I wish to point out that he had no official position in France.
Before his departure M. Spengler was obliged to send all his possessions to Germany.
My personal status is as follows: I have been permanently exempt from military service
since 1938 due to a heart condition. I am a professor at the Conservatoire although at
present suspended on half salary, the full salary being 36 000 francs per annum. My
solo work brings me considerably more. My last income tax return shows the figure of
160 000 francs for the year 1943.

According to the judgment, bearing the later date of 5 February 1945 and signed
by the Minister, René Capitant, Fournier was suspended from teaching and
public performance for one year as from 15 December 1944 (four days after the
hearing). However, on the file copy of this document the words 'one year' have
been crossed out by hand in ink, and 'six months' initialled RC written in the
margin. Also in the file and dated 11 December 1944 (the day of the hearing) was
a letter to the Ministry from the Director of the Conservatoire, Claude
Delvincourt, enclosing a petition from twenty students in favour of Fournier. The
original sentence had been light; the revised one was minimal. Why the
handwritten amendment contrary to all judicial practice, even given the chaos of
the time?

Although generally speaking the *épuration* punished above all the
unimportant and the young, and was 'more indulgent to the notables',[5] in the
entertainment world this was not always the case: some actors and musicians
escaped all censure when others were sent to prison. We may discount Fournier's
disability which was irrelevant: France still counted a great many wounded from
the First World War. On the other hand, the fact that Lyda had Jewish blood had
made her vulnerable throughout the Occupation and the protection she enjoyed
from distinguished German friends might well have melted away under the
increased savagery of the Gestapo as the Allies were closing in. It is difficult, Paris
being Paris, to believe that even this well-kept secret (few people knew her father
was Jewish) was not aired in some corridors; equally difficult to imagine that it
was not mentioned when Fournier and his father visited General Koenig,
supreme head of the FFI, and laid Pierre's case before him: we know that Koenig
was sympathetic.[6] Lastly, there remains the testimony of contemporaries that
apart from his stature as an artist, Pierre Fournier as a person was held in very
high regard. It is more than likely therefore that the sum of these considerations
led René Capitant to take out his fountain pen and amend the judgment in
Fournier's favour. On whose authority? De Gaulle is known to have had a
'hands-on' approach to these matters, so it may not be unreasonable to hazard
the opinion that the permission came from on high, through the sympathetic
hands of General Koenig, De Gaulle's Chief of Staff. The death of René Capitant,
however, robs us of any certainty.

In the end punishment fatigue set in, 'a combination of impatience and
lassitude'.[7] Some sentences were not fully served. The soprano Germaine Lubin,
condemned for life to loss of civil rights and confiscation of property

(*dégradation nationale*), saw her sentence cut to five years. Antoine Pinay, a Pétainist in 1940, became a minister in 1948 and later a reassuring national figurehead. The special courts, 'barely registered by public opinion'[8] were dismantled in 1951.

Notes

1. Herbert Lottman *The People's Anger*, London: Hutchinson 1986.
2. This episode has a postscript. Some time later, Sergeant M. was prosecuted for an offence in common law. Called as a witness for the defence, Lyda testified that on his visit to rue Lesueur he had shown her no violence. The sergeant thanked her afterwards: '*Vous avez été très chic, Madame.*' ('That was very sporting of you, Madame.')
3. The listed artists were Jean Doyen, the Loewenguth Quartet, Ginette Neveu (with the note '52 broadcasts'), Pierre Fournier ('83 broadcasts'), Marcel Dupré [the composer and organist] ('concert at Notre-Dame organized by the Germans') and Charles Panzéra [the Swiss-born baritone] ('119 broadcasts'). The name Claude Crussard is crossed out.
4. The judgment is headed 'Ministry of National Education: Fine Arts and Performing Arts'.
5. J-P. Rioux *The Fourth Republic 1944–1958*, *Cambridge History of Modern France*, Vol. 7. *Editions de la Maison des Sciences de l'Homme* and CUP 1987, p. 36.
6. General Koenig commanded a Free French brigade which in 1942 at Bir Hakeim in Algeria held out for fifteen days before Rommel's forces broke through; he lost a quarter of his men. In 1944 he became supreme commander of the FFI (Forces Françaises de l'Intérieur).
7. J.-P. Rioux, op. cit., p. 35.
8. Id.

11 New Horizons

Although conscious in his own way of the family stress of 1944–45, the seven-year-old Jean Pierre nevertheless enjoyed a sense of security. By his own account he was petted by his mother under the amused and indulgent gaze of his father. Increasingly taken up with his career, however, Fournier left the boy's education entirely in the hands of his wife. He had had an absent father between the ages of eight and twelve during the First World War; he was to be an absent father himself for considerably longer.

Sometimes it was as if he needed to stifle his natural warmth. When as a small child Jean Pierre once went up to him wanting a cuddle, Pierre appeared distant. Lyda reproached him 'Why don't you act like a tender father towards the little one? He needs your affection.' Smiling at his small son, Pierre answered 'Because I'm a cold Frenchman.' Then suddenly, in contradiction of his own words, he swept the child up in his arms.

Besides the piano, Jean Pierre started the cello, and Fournier laughed to see him holding the bow quite naturally, mimicking the father. The Prelude of Bach's First Suite was to be the apogée of Jean Pierre's cello career, after which he focused his energies solely on the piano.

By mid-June 1945, Fournier's suspension was over and the family took a summer holiday at the Hotel Sarciron at Le Mont-Dore. In the local cinema they caught sight of André Gide, an unmistakable figure 'with his little cap and grumpy expression'[1] who had once reminded Ilya Ehrenburg of an Ibsen pastor. Fournier approached the writer with caution. Gide at the time considered himself something of an authority on Chopin and, although he played the piano badly, he was filmed coaching a young pianist bar by bar through a Chopin piece. Fournier mentioned his love for the composer. 'What instrument do you play?' asked Gide. 'The cello' answered Fournier without irony. 'Would you like some music?' A happy routine was then established: every day the old writer listened to a Bach Suite in his room; afterwards the two spent the afternoon at the local 'flea-pit'.

When Gide produced a German review with an article he needed in translation, Lyda offered to help. Gide hesitated: it was a difficult text on philosophy. Lyda ploughed her way through it in French. The old misogynist thanked her with admiration and some surprise.

At the end of the holiday Jean Pierre left his toy bear at the hotel. A few days later it arrived in Paris, forwarded by Gide with a note and Shakespeare's most celebrated stage direction: 'Exit, pursued by a bear.'

World travel picked up after the war and Jascha Heifetz was one of the first to come over from the States. He was in Paris to play for the GIs at the Palais de Chaillot and spent the evening at rue Lesueur. The next day he brought Jean Pierre a colossal toy car. Hearing about Pierre's suspension, he declared a little rashly that no such thing could ever happen to an artist in America. He listened to Pierre playing Bach's D major Suite and as he left he whispered to Lyda 'Your husband is a prince.'

Another renewed contact was with the cellist Pablo Casals, at the Hotel Claridge in Paris the following year. Fournier mentioned a news item which had disturbed him: a massacre by partisans of a trainload of unarmed franquist soldiers returning to Spain from the eastern front. Casals was jubilant. 'They should be exterminated' he said. Fournier was shocked. The corollaries of total war were beyond him.

When he returned to his duties at the Conversatoire, one of his students, Madeleine Bourreil, shyly approached him to say how sorry she was 'about... everything'. He told her not to worry: he was going to London.[2]

*   *   *

In London Fournier was frank about his Occupation concerts, and found an evenhandedness, an unwillingness to condemn, which touched him and led to a lasting attachment to Britain. Another reason he liked visiting the UK was the audiences. Like Prokofiev earlier, he had little patience with the insincerities of the artists' room after a Paris concert.[3] These moments caused his expression to freeze, he forgot names, and his son once heard a wailing voice complain 'Your father didn't look at me when I was speaking to him!' Fournier's absent-mindedness was a wall which protected his privacy. Many times he referred an interviewer to Jean Pierre 'who would explain much better than he would himself'. This allowed him to avoid reminiscing in public, which he detested.

More congenial to him than sophisticated gatherings were the small provincial music clubs run by enthusiastic music-lovers.[4] Touring the British Isles he found the same sincerity when, journeying happily to Sheffield, Newcastle, Liverpool or Dublin, he shared the bill with the great Benno Moiseiwitsch and played poker with him in the train.

With its comforting associations in life as well as music, London held a special place in his affections: the concerts with Schnabel which sparked off his international career, the unsnobbish audiences, the pupil-friends whom he preferred to call his 'young professionals', the tolerant atmosphere in which he could shed some of the tension of Paris while keeping a vigilant eye open for the latest good restaurant. At Abbey Road in October 1949 he made one of his happiest recordings: the Dvořák Concerto with the Philharmonia and Rafael Kubelik.

To London he brought something quite new, and soon built up a faithful audience. In the words of Amaryllis Fleming:

> When Fournier first appeared in England after the war, the colour and nuance he produced with the bow, and the subtlety of emotional shading, particularly with his vibrato, was a total revelation. It was like the *chiaroscuro* of an Impressionist's brush.[5]

In Zurich also the public took him to its heart from the first post-war concert in 1946, later bursting each time into instant applause at the first glimpse of the cane and cello.

Fournier's return to the French concert platform took place in the autumn of 1946 at the Champs Elysées Theatre with the OSCC (*Orchestre de la Société des Concerts du Conservatoire*) under Charles Munch. During the Sunday evening rehearsal there were rumours that a demonstration might disrupt the concert and the musicians refuse to play. Well in advance, Louis Beydts' friends, Michel Girard and Jean Pétin, posted themselves outside the theatre. When Fournier appeared on the platform, Jeanine Krettly and her husband heard a few boos, countered with cries of '*Ce n'est pas trop tôt!*' ('And about time!') After that the concert went off peacefully. Friends gathered at rue Lesueur afterwards: the critic Claude Rostand, the journalist Philippe Boegner, Dr Jacques Landolt and the lawyer-photographer Roger Hauert. When the party was in full swing Lyda suddenly noticed that Pierre had disappeared. She found him lying on the bed, white-faced, sweating, breathing with difficulty. Dr Landolt drove him to see the cardiologist Professor Delamare. Fournier was told that polio had left him prone to tachycardia and this would need monitoring. In the event it was not until 1983 in Atlanta that the trouble would return, obliging him to spend a day in bed.

* * *

In Europe music was returning to life, but not without difficulty. Even some of the greatest orchestras had problems getting back to their pre-war form. Often they were overworked: in 1947 the Berlin Philharmonic, touring the British zone in Germany, gave a concert a day for three weeks. But the wheels were turning, rather hampered in Paris, Poulenc noted, by the purges. Indeed, Poulenc has left us his own view of the musical scene in Paris at the time. He deplored the fact that union rates were killing off the music societies (Sérénade, Pleïade), and complained that the Opéra was in upheaval since its Director, Jacques Rouché, had left. But there had been a bonus: the appointment of the composer Claude Delvincourt to the Conservatoire where Darius Milhaud, returning from the USA, was to take up a composition class. However, Poulenc was irritated that instead of resounding with music, Paris was bristling with society events. He observed London with some envy: at Covent Garden a new generation of young music-lovers were 'screaming with enthusiasm' as they discovered *Pelléas*.[6]

On an early tour of the Netherlands, Fournier was unable to find a hotel room in Amsterdam. His old friend from student days, Etiennette Tombeck, now Mme

Correa, offered to put him up. The flat was on the third floor with no lift. Climbing the steep staircase Fournier asked her if she was angry with him. She knew he was referring to his wartime concerts. 'Let's forget it, mon petit Pierre' she answered. Forty years later, recalling her return to France at that time, she said 'I could hardly recognize the place. It was then that I understood how much, after the exodus, people wanted an end to the fighting.' Of Fournier she said 'He needed to avenge his disability.'[7]

The atmosphere at rue Lesueur was full of life when Fournier was at home, practising and teaching – dinner parties, games of 'murder' and lots of visitors – but when he was on tour Lyda found his absence oppressive and she tended to press Jean Pierre to stay at home. He was studying the piano with Marie Obolenska, a grumpy lady of the minor nobility who had been Lyda's first teacher in St Petersburg.[8] Obolenska visited the house twice a week. Once, when Etiennette came to lunch, Jean Pierre played his party piece. 'Don't do your infant prodigy number' said Lyda with feigned severity.

On a visit Schnabel caught sight of Jean Pierre's music on the piano. What followed was a surprise performance of Czerny's exercises.

Jean Pierre had little time to be lonely, with his school friends from the Cours Hattemer coming and going. His cousin Philippe Fournier was entrusted to the family for several months while his parents Paul and Anna were in the Far East. But Jean Pierre was not allowed to enter the Paris Conservatoire. Lyda had reservations about a certain harsh and percussive style of piano playing which had little feeling for legato or for the depth of the instrument, and which she saw as widespread enough at the Conservatoire to put her off. She made an exception of the pianist and teacher Marcel Ciampi (1891–1980), but that didn't make her change her mind: Jean Pierre was kept away. He was to study later in Geneva with Nikita Magaloff and have some lessons with Cortot.

The Prague Spring of 1947 gave Fournier his début with the Czech Philharmonic in a performance of the Dvořák Concerto with Rafael Kubelik. He enjoyed the effervescent cosmopolitan atmosphere of a place full of artists – David Oistrakh, Emil Gilels and Shostakovich among them. He was to return the following year to find that all the fizz had gone: the communist threat was becoming a reality.

Notes

1. Pierre Fournier, Radio Suisse Romande, 7 April 1975.
2. Madeleine Bourreil in conversation with the author.
3. Prokofiev complained 'All these countesses, princesses and silly snobs make me angry. They act as if everything in the world was invented to amuse *them*.' (Nicolas Nabokov *Old Friends and New Music*, London: Hamish Hamilton 1951, p. 112.)
4. '*Ce que l'on oublie toujours, c'est l'importance des amateurs.*' ('What one always forgets is the importance of amateurs.') Said by Francis Poulenc to Tony Mayer, and recounted by him to the author.
5. Amaryllis Fleming, Pierre Fournier Celebration Concert, Royal College of Music, 16 February 1987.

6. Francis Poulenc to Darius Milhaud, 25 July 1949, in *Francis Poulenc 'Echo and Source': Selected Correspondence 1915–1963*. Tr. and ed. Sidney Buckland. London: Gollancz 1991, p. 188.
7. The late Etiennette Tombeck-Correa in conversation with the author.
8. Obolenska, like Artur Schnabel and Leonid Kreutzer, had studied with Yessipova, pupil and later wife of Theodor Leschetizky.

12   'Four Spirits'

Certain moments in music – a season, a festival or a single evening – remain etched in our memories when transcendental artistry and a sensitive audience converge. In the years following the Second World War there were a number of such moments with the return to London of the great international figures previously scattered by persecution and war: Kirsten Flagstad, Jascha Heifetz, José Iturbi, Andrés Segovia, Yehudi Menuhin, Pablo Casals, Victor de Sabata.... There was the birth of new festivals such as Edinburgh and the revisiting of old ones: Salzburg, Bayreuth and Glyndebourne.

In spite of the austerity, London in the late forties had a certain freshness of spirit; status and greed still more or less knew their place. Any fanatical pursuit of success was seen as vulgar, and as the poet John Heath-Stubbs recalled, 'a certain innocence co-inhered with the squalor.' George Melly, remembering the 'Bohemian no-go area' of Soho, called it 'an innocent time'.[1]

An antidote, first to danger and then to drabness, the arts drew an ever-growing public. At the height of the war the National Gallery had provided thousands of Londoners with an oasis of music for the price of a shilling. After the bombing of the Queen's Hall, the proms continued in the echoing Royal Albert Hall for an audience which included many servicemen and women discovering orchestral music for the first time. With the war ended, the same public heard Furtwängler, Casals, Bruno Walter, Richard Strauss. The excitement of these and other discoveries was far more important to the concertgoer than any particular artist's possibly dubious involvements under the enemy's boot: the matter simply did not enter into the enjoyment of music. It is an interesting fact that the most concerted antagonism towards such artists came from prosperous musicians, safely ensconced in the United States, 'non-heroes demanding heroism of others',[2] rather as if direct contact with Hitler's bombs had paradoxically left the Londoner less judgmental. Among artists in Europe there was a certain solidarity. The German baritone Hans Hotter recalled many years later 'We artists were close... After the war we all had problems.'[3]

Musical contacts had already been established between the UK and France before the war ended. The BBC's Head of Music asked Tony Mayer to suggest six French artists – three conductors and three instrumentalists – for a series of broadcasts of French music. As a result Charles Munch, Paul Paray and Roger Désormière, the violinist Ginette Neveu, the pianist Nicole Henriot and Pierre Fournier all came ('very willingly indeed' Mayer says) to London. By the end of the series Mayer had become, in his own words, 'the world's expert on the layout of the area around Victoria Station'.

But there was a gap in London's musical life and Mayer decided to fill it. As he remembers 'With the help of the ardent francophile Felix Aprahamian [later deputy music critic of the *Sunday Times*] and a micro-grant of about £400 per annum from the National Committee, [he] founded the London concerts of French music under the auspices first of the National Committee itself, then, after the Liberation, of the French embassy. All the posters were in the French colours.'[4]

The first concert, on 25 June 1942, was devoted to Debussy. Between *Fêtes galantes* and *Chansons de Bilitis* sung by Maggie Teyte, the lights were turned down for the flautist Gareth Morris to play *Syrinx* offstage. The critics approved:

> If the French Committee for National Liberation orders all its affairs as beautifully as the Wigmore Hall concerts [...] then the outlook for Europe becomes brighter. [The] new series began with an evening of Fauré, in which everything had been perfectly planned: music, artists, provision of a well-printed booklet containing all the Verlaine poems whose settings by Fauré and Debussy are to be heard during the cycle. Miss Kathleen Long bore the weight of the programme....[5]

The Times considered that 'the great public [had] still to be won over to a taste for the Gallic temper in music' but that it could 'learn sensibility from French composers'.[6]

From 1942 to 1966 there were 112 concerts, and few works were repeated. During the war the performers were British: Benjamin Britten played the celesta in Darius Milhaud's *Machines agricoles* for a fee of £3. He returned ten years later to accompany the tenor Peter Pears. When the war ended French artists came to Britain and Fournier was among the first invited. He gave the Couperin *Pièces en concert* and Haydn's D major concerto with the Leighton Lucas Orchestra on 5 April 1946; a recital came later: Fauré, Debussy, Poulenc and Honegger with Ernest Lush on 15 November 1951. On the first of the two occasions, Gendron remarked to Tony Mayer that it was obvious that talent was not enough for an engagement: 'you also had to be a collaborator'.[7] Gendron's old bitterness against Fournier had not been alleviated by early professional setbacks in Paris: the younger cellist 'tried to overreach himself, whereas Fournier always knew how to wait'.[8]

Among artists returning to Europe in 1946 was the Austrian pianist Artur Schnabel, leaving New York and his Central Park apartment for the Hyde Park Hotel and Kensington Gardens, almost within shouting distance of the Royal Albert Hall. Here Walter Legge had organized a series of Beethoven concerts. Besides the five piano concertos, Schnabel gave the Triple Concerto with Fournier (who was already under contract with Voix de son Maître in Paris) and Legge's newest find, the Belgian violinist Arthur Grumiaux; Alceo Galliera conducted the Philharmonia.

...M. Arthur Grumiaux, a young Belgian violinist with a classical outlook and an almost feminine delicacy, and M. Pierre Fournier, the French cellist with a more romantic temperament...[9]

Fournier's partnership with Schnabel (who had already heard about him from Joseph Szigeti) was a turning point in his career, comparable only, all things considered, with his joining the Krettly Quartet as a very young cellist in 1923. It was the catalyst which sparked off a major international career and world recognition. Musically Schnabel and Fournier did not always agree (Fournier sometimes found Schnabel's tempi in Beethoven and Brahms too hurried) but they resembled each other in one respect: a critic wrote of Schnabel 'The source of many of [his] most wonderful effects is almost sinister in its simplicity. He plays what is written.'[10]

For Fournier 1947 was a golden year confirming all his hopes. It marked both the inauguration of the Edinburgh Festival and the conjunction of two anniversaries: the 150th of Schubert's birth and the 50th of Brahms' death. Rudolf Bing, founder of the Festival, and his assistant and later successor Ian Hunter had already worked together the previous year. They decided to form a piano quartet with Schnabel, Szigeti, William Primrose and Fournier to perform the entire chamber music of Schubert and Brahms. And since the year was also the centenary of Mendelssohn's death, his D minor Trio was included in the series.

In his autobiography Szigeti was to write of Fournier at this time:

The rediscovery of Fournier's immense talent when we started rehearsing for the first Edinburgh Festival (1947) was a revelation to me. I had last heard him in the middle 1930s and was now tremendously impressed by the Apollonian beauty and poise that his playing had acquired in the intervening years.[11]

In August the quartet rehearsed at Sils Maria in the Engadine. Listening in the Waldhaus garden, Pauline Mayer could detect Szigeti's intensity and the bossiness of Schnabel who, for Lyda's taste, talked too much. Pauline noticed the charm bracelet with two little cellos on Lyda's wrist. 'Piatigorsky and Fournier' Lyda explained helpfully, rather like the man pointing to the Tour Eiffel and saying 'Paris'.[12]

On sunny afternoons at the Waldhaus Fournier found long rehearsals more oppressive than usual. His older partners Schnabel and Szigeti seemed endlessly entwined in philosophical discussion while he looked mournfully out of the window, longing to be out of doors in the sparkling landscape of the Engadine.

Otto Klemperer arrived uninvited at a rehearsal and told Schnabel he was playing too loud. Fournier was not surprised: he had already experienced the conductor's odd behaviour two months earlier at Baden-Baden. While rehearsing the newly-written Martinů Concerto, Klemperer had appeared so confused and lost that Fournier had substituted the Haydn D major Concerto to avoid embarrassment. (The Haydn was given without a rehearsal and received an ovation.[13])

The quartet had a triumph in Edinburgh. The four strongly contrasted temperaments had been closely watched by the critics for signs of inflated egos, but Neville Cardus wrote that 'they played ... like four spirits, not merely like four consummate musicians'.[14] It was music-making no listener would forget, 'peaks of experience' in Szigeti's own words.[15] They also appeared as soloists, and on 2 September Fournier played the Haydn D major Concerto with Sir John Barbirolli and the Hallé Orchestra. Robert Ponsonby, later to become the festival's director, spent an evening at the Caledonian Hotel with Pierre and Lyda, talking about the Ealing comedies which Parisians were queuing to see in the rue Marbeuf.

Notes

1. John Heath-Stubbs *Letter to David Wright* from *Collected Poems 1943–1987*, Manchester: Carcanet Press 1988. George Melly Introduction to Daniel Farson's *Soho in the Fifties*, London: Michael Joseph 1987. Both cited in Andrew Sinclair *War like a Wasp*, London: Hamish Hamilton 1989.
2. Yehudi Menuhin *Unfinished Journey*, London: Macdonald and Jane's 1976.
3. BBC Radio 3, 3 March 1989.
4. Tony Mayer to the author, 1995.
5. *The New Statesman and Nation*, 11 September 1943.
6. *The Times*, 6 October 1943.
7. Tony Mayer in conversation with the author.
8. Gabriel Dussurget in conversation with the author.
9. *The Times*, 1 June 1946.
10. *Musical Times*, No. 1240, June 1946. ('W.G.'.)
11. Joseph Szigeti *With Strings Attached*, New York: Knopf 1947. This quotation appears in the 1949 edition, p. 358.
12. Pauline Samuelson in conversation with the author.
13. *Badener Tageblatt*, 6 June 1947.
14. *Manchester Guardian*, September 1947 (Neville Cardus).
15. Joseph Szigeti, op. cit.

13   Old Friends

On 10 February 1948 in Zurich with the Tonhalle Orchestra under Volkmar Andreae, Fournier gave the first performance of Othmar Schoeck's concerto which was dedicated to him. This work, which is nearly forty minutes long, is scored simply for cello and strings. It has a fine singing line for the solo cello – perhaps unsurprising coming from Schoeck, a leading Swiss composer known for a very large output of lieder and an abundance of melody in his work.

At about this time Lyda received a call from Switzerland. A Dr Niehans[1] hoped that she and the maestro would come to the Montreux Palace to meet an old friend after many years. This turned out to be Wilhelm Kempff who was as surprised as they were themselves, and wept to see them again. Emaciated and with sores on his hands (the result, it was said, of malnutrition), he had been invited by Niehans to recuperate in Montreux. Beethoven was the natural outcome: an impromptu recital by Kempff and Fournier in the hotel drawing-room and, around the decorated mahogany piano, Helen Kempff, Elisabeth and Wilhelm Furtwängler, Richard and Pauline Strauss and the Prince and Princess Adalbert of Prussia.[2] Afterwards Strauss presented Fournier with an inscribed copy of his *Orchestral Studies* in celebration of Fournier's interpretation of *Don Quixote*. A few days later the Prince wrote to Lyda from La Tour de Peilz suggesting a present for Jean Pierre: a coin minted in 1913 under his father's reign, as a souvenir of the Beethoven evening and of a conversation about Berlin in pre-Nazi days, a place where Lyda 'felt so much at home'.[3]

'As an insufferable brat of ten', Jean Pierre recalled, 'I had the impudence to tell the Princess that she had marvellous legs, called the Prince "Your Majesty" and said I hoped he would return to the throne of his ancestors.'[4]

All over Europe artists and friends were picking up the threads. Wilhelm Kempff came to stay at Château Banquet. An early riser, he would sit wrapped in a kimono, writing letters on the balcony and watching the sun rise over the lake while his hosts were still asleep. Jean Pierre remembers a stay at Starnberger See with Wilhelm and Helene Kempff, and being offered *Kaffee und Kuchen*: 'mountains of pastry and Teutonic cakes filled with cream…'.[5] Over the years Kempff took an avuncular interest in Jean Pierre and was dismayed when he heard from Lyda that her son had lost his virginity with a *demi-mondaine*. In a three-page reply Kempff expressed his sadness that Jean Pierre's young soul hadn't been awakened by the kind of romantic flame which exalts body and spirit, rather than by a primitive, barrack-room impulse....

At the piano Kempff appeared to lose touch with mortals. In the course of a musical evening given by the journalist Philippe Boegner (one of the founders of *Paris Match*), Kempff lost all sense of the passing of time: Beethoven's last Sonata (Op. 111) was followed by Brahms' Handel Variations, an English Suite of Bach and some Schubert Impromptus. By this time all the guests were manifestly wilting. Lyda Fournier urged Nikita Magaloff to take his turn at the piano with the dazzling Chopin A minor Study (Op. 25/11) ('You play it better than anybody'), and the atmosphere lightened in front of a surprised but admiring Kempff.

The Fourniers were in the Deutsche Grammophon recording studio when Kempff was asked for a retake to correct a few blemishes in a Beethoven sonata. Kempff closed the piano, stood up and said 'I absolutely refuse. We'll leave it at that, then Gieseking [the Debussy specialist and Kempff's exact contemporary] can have another lovely day.' Like Kreisler, Kempff disliked recording.

While the intense activity of touring was Fournier's very lifeblood, there were moments when the pace overwhelmed him and he would fantasize about a less hectic life (which in reality would have appalled him): 'A very tiring journey to Spain... tomorrow a Conservatoire professor *once again*!' Tours resulted in missed lessons and soon he was to give up his official teaching post. Unburdening was sweet; in April 1948 he wrote:

> I feel I am condemned to hard labour... Tunis and Algiers, then Copenhagen and Stockholm.... You don't know how complicated my life is, with my own work, travelling, the Conservatoire, my pupils and all the rest.... I very much hope that with you I shall always find that understanding from the friend which you must always remain for me, as I shall for you.[6]

The recipient of this letter was Amaryllis Fleming, the flame-haired cellist daughter of the painter Augustus John. She had heard Fournier for the first time in 1946 at the Royal Albert Hall and, spellbound, had decided on the spot that she would be his pupil. From becoming her teacher Fournier, captivated and flattered by the admiration of a beautiful young musician half his age, rapidly became her lover – a situation just about tolerated by Lyda, no doubt aware that the affair would not threaten her marriage.

As a teacher, Fournier concentrated on the use of the bow as much as the left hand, an aspect of cello-playing which he was shocked to find was neglected in England where most of the attention seemed to be given to the left hand. Having himself learnt more from violinists than from any cellist, he put Amaryllis on to the Ševčik violin exercises, transposed by Feuillard, which he practised himself. He also taught her how to achieve beautiful phrasing by varying the vibrato. Through the right mental approach to difficult passages he made them clearer and easier. His fingerings were always chosen for clarity and musical expression.

The unmechanical variations he applied to scales and exercises were an example of the tireless work at technical minutiae that went into producing an effortless performance.

Under all the tenderness of a love affair, there was in Fournier a steely core: any attempt to interfere with his freedom or impair his relative peace with Lyda (which he carefully protected with *poste restante* addresses) met with intense irritation on his part. Inevitably his baroque arrangements broke down more than once. In Amaryllis's case her formidable mother, Eve Fleming, found out and, in a scene straight out of a boulevard comedy, her half-brother the explorer Peter was delegated to vet Fournier's intentions (which were non-existent). In the event the combined forces of the Flemings were too much for him. But his affection for Amaryllis lasted long after the affair was over: she was, as he once put it, echoing his childhood loneliness, '*la jeune fille que je n'ai jamais rencontrée.*'[7]

*   *   *

May 1948 brought a Paris recital with Ernest Lush and an accolade ('in Fournier France has the successor to Casals'),[8] after which he went on to complete his Beethoven sonata recordings with Schnabel, begun the previous year. He was exhilarated by the whole experience and on reaching the last (D major) sonata, told a friend 'This is going to be special.'

In the summer of 1948 the Furtwänglers were at St Moritz and Jean Pierre was introduced by his parents. Some years later, visiting the Furtwänglers at Clarens, Fournier played sonatas with the conductor. Jean Pierre turned two pages at once. 'Das ist nicht *richtig*!' roared Furtwängler, but when the music was ended and he saw the effect on the trembling Jean Pierre, he quickly consoled him.

Notes

1. Paul Niehans, the advocate of free cell therapy, who gave a roof to Furtwängler in 1945.
2. Prince Adalbert of Prussia (1884–1948) was the third of Kaiser Wilhelm's six sons. Hated by the Nazis, the princes had been disbarred from front-line duty lest they became figureheads for an opposition to Hitler.
3. Prince Adalbert of Prussia to Lyda Fournier, 25 February 1948.
4. Jean Fonda Fournier Archive.
5. Id.
6. Pierre Fournier to Amaryllis Fleming, 26 April 1948.
7. Fergus Fleming *Amaryllis Fleming*, London: Sinclair Stevenson 1993, pp. 78–79.
8. *Le Figaro*, 27 May 1948.

14 New World and Old Scores

On 13 November 1948 Fournier gave his début recital at New York Town Hall with the pianist George Reeves. In the preceding weeks he had felt both invigorated at the thought of breaking new ground, and plagued by his usual doubts and fears. 'I feel lost in this huge city' he wrote to a friend, arriving in New York; so much depended on the opening concert.[1] Besides two works by Bach – the Chorale *Nun komm' der Heiden Heiland* (BWV 599) and the unaccompanied Suite in D (BWV 1012) – he had chosen sonatas by Locatelli, Brahms (Op. 99) and Debussy, and Paganini's Variations on One String. The notorious critic Virgil Thomson (in Poulenc's words 'dreaded like Stalin') wrote in the *Herald Tribune*

> I don't know his superior among living cellists... Some play louder, many exploit a more obvious sentiment. I do not know any who gives me more profoundly the feeling of having been present at music-making... taste and musicianship of the first water....[2]

For another critic Fournier's handling of the Debussy sonata with its changes of atmosphere was 'defined and yet of ephemeral delicacy'.[3] Here, rather than with praise for his 'prodigious feats of virtuosity' displayed in the Paganini, the writer touched on the most personal of Fournier's gifts: the ability to shift from mood to mood with the agility of the human voice. 'I've had the luck', he rejoiced the following day, 'to get the best reviews in the biggest papers... I had been so full of despair, and now there is sunlight everywhere....'[4]

A second recital followed after New Year 1949, and included the sonata dedicated by Martinů to Fournier. The composer took his bow from the audience after the final *moto perpetuo* had brought many people to their feet. 'Composer and performer were so close in style, it was hard to say where Fournier ended and Martinů began.'[5] 'Elasticity of phrasing', 'weightiness conspicuously absent': the American critics were struck by Fournier's approach, a change for listeners accustomed to their huge orchestras' overwhelming and rather plummy sound born of a different string tradition. Fournier's finesse was to appeal to connoisseurs, musicians and critics, but by its very nature fail, as did his personal dignity, to turn him into a media figure with the wider American audience, *le gros public*.

Shortly after their first meeting, some time between 1925 and 1928, Francis Poulenc had told Fournier that he wanted to write a cello sonata, but the idea remained in the back of his mind until 1940 when, staying at Brive with Marthe Bosredon, a fine amateur pianist, he started sketching out the work. He had difficulties with string writing (he preferred wind instruments) but he struggled on, reporting to Pierre Bernac in 1945 that the first movement was 'a problem'. He contacted Fournier again, asking him on the telephone if he would like to give the first performance.

> I said yes at once and he added 'but it isn't yet written. As I write badly for strings, could you come over and look at the sketches?' He lived near the Luxembourg Gardens in Paris. From then on we saw a lot of each other and I was able to help him. The cello part he showed me was extremely difficult. He asked my advice about all the bowing and fingering problems. I didn't touch the shape of the work but I suggested small changes here and there to make it less awkward to play. He said yes to everything.[6]

The Sonata, dedicated jointly to Bosredon and Fournier, had its first performance at the Salle Gaveau on 18 May 1949 with the composer at the piano; the other works in the programme were Bach's D major Suite, the Debussy Sonata and Stravinsky's *Italian Suite*. It was a typically Parisian event with the usual mixture of genuine and sporadic music-lovers, composers, friends, film stars and society hostesses: Jean Cocteau, Georges Auric, Henri Sauguet, Gérard Philipe and Marie-Blanche de Polignac, a willowy figure rather unsteady on her feet, supported by Nadia Boulanger and the mezzo Marya Freund. 'Here comes the countess between her two nurses' whispered Michel Girard to Lyda.

The first London performance of the Cello Sonata was given at the Wigmore Hall on 15 June 1949. Poulenc, whose usual concert partner was the baritone Pierre Bernac, wrote to Darius Milhaud in July 'I was in England with Fournier with whom I was unfaithful to Bernac this spring because [sic] my Sonata.' He remembered the recital at Gaveau 'played in such a special style (quite simply what is written) that it met with all the success of... a first performance.'[7]

*   *   *

Like Mahler, Elgar was slow to win the hearts of the French, so Amaryllis had some difficulty in persuading the sceptical Fournier that the Concerto was worth adding to his repertoire, but when he explored the score he changed his mind. Felix Aprahamian watched him sightread the work, respecting every indication, every nuance, and asked him 'How do you make it sound so *English*?' Sir Adrian Boult was conducting when Fournier played it for the first time as part of the Elgar Festival at the Royal Albert Hall on 7 June 1949. Douglas Cameron thought that of all the foreign cellists he was the only one to 'get it right'.[8] *The Times* found that he 'gave to it an almost classical calm yet did not miss, as some players [did], either the wayward and elusive charm or the half-concealment of the deep emotion...'.[9] At York Minster he gave the Concerto with Sir John Barbirolli, for whom he had a great affection. A cellist himself, Barbirolli suggested a fingering in the last movement which Fournier was happy to adopt. In Paris the work, under André Cluytens, had only a mixed reception.

With broadcasts for the BBC's new Third Programme, European tours and the sight of ravaged Berlin, the pace was not to flag for many years. The hazards of travel, together with lower orchestral standards than we have today, led to some uncomfortable moments. In Paris the OSCC conductor André Cluytens was late returning from Milan, missing a first rehearsal for a concerto and *Don Quixote* before a Saturday public rehearsal and a Sunday afternoon concert. The concerto was not even run through, and the entire Friday session was taken up with the orchestra sightreading the Strauss piece.

On the other hand it was not all hard work. At Bryanstone Summer School Antony Hopkins conducted a cello band led by Fournier and Martin Lovett, in his *Sinfonietta for a Lot of Cellos*, 'a fun piece with a challenging top line for the master and easier-to-very-easy parts below.'[10]

In September 1949 Fournier heard that Gaspar Cassadó's American tour had been cancelled by Columbia Artists following a correspondence in the *New York Times* and much agitation behind the scenes. During the war Cassadó had toured Germany, Italy (where he lived) and Spain. His press release for the US tour had mentioned his association with Casals, his teacher. Inflamed by this, the cellist Diran Alexanian, who had moved to the States in 1937, protested in a letter to the *New York Times*, having first written to Casals 'To inquire as to his [Casals'] present estimate of Cassadó as a human being' and enclosing Casals' reply for publication. Referring to Cassadó's tours in Fascist countries, Casals wrote:

> Without a scruple [Cassadó] presents himself in America and is *received*. This is deplorable. The presumption of Cassadó has no limit... knowing that I am undergoing exile for having played the opposite card he uses my name to cover himself. A revolting cynicism![11]

Hearing that the tour had been cancelled, Fournier wrote to Cassadó offering his help with a recommendation to his agent, Jack Adams. Cassadó wrote back on 25 September:

> *Cher ami,*
>
> I very much appreciated your letter, especially at such a disconcerting moment in my life when I have been accused of certain crimes I did not commit. And the saddest thing in the whole matter is that one of the strongest forces against me is my own Master. It makes a fair and logical defence impossible for me, since one cannot plead against one's Master.
>
> As you may imagine, my Master's horrible accusation in a letter to an 'individual' in New York, published in the *New York Times* after recital last season, has spread about such a disastrous opinion of me that the atmosphere is unbearable. And I must stay impassive because if I were to defend myself with any justice I should begin by calling my Master to account. And that I shall never do.
>
> Dear friend, thank you from the bottom of my heart for your offer [the recommendation to Fournier's agent]. For the moment I can't see clearly. Let us hope that time will do justice to the truth which, through the force of logic, must always win in the end. All this has cost me a lot of pain and my time in New York has done my

health no good. I know the world is selfish and spiteful but I cannot take in what my Master has done. It is beyond my comprehension.[12]

Drawn up against Cassadó, besides Casals, was a coterie of New York musicians using the Master's renown to reinforce their boycott of suspect European colleagues. Their campaign, which neither Bruno Walter nor Yehudi Menuhin would join, was directed principally at Furtwängler. Fuelling this was the fear that European artists would overrun the US concert circuit, 'the land of milk and honey' which Heifetz wished to defend when he urged Menuhin 'We Americans must stick together.' As for Casals, he had, in his own words, 'nothing personally against Furtwängler' but he needed his court of admirers and to his credit he admitted as much. He turned down a recording of the Brahms Double Concerto with Menuhin and Furtwängler, explaining that his only reason was the fear of his followers' incomprehension.[13] It was Menuhin who pointed out to Casals the injustice done to Cassadó, and brought about the final reconciliation between the Master and his 'most beloved pupil'.

Against this troubled background Fournier prepared to make his Carnegie Hall début on 3 November 1949 with Stokowski and the New York Philharmonic. The knives were out. On the morning of the concert Jack Adams received anonymous telephone calls warning that 'if the collaborator Fournier [appeared], not only would there be a demonstration but he would be prevented outright from performing'. Cassadó had been threatened with physical violence and Adams was taking no chances. Without telling Fournier, he called Stokowski who in turn contacted his friend General Omar Bradley in Washington. The demonstration was called off. Fournier heard of all this just as he was about to walk on to the platform, but he managed to steady his nerves. 'Admirable playing' purred the *New York Times*. At his début recital the previous year, when all the praise was still to come, there had been not the whisper of a protest.

The accusing finger was aimed not only at Cassadó but at Fournier and even Lyda as well, and on a personal level which enraged her husband. Fournier started proceedings for slander against Alexanian through his Paris lawyer Roger Hauert. The affair went as far as a face-to-face confrontation, but no further: Fournier had little taste for litigation, and Alexanian retracted his statements. In time the two made their peace and Alexanian even visited the Fourniers in Geneva in 1957.

But there had been another cloud over Fournier's Carnegie Hall début: cello trouble. The Gagliano, bought from his old teacher Paul Bazelaire for one and a half million old francs in gold pieces, had become slightly unstuck and the humidity of the Philippines had made matters worse. Another instrument was needed for the Schumann Concerto in New York. Happily the dealer Emil Herrman came to the rescue with a Stradivarius. Schnabel was in the audience at Carnegie Hall. 'What instrument was that?' he asked after the concert.

'A Stradivarius', Fournier answered, all smiles.

'I preferred the one you had last year', muttered Schnabel. This was what

Fournier called his 'bon vieux Miremont'.[14]

In 1949 Gregor Piatigorsky made a sensational return to Paris at the Champs Elysées Theatre, all seats sold. Pierre was on tour and, avoiding the chit-chat in the stalls, Lyda chose to sit with a friend in the circle. On the stairs she passed the *Figaro* critic, Bernard Gavoty, and told him that he was going to have a treat: 'Grisha is playing all his favourite pieces.' When a disappointing review appeared in the paper the following day, rumour blamed Lyda, ex-Madame Piatigorsky, who was believed to have sat next to the critic and inspired his harsh words about her ex-husband. The truth was that nothing more than a similar hairstyle had caused Mme Gavoty to be mistaken for Lyda. It took sixteen years and an explanation in Moscow for the misunderstanding to be cleared up, and a further four years before Piatigorsky could be persuaded to return to Paris.

*　*　*

Fournier's partnership with Sir Thomas Beecham was brief and unmemorable. Things went badly from the start. The 1950 Edinburgh Festival was planned to include a performance of the Virgil Thomson Concerto, but Fournier disliked the work which he found puerile. The score posted to him went astray and he had to be sent another. Writing to Beecham to ask for his opinion of the work, Thomson added:

> Fournier is now trying to imagine that he could not possibly learn it by August, which is merely a French nervous anxiety on his part. I am writing to him that he has been engaged to learn it and that he is expected to do so in spite of constant touring. I should like to assure you, however, that if Fournier gets difficult, I shall be more than happy with any cellist of your choice. His proposal to me that the performance be postponed till next year seems to solve nobody's problem but his, since the work has been accepted by you and by the [Edinburgh] Festival committee. Please do exactly as you like about him. In any case he now has the entire work and has had two-thirds of it since November.[15]

Fournier escaped the Thomson Concerto. At the Usher Hall on 24 August, with Beecham and the French Radio Orchestra, he gave Bloch's *Schelomo* and the Boccherini B flat Concerto. It was not a happy evening, while Fournier's impression of Beecham was 'a spoilt child on a grand scale'.[16]

Notes

1. Pierre Fournier, 9 November 1948.
2. *New York Herald Tribune*, 14 November 1948.
3. *New York Times*, 14 November 1948.
4. Pierre Fournier, 14 November 1948.
5. Louis Biancolli, [?], January 1949.
6. Pierre Fournier, *L'Ame et la corde*, No. 5, November 1983.
7. Francis Poulenc to Darius Milhaud, 25 July [1949]. Cited in Buckland, op. cit., p. 177.

8.   Derek Simpson in conversation with the author.
9.   *The Times*, 8 June 1949.
10. Antony Hopkins to the author, 13 August 1991.
11. Pablo Casals to Diran Alexanian, Prades, 1 February 1949, published in the *New York Times*.
12. Gaspar Cassadó to Pierre Fournier, 25 September 1949.
13. Yehudi Menuhin, op. cit., pp. 230–231.
14. See p. 128 note 5.
15. Virgil Thomson to Sir Thomas Beecham, 5 March 1950. *Selected Letters of Virgil Thomson*, ed. Tim Page and Vanessa Weeks-Page. New York: Summit Books 1988, pp. 242–243.
16. Jean Fonda Fournier Archive.

15   Handwriting

Under the stress of touring Fournier took much comfort from friendship, and particularly the serendipity of a new encounter: he was also a considerable letter writer. Even when business would have warranted a secretary and a typewriter, he preferred to write all his letters by hand. Deprived of companionship in childhood, he seldom took friendship for granted. The exception was Tony Mayer, whom he treated with the casualness of a younger brother secure in support and affection, a habit which started in adolescence. This being so, he tended to study a new friendship as one might a fragile object discovered by chance. One such meeting elicited:

> I think of you as somebody to return to, the world being so full of mediocre, ugly and materialistic people. My long experience of travel makes me value a meeting such as ours. Having only approached you, I so much want to know you. Why should I not tell you? Have we not agreed on complete honesty between us?[1]

The sensitivity which prevented him from playing the mindless predator equally meant a lightning response to the beauty, charm or talent – usually all three – with which he was so often surrounded. One male pupil recalled the way his eye could acquire a special glint when an attractive girl student entered the room, a glint far from lost on Lyda, who habitually sat in on these sessions.[2]

While touring, confidences were shared in ink. In spring 1950 Fournier wrote to Amaryllis Fleming:

> The older I get the more I need the reality of your existence. Sometimes I wonder if everything is real, changing cities and countries all the time and finding oneself alone nearly everywhere.... I have such an anxious disposition, eating my heart out with self-doubt, afraid of disappointing each time I play, and with a ruthlessness towards myself which is often discouraging. You do me so much good with your presence, since everything seems natural to you....[3]

A fortnight later he wrote from the train between Vienna and Innsbruck, mentioning two successful Beethoven concerts with the pianist Paul Baumgartner. He had seen Vienna's rebirth, and while awaiting his South American tour as 'a great adventure with no notion of the result', he felt he was 'getting older without experiencing youth'.[4]

If the Beecham–Fournier partnership was a misalliance, Fournier and Sir

Malcolm Sargent worked happily together: for one thing Sargent understood a chronic problem for cellists, the fear of being drowned by the orchestra. On the South American tour, Fournier played the Dvořák Concerto with Sargent at one of the two spectacularly successful concerts organized by Amigos de la Musica in Buenos Aires. Nearly 4000 people, some of whom had queued since early morning, packed a giant cinema and later blocked the street in their enthusiasm.

In early December Fournier was in Vevey, playing nearly every day. Throughout his travels he kept in touch with Lyda and Jean Pierre and, in spite of the constantly disrupted family life and his own defensive postal arrangements, there was a remarkable closeness between the three widely differing personalities, a triangle of complicity welded by music.

He remembered Jean Pierre's birthday:

> I am so glad to know you are happy and having fun with your dear boxing partners. You'll be a champion for your 13th birthday which I'm sorry not to be celebrating with you all. Your dear Citroen[5] is running beautifully like a real Swiss watch and I hope to finish my journey on the 19th without any problems. You'll see when you come to Vevey what a charming hotel the Trois Couronnes is…. The view is marvellous and it is right on the lakeside.
>
> I'm sure you are working well… the finest present you could give me at New Year would be if you were first in your class. Tomorrow I'm going to the funeral of dear Lipatti who died on Saturday after a long and cruel illness.[6] It is so unfair that the best leave this world which is so full of nasty people.
>
> *Au revoir mon chéri, je t'embrasse bien tendrement*, Papa.[7]

In New Year 1951 Fournier returned to the New York Town Hall to play two concertos with the Little Orchestra Concert Society and Thomas Scherman. Virgil Thomson rose above any residual irritation over the matter of his own Concerto, and wrote of the Elgar performance that in less elegant hands it could easily turn to groaning; of the C.P.E. Bach A major Concerto he spoke of 'gracious technical ease and impeccable musicianship'.[8]

At Sils Maria Fournier made new friends: the pianist Walter Gieseking and the American contralto Marian Anderson. 'A voice like yours is heard once in a hundred years', Toscanini had said to Anderson in 1935, but in spite of petitions and protests from newspapers and prominent figures, for many years doors were closed to her because she was black.[9] Following the holiday at Sils, Fournier hoped to invite Anderson to a New York party arranged for him by an old friend, Cornelia Possart. When the suggestion met with a flat refusal he was so angered that he put down the receiver and never spoke to Cornelia again.

*   *   *

The Hungarian conductor George Szell's first visit to the United States in 1930 had been arranged by Artur Schnabel who now introduced Fournier to Szell. The conductor told Fournier later 'Schnabel never stops talking about you.' Szell had taken over the Cleveland Orchestra in 1946 and was turning it into one of the best in the world, in some opinions *the* best.[10] In due course Fournier was engaged to play *Don Quixote* at Cleveland. Szell was known to be difficult; conspiratorial and hypnotic on the rostrum, he was admired and feared by his players, but never loved. He had ways of testing his artists. Just before the Severance Hall début (*Don Quixote* was programmed in the second half), he asked Fournier to open the concert with an hors d'oeuvre, a 'special homage' as he called it, the sixth Bach Suite, the entire work in front of the waiting orchestra with Szell himself sitting on the rostrum beside him. It might have been less than a success but Szell knew what he was about: this concert sealed a rewarding partnership and Fournier returned to Cleveland many times, with a concerto of his choice and… *Don Quixote*.

Fournier's sister Cécile, the companion of his first out-of-town engagement in 1923, had married the Swiss banker Walter Niklaus and lived in New York. It was in her apartment that he stayed briefly in early March and was joined by Nikita Magaloff. The two men relaxed by making music together and playing bridge. Fournier fancied a bottle off a top shelf. Obligingly, up the stepladder went Magaloff, and down came not one bottle but the contents of a well-stocked bar…. Lunch over, Magaloff decided he would like to be entertained, preferably with a Bach Suite, and ideally the C minor which he was least familiar with. Fournier began to play. After a little while it was obvious that his listener was sleeping soundly, so Fournier played some other pieces then quietly started on a few exercises. The Russian voice boomed out of the armchair 'What are you doing, playing things I didn't ask you to play?'

Writing years later from El Paso, Fournier recalled this congenial break in the long and monotonous habit of hotel rooms: 'I often think of our stay together, of our broken bottles and our sleepy Bach Suites.'[11]

Still in the spring of 1951 Fournier was in Chicago, teasing Magaloff (it was a habit):

> How were the last days in NY? I suppose you are quite beyond yourself and those ladies of the Waldorf will tear you to pieces on Thursday! I shall look after your remains on the plane [Nikita hated air travel]. The concerts with Szell were a great success and I had splendid reviews. His *Don Quixote* is inimitable and I could never have as much enjoyment playing this work with anyone else. The enclosed [a publicity handout in which Szigeti spoke of Magaloff, his son-in-law, as his favourite partner] will put you in a good mood… I have worked hard for you on Szell who is the most *difficult* man I know! He has great confidence in me now and I think that might help… I wonder what La Claudia [the critic Claudia Cassidy] will be writing about me… I haven't seen Kubelik who is ill and who will only be submitting himself tomorrow.[12]
>
> I am terrified by the weight of my luggage for Saturday. Try to call your anonymous TWA friend for La Guardia because I've bought a tape recorder which weighs a ton! The news from Paris is still restless and it upsets me a lot.[13] Some people are coming on Saturday for a *drink* at 11.30. You come too. *Je t'embrasse*, P.[14]

From Zurich he sent Magaloff a postcard:

> Your letter was very comforting because I thought you had forgotten all about our New York days! It's a pity to follow each other everywhere (I leave for Finland next week) and never to meet. I don't yet know if I'll go to South America. I don't share your idea

of a holiday, at least not with my anxious nature, because I feel well only when I play all the time. I don't like your friends of the No Concerts and Co. [New Concert Artists Corporation]. When will you be slinking around Paris again? *Affectueusement*, Pierre.[15]

And a month later from home:

You're an angel to write me such a good, long letter... you're also the perfect *personal representative*. I found it on my return from a long journey... Berlin, Stuttgart, Vienna, Innsbruck, Bolzano and... five concerts in six days in Yugoslavia, two at Belgrade, two at Zagreb and one at Lublyana. Enormous success there and a charming welcome from people who are *so* unhappy. What I saw there confirmed my belief that our hemisphere is better... all those regimes mean a return to the Middle Ages and the establishment of kingdoms where men are reduced to the state of ants. Now I am steeling myself to lose all the benefit of that journey on the evening of 9 May, day of madness with my Paris recital... I find your decision not to go to America premature. No news from there. Mr Adams hasn't sent me the Heralds I was expecting and I hope he is not suddenly going bankrupt.[16] At Bolzano I spent an evening with A.P. de Bavier who treated me to a clarinet festival in my room, complete with demonstrations of himself at the rostrum. It was marvellously comic.[17] I saw Igor Markevitch in Vienna: I had applauded him enthusiastically after his wonderful performance of the *Three Oranges*, but he really didn't need to *lie* to me so blatantly when, on the evening of my recital, he pretended to have heard half of it, which was untrue because he was glued to your dear Michelangeli who doesn't appeal to me as a man, not one bit!

I think so often of you, of our evenings, our lunches, our chat, our gossip, in fact everything which made my NY life happy like an island in the middle of hell... I miss you. I'm so delighted at everything good which can happen to you, because you deserve the very best from every point of view. I embrace you as well as Irène, and I await the real joy of seeing you again soon. Lyda digested Yugoslavia very well!!![18] She sends her love too.

With a typically Fournier tongue-in-cheek afterthought, he ended:

I shall write to M. Amélie to give me your two Brazilian concerts. In exchange I'll give you two very fine engagements at Montluçon and Cherbourg! P.[19]

In spite of all his misgivings, the South American tour took place in the autumn and he was met at Buenos Aires airport by Toto and Germaine Baehr whom he had already met in Paris. Everything contributed to his pleasure: new friends, enthusiastic audiences, the warmth and hospitality of the three leading hostesses, Gloria Alcorta, Inez Bonadeo and Huguette Guthmann, as well as the soothing effect of exotic affluence after the austerities of Europe. The public was very keen: queuing often started at 5 am. The Teatro Opera ran free concerts; there was a wide choice of other halls, the concert club La Wagneriana at the Coliseo theatre, the Amigos de la Musica run by Eleonora Hirsch de Carabajo at the Teatro Colon, and the Teatro Gran Rex. In the relaxing atmosphere Fournier practised in front of an open window in the Baehr drawing-room with its balcony overlooking the street.

Huguette and Gaston Guthmann gave a large party after the Dvořák Concerto at the Teatro Gran Rex, with Rudolf Firkušny and Rafael Kubelik among the guests and impromptu *Hausmusik* afterwards. Huguette complained of having been too long away from the piano. 'Take it up again' Fournier told her, 'and we'll play the *Elégie* together.' After a dinner party the following year they dressed up as tramps and to Huguette's accompaniment Fournier played the entire piece out of tune.

'My thoughts turn to you' he wrote to Magaloff from Bogota:

> ...since you must be back from South Africa... I was talking to Dr Mendel about our jolly time in New York together.[20] I'm satisfied with my tour in spite of inevitable ups and downs and some great fatigue.

A stagehands' strike having closed the 3900-seat Teatro Colon in Buenos Aires for opera, the management substituted a series of recitals: Claudio Arrau, [Andrés] Segovia, Alexander Brailowsky, Yehudi Menuhin, the young William Kapell[21] and Fournier. 'The Brazil and the Argentine went well' the letter continues, 'Two recitals at the Colon full for the first time ever with a cello, hence an excellent impression on Quesada [concert management].'

Through a happy coincidence Fournier, Szigeti and Backhaus, touring separately, found themselves in Bogota together, an opportunity seized by Amigos de la Musica; the result was an impromptu Beethoven concert.[22] The three also gave individual recitals. 'I expect to play before 23 people' Fournier continued, characteristically expecting the worst. 'Next I go to Puerto Rico, 2 or 3 concerts in Caracas, 2 in Mexico and 2 in Havana, then Paris on 23 October...'. In Caracas his concert with Klemperer was sold out, but on the night he had the galling sight of a hall only three-quarters full. 'They have paid their subscriptions but they prefer to stay at home and play poker' he grumbled.

> From Lyda, good news with many variations on the eternal theme 'jealousy' and, like most women but just that bit more, she *doesn't know* how much one is alone.
>
> I often miss you, I wish I could run into you suddenly and at last relax with a friend. Joska Szigeti is very unhappy and is dragging his convict's lament around everywhere.[23] I went to one of his concerts in Caracas, very beautiful and so musical all of it.... *Mille affections pour vous trois et je t'embrasse avec une fidèle tendresse.*[24]

Notes

1. Pierre Fournier to CA, 9 November 1948.
2. Jonathan Williams in conversation with the author.
3. Pierre Fournier to Amaryllis Fleming, 10 March 1950.
4. Pierre Fournier to Amaryllis Fleming, 24 March 1950.
5. This car, of the gangster film type and a metallic grey, was the object of a family joke: it had been chosen by Lyda because it reminded her of Pierre's rather shiny alpaca suit.
6. The pianist Dinu Lipatti (1917–1950) had died of leukaemia on 2 December.
7. Pierre Fournier to Jean Fonda Fournier [?] December 1950.
8. Virgil Thomson. *New York Herald Tribune*, 26 February 1951.
9. In 1939, furious against the obstacles to Anderson singing at an Easter concert at Howard University, Washington, Eleanor Roosevelt resigned from the organizing society, Daughters of the Revolution. Taking part in the concert himself, Heifetz felt ashamed (but didn't cancel). In the end Anderson sang, on Easter Sunday at an open-air concert at the Lincoln Memorial, for an audience of 75 000 people.

10. A precocious talent, Szell performed a Mozart piano concerto at the age of ten; at seventeen he became assistant to Richard Strauss at the Berlin State Opera, and at nineteen succeeded Klemperer at Strasbourg.
11. Pierre Fournier to Nikita Magaloff, 9 November 1957.
12. Claudia Cassidy was the critic of the *Chicago Sunday Times*. A fervent admirer of Furtwängler and angered by the campaign of hatred conducted against him by a group of soloists and resulting in the cancellation of his Chicago contract, she was harsh towards Rafael Kubelik who replaced him. Kubelik had consulted Pierre and Lyda before accepting the post. He was under consideration at the time in London, Zurich and Amsterdam, but the cold war made life in the US a less stressful option for the Czech conductor and his wife. Years later he returned to Chicago to be very well received by La Cassidy.
13. Lyda, back in Paris, was feeling out of things with Pierre still on tour.
14. Pierre Fournier to Nikita Magaloff, 12 March 1951.
15. Id., 21 March [1951].
16. Jack Adams, manager of the NCAC, took the Paris Orchestre National and Charles Munch to court for refusing a strenous tour by bus with an excessive number of concerts. He lost the case.
17. Antoine-Pierre de Bavier, a remarkable clarinettist who recorded the Mozart Quintet with the Quartetto Italiano and lived in Bolzano. He had studied with Furtwängler and later became a notable choral conductor.
18. The unsettled political climate made Lyda more nervous than usual in Pierre's absence.
19. Pierre Fournier to Nikita Magaloff, 28 April 1951.
20. Dr Bernardo Mendel, guiding spirit of Bogota's musical life at the time.
21. William Kapell (1922–1953), brilliant young American pianist who partnered Heifetz. He was killed in an air crash near San Francisco at the age of 31.
22. The F sharp major Piano Sonata Op. 78, the F major ('Spring') Violin Sonata Op. 24, the A major Cello Sonata Op. 69 and the D major ('Ghost') Trio Op. 70/1.
23. Not only did Szigeti have bow trouble and agent trouble, but he had been detained on Ellis Island while awaiting US citizenship.
24. Pierre Fournier to Nikita Magaloff, 24 September 1951.

16 Kaleidoscope

At this point Fournier's life had come to resemble a great stretch of mosaic, with the division of his time into a multitude of contiguous fragments, the components of a single artefact: the constant making of music interrupted by travel. He was the willing prisoner of a continuum of musical works, fellow artists, cities glimpsed rather than visited and, only briefly registered, hundreds upon hundreds of faces.

At a Caracas hotel in September 1951 a young man with a gold chain gleaming on his chest called, hoping for an audition with Klemperer. Fournier arranged this for him and the young pianist, Alexis Weissenberg, played Schumann's *Kreisleriana*. 'He plays too fast' was the conductor's terse comment, but Pierre and Lyda were impressed with him. On a visit to rue Lesueur Weissenberg entertained them with his own hilarious version of the musical *New Faces*, in which he played both lead and chorus. Fournier, who was under contract with Decca at the time, suggested a joint recording of the Rachmaninov Sonata and sent him the score. There was no reaction from Weissenberg, so Fournier assumed that chamber music didn't interest him.

A conductor much admired by Fournier, if largely ignored today, was Dmitri Mitropoulos. Helped by Saint-Saëns and taught by Busoni, he had been Erich Kleiber's assistant at the Berlin State Opera. He possessed a prodigious memory, conducting *Wozzeck* without a score and, from the keyboard, the Krenek Concerto and Prokofiev's Third. He was also known for great personal kindness.

Rehearsing the Martinů Concerto with the New York Philharmonic in November 1951, Fournier noticed that Mitropoulos had no score on his desk and remarked upon it. 'Don't you trust my memory?' asked the maestro. 'Yours, yes' answered Fournier, 'but not mine!'

The New York critics turned their spite and sarcasm on to Mitropoulos, ostensibly for his choice of contemporary music – Bloch, Milhaud, Nabokov, Hindemith – but to a large extent on account of his homosexuality for which he became the target of much innuendo.

Other journeys this year took Fournier to Milan, to give *Don Quixote* with Karajan at La Scala (where he lost his heart to Ingrid Bergman in the Honegger-Claudel oratorio *Jeanne au bûcher* directed by Rossellini), and to London where he gave the Elgar Concerto in the Royal Albert Hall.

In 1952 the Berlin Philharmonic came to Paris. There was a flurry of letters between Furtwängler and Lyda in the New Year; also some confusion as to whether a major lieder singer would take part in one of the two concerts. Furtwängler preferred symphony concerts to galas with soloists. 'I have, as you know, refused them all up to now' he wrote. 'If there is to be a soloist at all, then it will have to be an instrumentalist who can, if possible, give a work which suits the framework of the concert; in this case PF would be the first person to come to mind....' The Brahms Double Concerto was planned 'with a first-class violinist (Schneiderhan perhaps...?'.[1] The first-class violinist materialized in the shape of the great Szigeti. 'A very thorough rehearsal will be necessary' Furtwängler continued, 'and a detailed discussion with both soloists of my idea of the work.... The whole thing is virtually a major symphony with the indispensible instruments.'[2]

The concert took place at the Paris Opéra on 3 May. At the first rehearsal with a piano, Fournier waited for the tempo. Furtwängler started at a very brisk pace. 'Listen to the cellist!' he called to Szigeti.[3]

While the Furtwängler negotiations were going on between Paris and Berlin, Fournier was at Essen, alternately playing and kicking his heels. With time on his hands the black dog of anxiety was scratching at the door. What seemed to him interminable Russian reminiscences when Lyda and Nikita discoursed for hours on Piatigorsky, Milstein and Horowitz, often left him feeling excluded; it took only a little inattention from those he loved for him to feel isolated. 'Although with Asian blood in your veins you are much more Lyda's friend than mine,' he wrote to Nikita,

> I am very often with you in thought and I thank you for your short letter, the only one, in fact... since our New York *ménage*. [Pierre was referring to their stay at Cécile Niklaus' apartment.] So you are in that country. For how long, and for how many dozens of concerts and tens of thousands of $? As for me, I am very content in Europe waiting for Mr Adams' Fine Tour (Fine Tour whose best concerts, NY Philharmonic, Cleveland, Chicago, were my doing not his).[4] I get bills from America [for musical directories and yearbooks] from various unions, and for countless *Who's Whos* eating into my coming earnings as a *middle-aged* cellist.

The acidulated note in this letter betrayed his growing conviction that he would have better stomached the idiosyncrasies of American musical life so alien to his nature – the preoccupation with stars, the emphasis on money, the involvement of socialites – if he had embarked on the experience as a younger man. He turned to teasing Magaloff:

> I know from Lyda that you boarded the plane like a hero and that the whole of Europe accuses me of cruelty to nervous transatlantic passengers.

After their stay together in New York, the two men had returned to Europe on a night flight. Magaloff had been particularly nervous when leaving the coastline which, as he declared at the top of his voice to the discomfiture of steward and passengers alike, he would rather fly along than leave behind. 'Did you have a drink?' asked the steward. Magaloff nodded weakly. 'Then you had better have ANOTHER.'

Fournier's letter from Essen continued and with anything new disaster tended to loom:

> Here I can't quite say that I feel at home, but nearly everybody is kind, I'm earning money and doing well....
>
> I leave on the 15th for a Portuguese adventure which looks perilous and according to unofficial reports we are in danger of missing the Madeira concerts because the Southampton hovercrafts leave late and the ones from Funchal wait for the sea to be as flat as a pancake before taking off, which is encouraging in this time of gales! We shall meet again at Ansermet's beard in early April which delights me.
>
> I heard with despair of poor Grisha's dental troubles. Are there any interesting obituaries over there?[5]
>
> I hope you won't think me gaga after this letter. I am bored to death at Essen. Lyda left me at Munich and is making jealous scenes by remote control which must amuse her, but myself considerably less since they are unjustified. If they weren't I should at least have *lovely times plus* scenes, which would be a compensation.

Lyda was often jealous, and not without reason. 'Lyda is upstairs having a *crise de nerfs*' Fournier said to one visitor. For his part he brooded on the idea that to a certain degree he was a substitute for the Russianness Lyda liked to have around her. 'I shall always be a bit *ersatz*' he said at a bad moment. Boredom at Essen had a lot to answer for.

> Tell me about your success which I hope is magnificent everywhere. I hope you have a lot of *cinq à sept* with Cornelia [Possart] in your Waldorf suite and that you also win a lot of money at bridge.
>
> I embrace you and order you to be very choosy conveying my regards over there. Embrace old Philipp for me.[7] What are your dates for Engadine [Sils Maria]? I suggest you *baise* [X]'s wife for a little peace, otherwise I won't stay.[8]

The Portuguese tour was a happy one and Fournier relaxed in Lisbon enjoying the hospitality of the British Ambassador Sir Nigel Ronald whose courtesy was 'so perfect and spontaneous that it might reconcile [him] to the atmosphere of embassies.'[9] [10]

*   *   *

While there is little noticeable mention of success in Fournier's letters, the ink flows freely on small problems: logistics, irritations with agents and managements (a recurring theme). Yet the list of engagements for 1952 speak for themselves: with Furtwängler in Paris, at the Lucerne Festival with Paul Sacher and the Collegium Musicum, the Amsterdam Concertgebouw with Rafael Kubelik, Berlin with Karajan (in East Berlin the two men saw Felsenstein's production of *Fidelio*), Boston with Munch, Los Angeles (he dined with the actors on the Hollywood set of the *Titanic*), Italy, Germany, Spain, Scandinavia and the Besançon Festival as the 15-year-old Roberto Benzi's first soloist.

Roberto Benzi and Jean Pierre Fournier were born the same day, 12 December 1937, and as a child prodigy Roberto visited rue Lesueur. It was roughly at the time of Fournier's Besançon concert with the young Italian conductor that the

15-year-old Jean Pierre made up his mind to be a concert pianist. It was no coincidence that relations with Fournier then became closer, the father confiding his anxieties in the son: not those concerning the boy's future (which he tended to consider a foregone conclusion), but instead his own. Two more opposing temperaments it would be difficult to invent. It was as if Jean Pierre's natural optimism and forcefulness offered his father a harbour for his angst.

The loss of Artur Schnabel who had died in August of the previous year (1951) gave Ian Hunter, Rudolf Bing's successor as the Edinburgh Festival director, the idea of reconstituting the Festival Piano Quartet. The trio of Szigeti, Primrose and Fournier was now joined by Clifford Curzon who had been Schnabel's pupil. The programmes included the three Brahms piano quartets. Schnabel had both listened to Brahms in his youth and played for him, and Curzon was a superb Brahms player.

Fournier admired the pianist and enjoyed making music with him, but there were conflicts, Curzon insisting on what appeared to the others as an inordinate number of rehearsals. Exasperated, Fournier wrote to Magaloff for 'some details about the infernal cycle of Vevey rehearsals'. Once again, the fear of physical stress was lurking under surface irritation. Where will they rehearse? Will they all be there? Where is Joska [Szigeti] going to stay? Did Nikita know the neighbourhood well enough to advise him about the nearest hotel?

> I would like to be *next door* [to the rehearsal hall] and not 2, 3, 4 kilometres away. I shall be without a car... I came back from Lorenzo Marques as early as the 8th because all the South African concerts were cancelled, the excuse being that they weren't sure enough of the dates. I was very disappointed! But the Portuguese were charming and sang your praises. What is more, I have completely won over M. Gadinho [impresario at Lorenzo Marques known for his lavish fees]. [...]
>
> I am outraged by the tone of the cable sent by Emmie Tillett (I don't know on whose authority) telling me that if I didn't rehearse enough I should be 'threatened with other arrangements'. I shall go to Vevey only if all the quartet members are there. Between ourselves, this atmosphere of threats is a real turn-off and this strange quartet won't see me around for long.[11]

Fournier believed that a stray remark of his, aimed at Curzon, had found its way back to Tillett: he had said that the quality of the rehearsals made up for their quantity.

In the autumn Louis Beydts, musical director of the Opéra-Comique, unable to attend a concert, wrote in his customary mock-heroic style:

> Good and dearly beloved Maître... Alas! the same evening the Opéra-comique is giving the first performance of a ballet by M. Jacque-Dupont (latest spelling)[12] and my duty as a civil servant obliges me to attend.... My spirit will be following your triumphant bow through the meanderings of the Cantor's inspired Suites[13] while my heart accompanies your own which it has never deserted.... A thousand sincere apologies and as many affectionate thoughts to all three of you, Louis.[14]

Beydts was ill and in answer to a letter from Fournier in July 1953 wrote of the boredom of convalescence. He hoped to find his friend 'in Paris, doing his scales to ensure the brilliance of his coming broadcast'.[15] Beydts had charm, elegance and wit, and being also of a rare discretion he left few records of his life and friendships. He was fond enough of Fournier for the Poulenc–Fournier duo to cause him to smart a little, but this never went far enough to spoil the relationship which was one of delighted camaraderie. Beydts died of cancer two months after this letter.

Notes

1. Wilhelm Furtwängler to Lyda Fournier, 11 January 1952.
2. Id., 2 February 1952.
3. Elisabeth Furtwängler in conversation with the author.
4. The last tour with Jack Adams, and very successful concerts with Szell, Mitropoulos, Munch, et al.
5. An allusion to an American acquaintance celebrated for both his health complaints and his longevity.
6. Cornelia Possart was the excellent amateur pianist already mentioned, whom Fournier first met at the house of his sister, Cécile Niklaus, in New York and was a frequent bridge partner with Magaloff. She had played with the Flonzaley Quartet.
7. Isidor Philipp (1863–1958), Hungarian-born pianist and teacher, studied with Saint-Saëns and taught at the Paris Conservatoire.
8. Pierre Fournier to Nikita Magaloff, 1 February 1952.
9. Sir Nigel Ronald, KCMG, CVO (1894–1973), Ambassador to Portugal 1947–1954.
10. Pierre Fournier to Tony Mayer, 1 March 1952.
11. Pierre Fournier to Nikita Magaloff, 15 June 1952.
12. Originally plain M. Jacques Dupont.
13. Beydts teased Fournier about 'all the repeats' in the Bach Suites.
14. Louis Beydts to Pierre Fournier, 6 October 1952.
15. Id., 30 July 1953.

17   L'Autre Pierre

For the composer Francis Poulenc 'Pierre I' was the baritone Pierre Bernac, his concert partner for nearly twenty-five years; 'l'autre Pierre' was Fournier with whom he toured Italy in the spring of 1953. 'You cannot imagine', the composer wrote to his friend Simone Girard[1] in March, 'how it constantly fascinates me to compare the two Pierres.'

> Fournier is a *love*, a real *love*, but he is not my Pierre I.... He is undoubtedly an admirable artist, the greatist cellist of our day... but he does not have all the multiple levels of my own Pierre, my irreplaceable counterpart. All the same, only someone of Fournier's stupendous class could make me take on a new duo. We caused a sensation with the Debussy, played the Schubert very well, the Schumann less well, the Poulenc quite well and the Stravinsky *very well*. Tonight in Bergamo, everything should go quite smoothly. At any rate it is very easy to play with Fournier. Like Pierre I he never falters. I repeat that he is adorable....

He adds a PS: 'The duo Four-Poul is much in demand but it will be *rarissime* and very expensive.'[2]

Arriving at Bergamo from Turin, Poulenc sent a postcard to Lyda in Paris:

> Lyda *ma belle*, the concert in Turin went very well after combined stagefright and a not-very-cosy audience. Arthur [Rubinstein] had one encore and atrocious reviews, [Robert] Casadesus one encore and a good press, Gieseking a mixed reception. Thanks to twenty people including [Igor] Markevitch we had 2 encores so imagine! We are putting out the flags. The programme is now Locatelli, Schubert, Poulenc, interval, Debussy, Stravinsky. Your little husband is as sweet as anything and *as good as gold*. When he gets cross with the station-master I calm him down. We are very comfortable at Bergamo. A thousand kisses to you, the son and the dog. Poupoule.[3]

A day was spent at Assisi and during Vespers at the Basilica Fournier noticed that Poulenc was in tears. Writing to Bernac, however, the composer deflected the spotlight onto *'l'autre* Pierre':

> My 24 hours at Assisi are intoxicating and are stirring that sceptic Fournier beyond belief. We get on *perfectly* and I have a great deal of esteem and affection for him. We are beginning to play very well. The recording for radio is good I think.[4]

To understand Poulenc's emotion we must return to 1936 when he visited Rocamadour, an ancient place of pilgrimage close to the Aveyron. A few days earlier he had heard of the death of his friend the composer Pierre-Octave Ferroud, decapitated in a road accident in Hungary. At Rocamadour, half-hollowed in the rock, is a chapel with a statue of the Virgin carved in black wood and said to be miraculous. For Poulenc this visit represented a mystical experience. Already the loss of his friend had caused him to re-examine his spiritual values; at Rocamadour he recovered the faith of his childhood. Not only did he return there in later years, but the event inspired his first religious music, the *Litanies de la Vierge noire*, which he began to sketch that evening. Assisi, seventeen years later, touched a raw nerve.

In July 1953 Fournier received the decoration of Chevalier de la Légion d'honneur. Poulenc wrote:

> *Ma beauté adorée*, I am sad not to be able to give you an extra kiss for your fête tomorrow (this one is for Michel Girard). Above all, and I'm not joking, may St Francis give you back your lovely peaceful face of Assisi. I am pleased with my work. I have just finished three movements out of four of my sonata for two pianos....
>
> ...Can you both come to lunch on Wednesday 24th with Pecci[5] and the beauties?[6] I hope so. A thousand affectionate thoughts for Lyda. For you... a naughty kiss. Poupoule.[7]

Poulenc had an unpredictable side. On one occasion in New York in Bernac's company, he left Fournier standing on the pavement as he sped off in a cab to a cocktail party given by the French coloratura Lily Pons, throwing over his shoulder 'He's a bad boy'. He apologized later for this little dart and dedicated his Cello Sonata to Fournier, telling him that this had provoked Gendron's fury and the remark that he, Poulenc, had dedicated it to Gendron's 'worst enemy'.

Generally Fournier found Poulenc very congenial company; he was funny and, usually, without malice. Both men were anxious and self-doubting; neither followed musical fashion. They had another unexpected thing in common: both were descended from eighteenth-century market gardeners.

*　*　*

Staying at any resort, however luxurious or beautiful, without his cello was not Fournier's idea of a holiday, so it was natural that at the Waldhaus at Sils Maria, a hotel particularly favoured by musicians, he played as often as he wished. One of his listeners in August 1953 was the German poet and novelist Hermann Hesse. Fournier played Bach Suites for him; conversation moved afterwards to the origins of Christianity. Hesse, the rebellious son of Pietist parents, was an agnostic. Fournier, brought up a Catholic, practised no religion but was drawn to the Lutheran faith by its simplicity and closeness to nature; the rigours of Calvinism were not for him. The two men talked of the link between Bach and Luther, and the dancing quality to be found in the Suites with their unique combination of the ascetic and the sensual.

'Still steeped in the wonderful Sarabande...' Hesse inscribed on the flyleaf of *Die Morgenlandfahrt*.[8] Fournier's fondness for the two Brahms sonatas puzzled the writer: they displayed a Germanism, he said, which didn't appeal to him.

Fournier's first recording of Strauss's *Don Quixote* was made this same year (1953) with Clemens Krauss and the Vienna Philharmonic. Glad to be working with the composer's friend and leading exponent, he arrived at the first session full of anticipation. He was disappointed: having apparently all but forgotten the piece, the orchestra was laboriously sightreading it. Krauss had to spend the entire session putting the players through the long Introduction while his soloist sat idly by.

Marking time in New York at the end of January, three days before his first Carnegie Hall recital with the Polish-born pianist Artur Balsam, Fournier confided in his sixteen-year-old son, setting a pattern for many years: 'I'm rather resigned, waiting for my recital, and what I hope for above all is a great artistic success.' He added some paternal advice:

> You must realize that this damned career is exhausting and means continuous labour because competition is so enormous and audiences so unfaithful. [...] You have to renew yourself repeatedly and never rest on passing laurels. Keep this in mind, you who live only for music and are so gifted. Follow your mother's marvellous instinct and don't procrastinate. Make the best of the quiet life you are blessed with to study as much as possible and store up the maximum of repertoire. Tomorrow I'm going to hear Brailowski in a Chopin recital, then on Tuesday Milstein and Ormandy in the Tchaikovsky. That will prevent me from moping before my concert. [...]
>
> The weather here is very fine, not very cold, and I pray heaven not to send a snowstorm on Wednesday! I shall cable on Thursday to say if it was a success. It's wrong to think a concert in New York is any bit more important than in any other city but you really do live entirely on your nerves beforehand!
>
> I'm as well as one could hope and have seen quite a lot of people as rich as they are boring, like the [Xs....] What matters is the great mass of ordinary people and not the rich snobs interested only in millionaire artists. [...]
>
> This week I shall buy you *Death and Transfiguration* with Furtwängler.
>
> *Je t'embrasse bien tendrement toujours*, P.[9]

*   *   *

In 1947 Fournier had gone to Berlin alone, sparing Lyda the sight of the ruined capital. Early in 1954 they went together for a concert with Karl Böhm and the Berlin Philharmonic. They also visited east Berlin to hear David Oistrakh, in spite of Böhm's warnings that Lyda's passport, which showed that she was of Russian birth, might have got her into trouble.

In May 1954 at the Salle Pleyel, Fournier and Kempff gave their first recital together. (It says much for Fournier's stamina that the night before, in London, he had played three concertos – Haydn, Dvořák and Elgar – at a sold-out Festival Hall concert in aid of a polio charity.[10]) This recital was the beginning of an outstanding partnership to be joined later in trios by the fine violinist Henryk Szeryng. Kempff and Fournier had widely differing natures. Never rattled by touring, Kempff didn't suffer from nerves, indeed on the platform he appeared to enter another world, moving serenely through even the occasional inaccuracies on a wave of spontaneous and poetic inspiration. Both artists had the deepest reverence for Beethoven and returned many times to Romain Rolland's study of the composer. Kempff said 'We know that everything is stilled in us when we play a Beethoven adagio.'[11]

Francis Poulenc was in the audience at this first recital. Remembering his Italian tour with Fournier, and clearly still under the cellist's spell, he wrote from Touraine:

Mon Pierre chéri,

This is a real love-letter. I have not stopped thinking of your concert. You were sublime and if I didn't have the hope of playing with you again I should have committed suicide at the métro Ternes out of despair and jealousy (nice headline). I found Kempff marvellous (although not as good as you) but I'll keep Debussy and Stravinsky for myself.[12] My dream would be to write something worthy of you at last, and to kidnap you. How many times in sad moments, which thank God come less often now, have I thought of our Italy, of 'my' Bach sonatas at Assisi. I can say this without lying: if I were a virtuoso I should like to be Pierre Fournier, for you possess something few people can boast: style.

My Carmelites are making good progress. I must play them to you. You'll see it's very good and I think you'll get a little shock. I'm coming back on Monday 6th. Get in touch with me. Don't let Lyda be jealous of this letter.

Je vous embrasse tous deux très affectueusement, plus le fils.[13]

Poulenc was under stress on several fronts: his health, a complicated relationship which he could neither sustain nor relinquish[14] and, above all, his opera *Dialogues des Carmélites*. The commission from the Italian publishers Ricordi both entranced and alarmed him, but rights difficulties had interrupted his work when it was at full throttle. He was to cut short a tour in November to undergo a sleep cure. Approaching this crisis, he wrote to Fournier in September 1954:

Quite definitely, my beloved angel, I do not like Dvorak's concerto although I couldn't write one myself sounding half as good, but you played it so well last night at Lucerne (I suppose it was live) that during the Andante 'it' stood up for joy – what would Marguerite Long or our biographers think if ever they read this? It can't be helped.

Mon Pierre, please forgive my silence but I have been very distressed for various reasons which I'll explain when at last we are on our own!

I'm as fit as the Pont neuf, I sleep, I look ravishingly well, and... I've grown a moustache which is driving all the women crazy about me. At last!!!

The Carmélites are finished. I am at this very moment putting them out of pain. You'll see: my last act is terrifying... the whole tragedy unfolds in an atmosphere of happiness and peace. Kisses at various degrees but warm ones for the three of you. Happily some people are beginning to take my music seriously. At last!!!![15]

In the turmoil afflicting Poulenc there is a disturbing coincidence: the nature of his friend Ferroud's horrific death in 1936 echoed in the opera's final, scaffold scene. The commission had erupted at another moment of personal crisis and its theme 'above all... grace and the transference of grace'[16] stirred Poulenc's deepest feelings. 'I thank God for it, despite the suffering involved. And yet with all that suffering, I will still be known as "the charming Poulenc".'[17]

After the sleep cure at l'Hay-les-Roses, he wrote again:

Mon Pierre

Your old phoenix is rising slowly from his ashes, a little each day. Last month spent in the Pyr[enees] with my neurologist friend [the Bordeaux specialist Dr Delmas-Marsalet] helped me so much. How did this ever happen to me? My concierge says it's my menopause; maybe it is but I still expect to be healthy enough to travel with my darling cellist. The Vivaldi concerto still intoxicates me. You are undeniably the greatest French instrumentalist and the world's greatest cellist. Upon this *je te baise...* on your forehead I mean. Kisses to Lyda and Bébé.[18]

Notes

1. Simone Girard was the organizer of the Avignon concert society.
2. Francis Poulenc to Simone Girard, March [1953], cited in *Francis Poulenc 'Echo and Source'. Selected Correspondence 1915–1963*, tr. and ed. Sidney Buckland (1991) London: Gollancz, p. 201.
3. Francis Poulenc to Lyda Fournier, [?] March 1953.
4. *Francis Poulenc. Correspondance 1915–1963*, réunie par Hélène de Wendel, Paris: Editions du Seuil 1967, p. 209.
5. Contessa Mimi Pecci-Blunt, a leading figure in Italian musical life, co-founder of the *Concerti di Primavera* which had links with *La Sérénade* in Paris.
6. Arthur Gold and Robert Fizdale, American duo pianists and authors. The Sonata had its first performance at the BBC on 2 November 1953.
7. Francis Poulenc to Pierre Fournier, 1 June [1953].
8. Hermann Hesse *Die Morgenlandfahrt: eine Erzählung*. Tr. by H. Rosner as *The Journey to the East: a Tale*. New York 1968.
9. Pierre Fournier to Jean Pierre, 31 January 1954.
10. The concert with Sir Malcolm Sargent and the London Philharmonic was in aid of the National Fund for Poliomyelitis Research, predecessor of the present-day British Polio Fellowship. Sargent's own daughter had been a victim of polio.
11. Wilhelm Kempff in an interview with Jürgen Meyer-Josten (Courtesy of Deutsche Grammophon.)
12. The Debussy Sonata and Stravinsky's *Italian Suite*, which Fournier and Poulenc had played together in Paris and on the Italian tour.
13. Francis Poulenc to Pierre Fournier, 31 May [1954].
14. The young *toulonnais*, Lucien Roubert, was to die of tuberculosis just as Poulenc was finishing the score of *Dialogues*.
15. Francis Poulenc to Pierre Fournier. 16 September [1954].
16. Francis Poulenc *Entretiens avec Claude Rostand*, Paris: Julliard, 1954.
17. Francis Poulenc to Henri Hell, [14 February 1954]. Buckland, op. cit., p. 216.
18. Francis Poulenc to Pierre Fournier, undated. [January 1955?].

18   Further Afield

In order to follow another thread in Fournier's life we must return to 1953 when he and Lyda were guests at the Chateau d'Etoy which the pianist Alexander ('Sasha') Brailowski and his wife Ella had taken for the summer.[1] It was their first meeting with Eugene Ormandy who was a fellow guest. Ormandy took a liking to Jean Pierre and made him presents of gramophone records. Fournier and Ormandy were to appear together at an OSCC concert in Paris the following year, and Ormandy was keen to meet the critics Claude Rostand and Bernard Gavoty ('Clarendon' of *Le Figaro*).

In October 1954 a dinner was arranged at rue Lesueur. Fournier fetched Ormandy at the Hôtel Plaza Athénée and on the way the conductor asked who were the other guests. Fournier mentioned the pianist Magda Tagliaferro, an old friend. Ormandy said he hoped fervently that she would not ask to play at Philadelphia. But when the guests arrived and Tagliaferro appeared, he stretched out his arms with the warmest invitation to do exactly that. It was a banal form of insincerity, but despite a lifetime in the profession, Fournier never learned to brush this sort of thing off, and he was furious. It was an intransigence which to a certain degree set him apart; it also brought several relationships to an end. '*C'était un pur*', Gabriel Dussurget said of him.[2] In the event the Dvořák Concerto with Ormandy was acceptable if a little detached; the sympathy had gone.

Their next joint engagement was also fated to present a problem. Fournier had not seen the last of the Virgil Thomson concerto which he had, up to now, succeeded in escaping. Now Ormandy was asking him to play it in Paris as part of a concert series called *Salut à la France*.[3] Fournier suggested that a French concerto might be more suitable in his native city. 'So you refuse?' asked Ormandy, hearing of the cellist's reservations. Bloch's *Schelomo* was accepted as an alternative but Fournier was never again invited to play with the Philadelphia Orchestra. With Fritz Reiner in Chicago he agreed to give the concerto (Reiner was adamant that there had to be an American piece); the addition of *Schelomo* was the carrot.

*   *   *

The first Japanese tour in November 1954 brought a gale of invitations to the theatre and to restaurants. After cushions on the floor, chopsticks and sushi, Fournier was tired and relieved to find that he could get some rest: the hotel was 'dead at 10 pm'. 'Kempff was magnificent' he wrote to Jean Pierre

> and just to play with him put me back into that European atmosphere which I miss in this remote country. You never know what the Japanese are thinking in spite of all their kindness, and their reactions are always devoid of emotion.

He had a concert nearly every day on this long tour, causing him to add 'My only consolation is to work very hard to get back my form and... my repertoire.' He longed for the weeks to pass 'until we two are together again'. Time and distance brought out the absent father:

> I am sad not to be able to do more for you on the spot, but already you know that nothing serious is ever done except by oneself and by daily work.

He promised 'ravishing Japanese binoculars':

> Tokyo is dreadful. I'm glad to be staying four days at Kyoto where the old Japan is still intact and which Kempff described with enthusiasm. Up to now the only visions of enchantment I have had are the photographs I've been swamped with. Like all artists I've been pursued and photographed all day long. After each concert two beautiful little Japanese girls in kimonos bring you breathtaking flowers and when I left my room it looked like an Easter altar. As for the workings of the tour I shall be getting into bad habits: nothing to worry about and every journey taken care of by the NHK who transport everything and look after the lot.

But what went to his heart was the stillness of the Japanese audiences:

> In no country in the world do they listen to you in so religious a silence....
>   I think of you all the time, hoping everything is going the way you deserve. I want to help you [...] on the threshold of the career which is taking shape before you.[4]

This tour was clouded by very sad news: the death of Furtwängler in Germany on 30 November. For Pierre and Lyda the world of music was to seem a duller place; they had also lost a very loyal friend.

*   *   *

In January 1955 Fournier heard from Bohuslav Martinů who was in Nice:

> The other day I heard the Cello Concerto on the radio.[5] I didn't recognize it and I asked Schott if it wasn't the first version material full of mistakes. And it was. He [sic] said he still hadn't received the second version. I thought this was fixed a long time ago. Besides I want to establish the concerto definitively and I have asked Strecker (Schott) if he would agree to publish a new edition and he accepted because he has now had several requests for this concerto. I'm going to work at it again and settle the scoring (without piano) and also the cello part. Where will you be in early September? Can you send me the score, I have a little time now and I could do it at once. Are you not coming to Nice? We'll be here until the end of July....[6]

On 19 June the composer wrote again:

I have received the score and I am terribly disappointed in my orchestration: it seems 1939 was not a good year for creative work. *Anyway* I'm going to do the scoring again and this is for my own conscience because... I want it settled for good. I shall reduce the orchestra so that the solo part is quite free. Of course the concerto is dedicated to you. What worries me is that there will be changes, and in the cello part as well, and for that I should like your advice.... I am sure the concerto can remain in the cello repertoire, but not in its present condition. Everything must be settled for good.[7]

On a copy of the 1931 printed score, Martinů made what is probably the first series of 'definitive' corrections, with comments, explanations, annotations and instructions to his soloist. One orchestral section is marked self-deprecatingly *'Beaucoup des bruit [sic] pour rien.'* ('Much ado about nothing.')

Fournier gave a first performance of the revised Concerto with the Bayerische Rundfunk in 1955, and another the following year with Rafael Kubelik and the Berlin Philharmonic. The work had a mixed reception in London in 1962.

*   *   *

Fournier's visit to South Africa in the summer of 1955 started with Angola and Mozambique, and with a problem: his visa forgotten in a drawer. Cancellation threatened and angry telephone calls followed until an impresario friend, Constantin Varella Cid, organized some breaking and entering to salvage the visa and save the tour.

A South African Airways captain refused to allow Fournier's cherished Miremont in the passenger cabin, and this resulted in the cello being flown to Durban by mistake. The Greek cellist Elephtherios Papastavro came to the rescue with his own Amati, saying Fournier was the only man in the world to whom he would ever dream of lending it.

The first visit to South Africa was to bring Fournier a new friend who was to become a frequent correspondent and confidante, Peta ('Peter') Fisher. A professional flautist by training and married to Cyril Fisher, she was the founder and director of Musica Viva, a concert society based in Johannesburg.[8] Known for her loyalty to artists, she persisted in honouring her commitments even at a difficult time when financial loss had been sustained after an astronomically expensive singer had decamped during a tour.

Fournier continued to voice his fears and desires and counter his sense of solitude through letter-writing. Secrecy was in his nature and, as practicalities had to be considered, accommodation addresses continued to be aimed, somewhat vainly, at domestic peace. The feverish mobility of his career did nothing to free him from the inescapable isolation of his childhood. On the plane from Geneva to London he wrote to Peta Fisher on 10 August. The journey from South Africa had not gone smoothly:

After 24 hours spent in Leopoldville in a terrible 'blue mood', we finally boarded another Sabena plane to Brussels where we had just the time to catch a train to Paris, every plane being full. And now I have just 2½ days with my family.

You make me confident regarding human beings who betray so often our hopes and illusions....

He would like to write more often but confided the first hint of the mounting crisis in his private life: 'My life has already started to be very complicated... music remains my only escape, the only safe road among so many dreamy paths.'[9] By the time he reached Stockholm in the last week of September (after London, Edinburgh and Montreux), he admitted to being

quite exhausted and taking as much rest as possible in complete solitude apart from a few concerts.

How is your season? Are you happy with your artists? I met Jean-Claude [Ambrosini] recently, for the first time since our return together and it was *so* good to remember... the wonderful friendship you gave us. But I can't say to anyone the 'unsaid', which I would like to with you, dear Peter. It seems very hard to open my heart in a letter and I am afraid to create complications around! But you must never forget that I shall be longing to find, close to you, these rare moments of communion which are treasured in my inner thoughts and for which I shall ever be grateful....[10]

A stop at Duisburg gave him a few days' rest after Frankfurt, Bielefeld and Cologne, and thoughts turned to Jean Pierre at rue Lesueur:

Mon cher petit Jean Pierre

I send you all my fond thoughts now that you are going to be alone again, and I hope that the week will go quickly until the joy of seeing you again when we get back. I arrived this morning, very glad not to have to move from the same hotel for a few days. The tour has been tiring and monotonous, the only 'entertainment' being the continual moving from place to place, but on the whole I have been pleased with the reception everywhere. The evening before last at Bielefeld, I played Don Quixote with only a single rehearsal, a feat impossible with any French orchestra! But here, even in the smaller towns, the level of musical culture is amazing, as well as the enthusiasm of every audience. The day before, the Frankfurt (Schumann) concert wasn't very pleasant, with the conductor [S.] so infatuated with himself like all those conductors with a job in America! He is at Pittsburg and was invited to conduct my concert. The orchestra very pedestrian and the hall horrible, acoustically. Tell *Maman* that I'll go and hear Janigro on Monday evening in Cologne: [he is] playing the Dvorak... I shall join her on the train.[11] That way we'll arrive together.

Remember me to [the pianist Friedrich] Gulda please, and spend your free time at concerts rather than at the cinema!! Work without tiring, and plan your practice time.... Above all check constantly with the metronome. I know from experience how important that is; you can get into bad habits if you don't watch the balance of movements which is the essential factor in success before an audience. Never get discouraged or tell yourself that this profession is slavery. The further you go and the more you think you are in command, the more you notice how fragile your form is without daily practice.... I have learnt that any development entails perpetually going back to the beginning, and memory can be a problem. Play your repertoire *slowly* and learn from my experience, an experience I only wish I could have conceived when I was your age. Develop your memory (yours is a gift), it is the greatest advantage in this career. I am, alas, a slave to it, often wondering how I can possibly hold so many works in my head....

Let me know everything that is going on because since I left it has been nothing but train timetables and hotels!

I embrace you very tenderly and I'll remember your camera which I shall buy this week.

A toi toujours en pensée. Papa.[12]

For the Edinburgh Festival of 1955 Ian Hunter formed a new ensemble, the Festival Piano Trio, with Fournier, Zino Francescatti and Solomon. Fournier appeared in five concerts which included chamber music, the Beethoven Triple Concerto and the Brahms Double. This star trio should have toured Europe and the USA, but tragedy put an end to these plans: the following year a stroke prematurely ended the great Solomon's career. Like Fournier, his partner on many occasions, Solomon had a deep respect for the spirit behind the music and a corresponding scorn for platform affectations.

Appearing in Stockholm in September 1955, but independently, Fournier and the violinist David Oistrakh managed to go to each other's concerts. While neighbours at a dinner party, they discovered that they both had a couple of days to spare. Oistrakh said 'Pity we can't make music together....' The director of the Swedish Radio overheard this and offered them the use of 'a big studio with a magnificent piano' for Oistrakh's pianist, Vladimir Yampolski. Here Oistrakh 'ran in' the new (First) Shostakovich Concerto.[13] Over tea Oistrakh mused, 'Pity we can't do the Double Brahms....' 'Give me five minutes' said the director who rushed to the library to fetch the parts. Fournier left his impression of this impromptu performance:

> I was very moved because it was an unforgettable session in the sense that perhaps through some mysterious instinct we had the same conception of the phrasing, the same breathing, the same contrasts. Oistrakh was pleased too. He said 'Pity we didn't record that.'[14]

Fournier asked him if he was free. He was. The next day Fournier telephoned Walter Legge ('a difficult man, but very intelligent'). That is how the recording with Alceo Galliera and the Philharmonia Orchestra was made.[15] 'David Oistrakh had infinite kindness' Fournier recalled later. 'He was never one of those triumphalist fiddlers. He spoke of musicians and of music with the deepest respect.'[16]

*   *   *

With the 1956 New Year greetings went a sad anniversary letter to Jeanine Pérès whose sister, Pierre's first teacher Odette Krettly, had died a year earlier of muscular dystrophy. Throughout his life he spoke of Odette with affection: his gratitude, he wrote, was 'stamped with the happiness of youth'.[17]

Respite was brief and in the last week of January Fournier was in the States. On his way to Houston and Lebanon, he paused in San Francisco and wrote to Jean Pierre, marvelling at the American landscape seen from the sky; on earth the picture did not enchant:

> ...in the small towns, nice people, all rather alike, with the same conversations, the

same parties…beginning 'It was a lovely concert' and ending 'I hope you'll come back soon', that is in 10 or 20 years!!

Changes of accompanist at each city (*'here…* charming and as helpful as one could wish') condemned him to repeated rehearsals of the same works, boring him dreadfully. He exhorted Jean Pierre to work relentlessly at his technique ('you have the rest'), because 'nowadays there is room only for the faultless – alas!' With languages this 'will open the doors of the future…'. Fatherly considerations led him to brood on age and how out of tune he was with America:

> You would like this country which is made for youth but can scare anyone older. I find that America and the Americans, saturated as they are with material goods and labour-saving machines, are bored, because apart from the *rush* to make money, they don't know what to do with themselves and haven't the wit to think.

The sense of isolation had returned:

> I have *no* news except a short letter from *Maman* and with the black mood I have been in since my NY concerts[18] I feel very much alone, hoping to find some news at Cleveland where I shall be on the evening of the 31st for the *only* interesting concert.

János Starker had been the subject of an article in *Time* magazine ('the greatest perhaps of all cellists') and Fournier took pleasure in his friend's success, urging Jean Pierre to read this 'very good article which [proved] that [Starker was] gaining recognition everywhere.' A telegram from Georges Soria[19] confirmed the dates for the Brahms Double Concerto recording with Oistrakh. '*Les shoppings*' and a rest from concerts appeared like an oasis. 'I have ordered your records – tell me what else you would like.' Fatigue, isolation and his 'American experience [which] came too late' permeate this letter.[20]

Taken up with his US tour in early February 1956, he had no time to ruminate on 'the many problems' of his private life, but only to 'think of his dear music'; no time, that is, until at Cleveland he put pen to paper in a disjointed letter to Peta:

> I hope everything is well [with] you and that you have no more trouble with your health. I make always plans for the future, building before 'getting old' on a ground already long prepared.

The ambient materialism grated on him and sympathetic human contact was scarce:

> I always think of you, Peter – distance and time don't exist for two human beings who seem to understand each other so well. I shall have a lot to tell you in September.

He added a line from André Maurois' life of George Sand: '*La vie est une longue blessure qui s'endort rarement et ne se guérit jamais.*' ('Life is one long wound which rarely sleeps and never heals.')[21] Approaching fifty, preoccupied with age and under emotional strain, he longed 'for a few moments of happiness with someone who [had] suffered a lot', then added 'Forgive these few inconsistent lines written in complete loneliness of soul.'

It is a surprisingly wretched letter coming from a man who enjoyed conviviality, food and wine, painting, travel, the company of friends and all the good things in life. But before a reader could suspect the onset of depression, the mood suddenly changed key, with revivifying thoughts of the coming South African tour and characteristics hints of discord with his agent (a chronic Fournier condition).[22] Life went on and there would be more travel: Paris, Turkey, then London for the Brahms recording with Oistrakh, the fruit of musical-love-at-first-sight.... Relieved of his sorrows, he was happily packing his suitcase once again.[23]

The young Mstislav Rostropovich made his triumphant Paris début at the Salle Gaveau in February 1956. Visiting rue Lesueur he brought Pierre and Lyda his photograph, a tin of caviare and a bottle of vodka. He told them he had two ambitions – to visit Casals at Prades and them in Paris. He then dazzled them at the piano with a study of his own in the manner of Prokofiev. They were totally captivated.

In those days Soviet artists needed special visas to perform in the west. At the embassy party Rostropovich asked Lyda to use her influence with Kiesgen to obtain some invitations he could then show Goskoncert (the Soviet agency). Meanwhile, threading their way between the guests, the KGB were watching. Each time one of them came within earshot Slava plunged into some wild new anecdote. In the end the minders were reduced to staring hungrily at the buffet.

While Fournier's letters during this period betrayed fatigue, self-doubt and loneliness, he was nevertheless at the height of his powers; the one was no doubt the price he was paying for the other.

In March he had a triumph in Brussels with Carlo Maria Giulini: 'the purity of sound, the emotion he communicates, the impeccable technique...'.[24] In June, a Paris recital with Ernest Lush compelled the critic Claude Rostand to hail him as 'the great Fournier, bearer of the most sublime messages of music'.[25] Another critic, Dorel Handman, recognized that 'the gods had given him everything: musicality, the ability to "sing" and to make one forget the strictures of technique.'[26] While Handman reproached Lush for 'not being more discreet', Rostand found him 'self-effacing'. Poor Lush! Clarendon (Bernard Gavoty) wrote of him '[Fournier's] excellent partner... who is not an accompanist but a pianist: a chasm separates the two'.[27]

*   *   *

Incredibly, in the midst of all this activity, the Fourniers moved house, leaving France in June 1956 to settle in Geneva. For some time Pierre had been tiring of Paris: the endemic restlessness, the changing musical scene and the old echoes of the war. He was privately under emotional strain, exacerbated by allegations about the family reportedly put about by Gendron whose old animosity was public knowledge. The move had been in the air for some time: it was finally set in motion by a new situation typical of post-war Paris.

Comfortable flats to rent were scarce in the fifties and there were few as yet for sale. The flat-hunter would expect an obstacle course strewn with phantom landlords, dubious intermediaries, promises, delays and Borgian family entanglements. He would also part with a considerable sum in key money. Against this background Pierre and Lyda suddenly learnt that their own landlord wanted to recover their flat for his son who, he claimed, was due to return from North Africa. (It was to emerge later that he had sold it instead to a third party.) A half-hearted search for another Paris flat ensued, but although Lyda doubted the wisdom of losing regular contact with Paris, their minds were made up. The financial advantages were obvious, but Pierre lacked foresight in money matters. While he was often to laugh off his motives for settling in Geneva, ('You can get direct flights everywhere'), his physical need for its solid peace was undeniable, although from time to time he would miss the charm of Paris, its bustle and beauty.

Before moving into 14 Parc du Château Banquet, the family took a furnished flat at 5 ru du Vieux Collège, on the edge of the old town. Lyda was quite sad to leave this temporary home and wailed '*C'était si cosy!*'

Many years later Fournier and Gendron met at a concert. Fournier was by this time an old man and Gendron, in spite of being very ill himself, clearly wished to make amends. After casting about for something to do, he did the best he could in the circumstances: he fetched Fournier a sandwich.

A month later after the move to Geneva, in July 1956, Fournier lost an old friend, the violinist Robert Krettly whose quartet he had joined at the age of seventeen. The work of those years had laid the foundations of his career and he never forgot what he owed to Krettly. From Montreux he wrote to the surviving Krettly sister Jeanine, remembering his 'companion and guide' Robert with the same gratitude and affection as their sister Odette, 'still alive at every step of [his] career.'[28]

*   *   *

In 1955 Peta Fisher, founder of the Johannesburg Musica Viva Society, approached Hans Kramer in Cape Town suggesting that he invite Fournier to give a recital. Kramer later joked self-deprecatingly about his financial qualms in those early days before the subscription concerts and the Cape Town Concert Club. This soon became a sought-after platform for top-flight musicians – Andrés Segovia, Irmgard Seefried, Alfred Brendel, Heinz Holliger and many others.

At the Temple Hall then, on 17 September 1956, Fournier gave a recital with Jean-Claude Ambrosini. Hans Kramer said of the cellist, remembering that time, 'One's contact with great artists is so brief that it tends to be intense; it was so with Fournier.'[29]

Like South America earlier, South Africa offered Fournier an irresistible mixture of music, friendship, distance and physical ease which swept away any possible scruples about apartheid, but the fervour he encountered when playing for a segregated black audience underlined the injustice like a reproach, and he was very moved.

In September 1956 he appeared with Sir Malcolm Sargent at the Johannesburg Festival (unsurprisingly in the Elgar Concerto) and performed Kodály's Op. 8 unaccompanied Sonata for the first time in a recital. Written in 1915, this work had been slow to attract major performers; any others would have been defeated by its difficulty. In the States only one cellist, George Neikrug, had played it before the composer's fellow countryman, János Starker, made it his own in 1948 with a prizewinning French recording followed by another in 1950.[30] It was he who persuaded Fournier, Tortelier and, in America, Zara Nelsova to take it up. Fournier liked the work which he adopted for his regular practice. Of a Paris performance in 1959 Claude Rostand was to write that it called for

> breathtaking virtuosity and all the resources of the instrument. In Fournier's hands this 'awkward' instrument shows extraordinary richness, diversity and power. A whole orchestra, including percussion, bursts out of this sonata, handled with stupefying mastery by M. Fournier and producing an astonishing tonal chemistry with rhythmic precision as delicate and exact as clockwork.[31]

Fournier had recorded the two Brahms sonatas with Wilhelm Backhaus in May 1955 for Decca. (This was at Backhaus' suggestion: Fournier's modesty would never have permitted him to make the first move.) Now Walter Legge of HMV planned to produce his own set with Fournier and Walter Gieseking. Beethoven, Debussy and Rachmaninov sonatas were also on the cards at this time, and trios with David Oistrakh. Sadly, four months after the move to Geneva these plans were cut short by the premature death of Gieseking on 27 October.

In November Fournier appeared with Ansermet and the OSR at the Victoria Hall in Geneva in aid of Hungarian refugees. This was the autumn when a mesmerized and impotent Europe watched the Soviet tanks roll into Budapest to crush the Revolution. Hungarians were fleeing in their thousands. From Paris Fournier wrote to Peta:

> The recent events, the [uncertainty] of the future are so depressing! I try to devote the best of myself to my professional activity, the only reason for my existence now, which can bring some security. My new flat is ready now in Geneva. On my return we shall move in. I hope my family will be happy then. For me there is no more happiness, real happiness – I wish that I shall be strong enough, morally and physically, to go on. Will you forgive me if the little bracelet I have sent you is not a heavy gold one!!! Consider it as a presence [*sic*] and accept my early but most tender wishes for everything you may desire. A very happy New Year also. With love, Pierre.[32]

Paris, with all its complications, was the city of his birth. Geneva represented something of a leap into the unknown.

Notes

1. This house near Chexbres in the canton of Vaud was owned by Guy de Pourtalès.
2. ('He was without guile.') Gabriel Dussurget in conversation with the author.

3. Two concerts at the Palais de Chaillot, and one (with Fournier) at the Opéra. The other soloists were the baritone William Warfield and the pianist Alexander Brailowski.
4. Pierre Fournier to Jean Fonda Fournier, 12 November 1954.
5. Martinů's First Cello Concerto, published by Schott in 1931 and revised in 1955.
6. Bohuslav Martinů to Pierre Fournier, 13 January 1955.
7. Id., 19 June 1955.
8. All Fournier's letters to Peta Fisher are quoted exactly as he wrote them, in English.
9. Pierre Fournier to Peta Fisher, 10 August 1955.
10. Id., 23 September 1955.
11. Antonio Janigro (1918–1989), Italian-born cellist and conductor, pupil of Alexanian. Especially associated with small ensembles, he was a duo partner of Dinu Lipatti and played in a trio with Paul Badura-Skoda and Jean Fournier.
12. Pierre Fournier to Jean Fonda Fournier, 'Sunday' [1955].
13. The work was dedicated to Oistrakh and he was to give its first performance shortly after in Leningrad with Evgeni Mravinsky. Mark Lubotsky, a pupil of David Oistrakh, remembers that in Fournier's opinion it was one of Oistrakh's finest achievements (Mark Lubotsky to the author).
14. Pierre Fournier, *L'Ame et la corde*, No. 5, November 1983.
15. At the Kingsway Hall, London, on 29 February and 2–3 March 1956.
16. See note 14.
17. Pierre Fournier to Jeanine Krettly-Pérès, 31 December 1955.
18. A Carnegie Hall concert with Charles Munch and the Boston SO had been poorly reviewed by Howard Taubman in the *New York Times*.
19. Georges Soria, French writer and historian, indefatigable worker in Franco-Soviet cultural exchanges.
20. Pierre Fournier to Jean Fonda Fournier, 26 January 1956.
21. André Maurois *Lélia ou la Vie de George Sand*, Paris: Hachette 1952, p. 332. In a letter from George Sand to the actor Bocage (Pierre-Francoise Touzé). She continues *'Je suis bien triste et bien sombre mais je n'en aime que mieux ceux qui méritent d'être aimés.'* ('I am very sad and very gloomy but hence I love all the more those who deserve to be loved.')
22. Amaryllis remembers meetings starting with a brief 'How are you?' followed by a diatribe against the latest agent or record producer to offend.
23. Pierre Fournier to Peta Fisher, 1 February 1956.
24. *La Lanterne*, Brussels, 13 March 1956.
25. *Carrefour*, 20 June 1956.
26. *Temps de Paris*, 13 June 1956.
27. *Le Figaro*, 12 March 1962.
28. Pierre Fournier to Jeanine Krettly-Pérès, 20 July 1956.
29. Hans Kramer in conversation with the author.
30. On Pacific and Period labels respectively. The Pacific recording won the Grand Prix du Disque and is still (1993) on 78 rpm; it was also reissued on LP. (János Starker to the author, 22 February 1993.)
31. *Carrefour*, 8 June 1959.
32. Pierre Fournier to Peta Fisher, 22 November 1956.

19   Not Only for Cellists[1]

By 1949, with increased solo work, Fournier was so often away from Paris that he felt it unjustifiable to hold on to his teaching post at the Conservatoire. He resigned, but continued to teach privately. In Geneva he was able to give his 'young professionals' sustained attention between tours; often they stayed at Château Banquet for a period of work. He also gave masterclasses at the Geneva Conservatoire and at Muraltengut in Zurich.

A new student could feel intimidated by the aristocratic figure whose old-fashioned courtesy made him sometimes appear distant. The more diffident of the two, however, was quite likely to be Fournier himself, hiding his natural warmth under a *vieille France* formality which was not coldness but respect. One Parisian student, Madeleine Bourreil, observed his hand trembling as he demonstrated a phrase.

Having met Fournier through Thomas Igloi,[2] Emma Ferrand joined the Zurich classes. 'They were quite demanding. For two weeks you had a lesson of an hour or so on alternate days and you never did a piece more than once, so you had to have a lot of them!' She observed that Fournier looked comfortable; there were no contortions. His hand was free; he used the fourth finger and thumb a lot. She noticed his subtle bowing technique and the vibrato used very sparingly, 'with flexible joints, never a roll';[3] 'an unagitated vibrato from the end of the finger',[4] 'more like a violinist's.'[5] 'He had a relaxed left arm with a powerful hand held in a natural, rather than a claw-like position'.[6] The right arm was Fournier's voice. 'The variations in speed and in the weight of the bow produced subtle reflexive changes.'[7] In Fournier's own words, 'It is the infinite variations in stress controlled by the bow which give warmth to your playing.' Or more simply 'You must speak with your bow'.[8] His own use of it was a supreme lesson in flexibility and eloquence: 'it was liquid.'[9] One of the exercises Fournier gave pupils to develop bow control was a two-octave arpeggio, up and down one string in a single bow, starting at moderate speed and becoming progressively slower and slower.[10]

Everything looked natural; his freedom of playing liberated the sound. It appeared effortless – a difficult achievement with a cello. He didn't 'tighten' with volume, or worry about technical problems. The First Shostakovich Concerto has a spectacularly difficult section towards the end, in which the soloist flies about the instrument at terrific speed. Fournier took his pupil's cello and gave a breathtaking demonstration of the passage but so effortlessly that one forgot the difficulty.[11]

*   *   *

Metaphors drawn from a lifelong passion for painting informed much of Fournier's teaching. He considered that vibrato was overworked by cellists and, drawing inspiration directly from hearing the guitarist Andrés Segovia, he believed that its use should be confined to 'the ultimate touch of colour, the last dabs of the painter's brush… like a sunbeam falling on a canvas and bathing it in sudden light.'[12] Time and again he returned to Giotto in Padua, to El Greco in Toledo and to the joy of Monet whose brush-strokes he translated into music. He numbered painters among his friends: Reuben Rubin in Israel, and in Mexico Leonardo Niermann who presented him with two pictures.

When Douglas Cameron asked Fournier to take on his pupil Derek Simpson, Fournier warned that he was the worst professor in the world, 'always away'. 'Yes, but you're the best cellist', Cameron replied. Of all the foreign exponents of the Elgar Concerto, Cameron thought that Fournier was 'the only one to get it right'.[13] The affinity between Cameron and Fournier was such that Derek made the transition between the two teachers with ease. Lessons at rue Lesueur, often punctuated by Jean Pierre's only too audible high spirits in the corridor, were 'three-quarters demonstration, one quarter words'. Derek found that he learnt through observing and recording infinite subtleties. 'I never heard him make an ugly sound.'[14]

Throughout his career Fournier revised his interpretations and this sometimes created problems. At one class, his students having been up late, dutifully marking all the bowing and fingering from the Fournier edition,[15] one of them played a passage.

'No! what are you doing? That is wrong!'
'But Maître, it says so in your own edition…'
'Well, that was some time ago. I've changed my mind.'[16]

He did exactly that with the Lalo Concerto, a piece which had won him the Premier Prix on leaving the Paris Conservatoire, and which he had subsequently made his own. There were too many markings ('It's impossible to play them all') and he altered or removed a great number, 'a relic of an age of pomposity and bad taste.'[17]

Fournier, who played his cello unfailingly every day ('Two days without it and I become irritable')[18] insisted on daily practice and, following his 'polyinstrumental' theory, recommended Sevčik's violin exercises. Gentle with hard-working pupils, he tended to suit the teaching to the student in an undogmatic way. 'Do what is comfortable' he sometimes said; at other times

'Don't be afraid of a little pain.'[19] He was kind to the less gifted, although they surely received less criticism and imaginative encouragement. A lively talent aroused the teacher in him, but anything brash, vulgar or artificial, sloppy thinking, unprepared work or a repetition of errors from an intensive earlier session brought out his sarcasm. Ralph Kirshbaum witnessed a pupil being handed back his part complete with markings, and told succinctly to 'go and learn it', and at least one arrogant student was shown the door.[20] Sometimes he complained 'They all make the same error at varying degrees.' By this he meant a tendency to rush at the arrival of a crescendo, swelling the tone and using excessive vibrato. He treated all his pupils, however, as colleagues with a modesty which astonished and could even embarrass. 'Do you think I ought to do the Prokofiev Sinfonia Concertante?' he asked a flabbergasted Julian Lloyd Webber. 'Rostropovich does it so well....'[21] At the Queen Elizabeth Hall on 5 October 1980, Fournier agreed to join the Aeolian Quartet for a performance of that Schubert C major Quintet (D 956), but only on condition that he played the second cello, to everybody's disappointment: they had been looking forward to hearing Fournier 'in all those glorious tunes'.[22]

Asked repeatedly by a French publisher to produce a definitive edition of the Bach Suites with his own markings, for a time Fournier declined. 'How can I? Each time I play them I have a new idea!'[23] The Suites were so much part of him that on the afternoon before a concert he was heard asking which of them he was playing that evening.

In a radio interview he was asked what advice he would give a young cellist. This was his reply:

> Start with the piano, early. It is good for your ear, for the
>   harmonic basis.
> Study all music, not merely the cello repertoire.
> Listen to singers and to other instrumentalists.
> Follow the composer's indications.
> Sing your music, interpret it, don't just play it.
> Work regularly every day.
> Don't get discouraged.
> Don't force the pace. Let your career develop naturally.[24]

Fournier believed that musicianship, like wine, should be laid down with wisdom and care.

Sceptical of supervirtuosi of the kind who are said to have reached the top by the age of thirty, he wondered where else they could go after that, but down. And why so often, emerging from one of their concerts, did he have an empty feeling? All the notes were there, but he had been left with nothing, having waited in vain for the phrase that tore at the heart, for the escape from reality. To their pyrotechnics he preferred 'a softer light, and playing which came from the soul and from intelligent thought.'[25]

* * *

Fournier enjoyed a family atmosphere at Château Banquet. Students would catch sight of a table laid for dinner with a *bonne bouteille*, a sign that Fournier knew when to stop work and turn to the serious business of enjoying life....[26]

Not long after Emma Ferrand's arrival in Geneva, Lyda and Pierre took her out to dinner with Thomas Igloi. It was a beautiful summer's evening and they ordered strawberries. Feeling a little shy, Emma was trying to find things to say to Lyda. When she returned to her plate the strawberries had vanished. All the time she had been talking, Fournier had been steadily eating them up.[27]

At the Wentworth Hotel in Aldeburgh many years later, Fournier's second wife, Junko, chided him at lunch for feeding scraps to the hotel cat. Throughout the meal, each time her attention wandered, he slipped another titbit neatly under the table.[28]

Like many musicians, he found crime novels the perfect antidote to platform stress, and was happy to settle down to a James Hadley Chase[29] in preference to the heavier delights of *War and Peace* or Romain Rolland's *Jean Christophe*, two works to which he often returned.

Above all it was the cello which had prevented him as a child from 'sinking into melancholy'. Incessant activity and travel were a compensation and provided escape. Even the introversion stemming from disability was turned to advantage: 'The withdrawal into oneself gives an inner strength which adds weight to any inspiration.' The key to his artistry lay in his early experience of quartet playing, what he described as 'discipline forged in friendship'.[30] One interviewer asked him if he had ever thought of conducting. He answered simply 'Doing one thing well in life is hard enough.'[31]

Notes

1. The title of this chapter may puzzle the general reader; for the Fournier student it should have something of a familiar ring, since he often urged his pupils to avoid confining themselves to the cello repertoire, but instead to study all music. Pianists know the value of thinking in terms of other instruments than their own; an imaginative masterclass can benefit any musician or music-lover. We shall return to this later.
2. See p. 157, note 19.
3. Emma Ferrand.
4. Julian Lloyd Webber.
5. Jonathan Williams.
6. Ralph Kirshbaum.
7. Derek Simpson.
8. See Appendix 2.
9. Julian Lloyd Webber.
10. Derek Simpson.
11. Julian Lloyd Webber.
12. Pierre Fournier, ORTF, *Radioscopie*, 5 July 1976.
13. Derek Simpson.
14. Id.
15. J S Bach, *Six Suites for Cello Solo*, ed. Pierre Fournier, New York: International Music Co 1972. Revised edition 1983.

16. Emma Ferrand.
17. Pierre Fournier to Jean Fonda Fournier, 21 March [1961].
18. On long flights he often did finger exercises.
19. Fergus Fleming *Amaryllis Fleming*, London: Sinclair Stevenson 1993, p. 79.
20. Ralph Kirshbaum.
21. Julian Lloyd Webber.
22. Derek Simpson.
23. He was later to change his mind. See above, note 14.
24. Pierre Fournier, ORTF, 5 July 1976.
25. Pierre Fournier, Radio Suisse Romande, 7 April 1975.
26. Julian Lloyd Webber.
27. Emma Ferrand.
28. John Owen.
29. Junko Fournier.
30. '*La discipline forgée dans l'amitié*', Jean Fonda Fournier Archive.
31. Pierre Fournier, Radio Suisse Romande, 7 April 1975.

Pierre Fournier in 1970

20   The Master

That he held a special place as an artist was clear from the very instant that the sound emerged from his instrument.

The late Henri Sauguet

When Henri Sauguet was asked what single quality Fournier's name evoked for him, he answered 'the sound'.[1] He didn't say 'the tone', implying something contrived, the result of hard work. The astonishing beauty of Fournier's sound, already remarkable in childhood, was part of himself. Like Kreisler, like Callas and like Kathleen Ferrier whom he worshipped, his 'voice' was so individual, so disturbing in its quality that even a single detached note out of context could be moving in itself: the emotion was an integral part of it. For many listeners it seemed that no more beautiful sound could be drawn from the cello, and it was all the more striking for the simplicity with which it had broken free.

Fournier came to be a soloist almost in spite of himself. Without Louise Maillot's support and encouragement to build up a solo repertoire (reinforced later by Lyda), he might have been content for the rest of his life playing the chamber music which suited his nature and had moulded him as a musician. The two guiding principles learnt during the Krettly Quartet years – fidelity to the composer and awareness of the other players – informed all his playing. He had an architectural grasp of works and took freedom within it, 'an amplitude and generosity of approach',[2] a certain liberty of phrasing, but 'only after ferocious self-discipline as regards the score'.[3] This freedom was lyrically described by an Italian critic years later: '*la fantasia quasi inarrivabile di un Fournier…*'.[4] World virtuosi, Fournier said, often wanted to set their stamp on works by distorting the music, whereas real personality in a musician consisted in persuading the audience to forget the instrument in favour of the music itself. 'With [Fournier] seductiveness [was] curbed by a sense of style.'[5] Although his technique was prodigious, the listener could be unaware of the fact; Fournier's own freedom liberated the music. 'He aimed to stir rather than to astonish.'[6] He played, he said, less for the applause of the public than for its silence.

Few things enchanted him more than what he called his musical *coups de foudre* (love at first sight), his encounters with musicians such as David Oistrakh, Sviatoslav Richter and Wilhelm Kempff, when the meeting of a kindred spirit and spontaneous music-making produced moments of unbridled delight. It had to be instantaneous: 'magic is there in the first moment or not at all.'[7]

Conductors sometimes obtained concessions – on a mutual basis it was understood! – and Fournier liked orchestral players, respecting them as professionals 'who had a difficult time, long hours, heard endless soloists and couldn't be fooled.'[8]

He saw much of his concerto playing as chamber music, particularly the Schumann Concerto which he described as 'a chamber concerto, a perpetual dialogue'.[9] He enjoyed being part of a small orchestra: it came, he said, with his training. 'Virtuosi going on for hours and hours perfecting their technique, that is not enough.'[10] Needing short pieces, or simply following his fancy, he poached liberally from violinists and singers: Brahms' *Feldeinsamkeit* for example, or Richard Strauss's *An einsamer Quelle*.

He found the career a lonely business, 'deprived of family for weeks at a time, carried by a certain egoism.... Alone when you come on to the platform, alone with your artistic responsibilities, alone again when you go off, and when people come with smiles to congratulate you, you are still alone.'[11] It is an illusion to think you can rest at the top of your career. There is no perfection: 'the closer you think you are to it, the further it moves away, like a mirage.'[12]

Chronically anxious ('I try to live with it'), Fournier learned from experience that a certain contentment before a concert could be a bad sign, whereas after a day spent worrying he would suddenly feel in control when he reached the hall. Asked if he thought about his performance when he went home he answered 'I always examine my conscience, and often sleep badly as a result!'[13] His greatest fear was not to be giving the best of himself 'when surrounded by great talent. It is such a responsibility: you are creating your own note.'[14]

In later years his son and frequent duo partner was aware of a stormier element entering his playing, as if he were sometimes turning away from the 'angelic' quality. At those times, less concerned with beautiful sound, he took risks in the search for a deeper musical insight.

It was Fournier's belief that however inspired the artist, the sublime in music could only be approached through ruthless self-discipline, hard labour and an unfettered mind. To a certain extent his brand of idealism and his distaste for publicity tricks circumscribed his career. This intransigence, a kind of fastidiousness of the soul, enhanced his artistry. Right or wrong he saw music as an instrument of reconciliation and the artist as healer in an altering world.

Notes

1.   The late Henri Sauguet in conversation with the author.
2.   *The Strad*, 8 May 1989.
3.   Pierre Fournier, ORTF, 5 July 1976.
4.   *Corriere della sera*, 11 May 1989.
5.   *Le Figaro*, 14 May 1951.

6. Alain Pâris *Universalia* Annual Supplement to *Encyclopaedia Universalis*, [Paris?] 1987.
7. Pierre Fournier, ORTF, 5 July 1976.
8. Pierre Fournier, Radio Suisse Romande, 7 April 1975.
9. *L'Ame et la corde*, No. 4, November/December 1982.
10. Pierre Fournier, Radio Suisse Romande, 7 April 1975.
11. *Harmonie*, February 1968.
12. Pierre Fournier, ORTF, 5 July 1976.
13. Pierre Fournier, Radio Suisse Romande, 7 April 1975.
14. Pierre Fournier, ORTF, 5 July 1965.

PART III
(1957–1986)

21   Force Majeure

In the spring following the move to Geneva, Jean Pierre was about to compete at the Geneva Conservatoire and had some lessons with Cortot. His father sent advice from Copenhagen:

> Remember that being gifted you will always be envied by those who have less talent. But you must forget your gifts and work only at complete mastery of your technique, at breathing and singing everything you play. What you may lose in useless speed you will gain in intensity of expression. This is the fruit of my belated experience…. Enjoy your freedom, but don't go too far!

The Vuillaume cello was giving trouble:

> I'll end up, unlike anyone else, by using new instruments – a paradox which may well lead to the truth, contrary to all habits and routines and pious notions. It is more of a triumph to make a career with a simple tool than with a priceless object.

He enclosed reviews: 'American rubbish for your enjoyment. I see they don't like the Brahms Double in New York, no doubt because I'm too French….'

Always the outsider when in the States, he observed with distaste the games others played, particularly one musician 'nursing all the committees, whose slave he is, like so many others. *Vive la Liberté*, again and again, instead of slavery to routine and money.' He ended his outburst with tender wishes 'for the 8th'.[1]

Throughout this spring of 1957 his letters were full of plans. He was happy at the success of a Paris recital with the performance of the Kodály Sonata, which he had given for the first time at a Musica Viva concert the previous year, as he reminded Peta.[2]

Before a performance of the Haydn D major Concerto with Hans Schmidt-Isserstedt at Montreux, Nathan Milstein appeared in Fournier's dressing-room between the rehearsal and the concert and told him that he must absolutely change the tempo in the first movement and play it *alla breve*. Fournier played a passage for him; Milstein approved. Fournier went on to play the concerto at his usual tempo. Milstein came backstage. 'You see?' he said, 'I was right.'

In October the first Casals Competition, postponed from June on account of Casals' heart attack in April, was held in Paris at the Salle Gaveau. Fournier served on the jury with Enrico Mainardi, Maurice Eisenberg, Gaspar Cassadó,

Sir John Barbirolli and Mstislav Rostropovich. At the finals, while the American cellist Leslie Parnas was in full flight in the Dvořák Concerto, a voice from the audience shouted 'The orchestra's too loud! You can't hear the cellist!' The voice was Paul Tortelier's and the problem a familiar one for all. Parnas won the competition.[3] In the restaurant afterwards wine flowed merrily and few were merrier than Mainardi and Rostropovich, but all were silenced when Casals made an announcement: 'I have married again.' There was a hush, followed by loud applause. 'I have married my pupil and colleague Martita Montañez who has given me back my youth.'[4]

*   *   *

Since a fall in 1953 Fournier had been trying to ignore the increasing pain and discomfort in his left ('good') knee, the result of forty years of overwork as this limb compensated for the paralysis in the other. At Munich airport in February 1957 he had missed his footing and fallen on the icy tarmac, damaging a tendon and tearing a ligament – a common enough accident with sportsmen and athletes but far more serious in his case. Ignoring advice, he had gone on to play with Kubelik and the Berlin Philharmonic, and continued to tour while walking became more hazardous, falls more frequent and the pain more acute.

Throughout 1957, however, he behaved to the outside world as if nothing was amiss. After a Paris recital and a long South American tour he wrote to Peta, sympathizing with her anxiety about her mother and speaking of his own, Gabrielle, 'declining in the total darkness of her brain'.[5] He had just recorded some pieces with Gerald Moore for EMI (his own arrangements of Bach chorales, and short pieces by Boccherini, Debussy, Ravel and Fauré). Before leaving for the States on 25 October he was off to 'Germany, Paris, Belgium and 2 concerts at La Scala'.[6] Anxious for a word from her 'written officially but not too officially' to his Geneva address, he added 'Life is so restless, so complicated, with heavy burdens on the shoulders and such loneliness, so often, in the heart.' Sandwiched between tender wishes to 'mon *grand* Jean Pierre' (symbolically underlined for his twentieth birthday) were the bitter thoughts which so often assailed him in God's Own Country. The previous year 'the cow of a critic on the *Boston Herald*' had mentioned 'a couple of technical slips ('one-twentieth of a second each' Fournier remembered, adding 'technical perfection is all they care about here'). There followed another outburst against what he saw as the American obsession with money and the insincerity he saw around him (which he quaintly called 'good boys' falsity'), momentarily personified by Munch who, 'after showing indifference at the rehearsal and concert, [and] completely drunk after Mrs Steinert's party, wanted to cable Geneva [i.e. Lyda] [and] was kissing all the women around and calling Ania Dorfmann chérie....'[7]

Beneath all his anger and distaste was the realization, as the pain in his leg became increasingly unbearable, that he would have to consult a specialist, and worse, he would have to lay his cello aside. Nothing could be designed to alarm him more. In Paris, nevertheless, at the end of December, he was writing his New Year letters as usual, planning concerts in the Netherlands, Switzerland, Scandinavia and Germany, six weeks in South America in June and July, followed by a tour in the States in the autumn. In an affectionate letter to Peta on 30 December, he spoke of being quite settled now in the Geneva flat at Château Banquet, but impatient to travel again. The best of what he would remember of 1957, he told her, was what he found in her company:

> At home I worry about my wife's health, so exhausted always. Here [in Paris] my mother's brain is more and more obscured. Elsewhere there might be some distraction, but empty and superficial. The truth remains in our dear music and the fight for creation....

His brother Jean, the violinist, was to play in Cape Town, but Peta's letter to him of 2 November remained *poche restante* for six weeks ('I saw the postmark!'). He hoped that Jean would be able to go 'in spite of this lost-in-pocket letter' adding 'I could play every day, and then I should perhaps forget the sadness around, and also my deep solitude.'[8] With the sharp pains in his knee it was now clear even to Fournier himself that some treatment was needed. All the practitioners, American, Swiss and French, were adamant that an operation was essential. Dr Philip D Wilson of the New York Hospital for Special Surgery went further: the knee was so damaged that the choice was between surgery and life in a wheelchair.

In Cologne on 26 January Fournier wrote to Peta 'for a very crucial reason':

> For years I have suffered from a bad fall which affected my *good* leg. Month after month my condition is worsening. I have to save this only leg....

The operation was planned for the end of April with two months in plaster and two months of physiotherapy to follow – a total of four months' inactivity. And Fournier being Fournier, he planned to appear immediately afterwards at a European festival 'to silence alarming gossip'. He wanted to bring forward his South African visit to early April, otherwise it would have to be postponed. 'Please do understand, it is *un cas de force majeure*.' He then put forward the name of the young pianist Marie-Thérèse Fourneau to replace him, but Peta was under no circumstance to mention this in her reply cable to be sent to Bremen. After that she could write *poste restante* to Geneva. As usual he offered no explanation.[9]

It was Geneva he needed to escape from, which was one reason for his decision to be operated on in New York. By 7 February the date was fixed.

> I hope you will understand, if I decided so it is for an imperative reason. I prefer to make no comment on my [morale]. I am facing an inner anxiety and I shall write to you from New York. *Let me hope that I shall come back to you.*[10]

Fournier was aware that he might never walk again. In a conversation with Bernard Gavoty he said later 'Being lame touched people's hearts; in a wheelchair I should have made them laugh.'[11]

The family leave-taking was painful. Lyda didn't accompany her husband to

New York. Withdrawn, he insisted on facing the ordeal alone, the crisis being far more than purely orthopaedic: he was emotionally at breaking point. Ease would now be scarce.

By 23 April 1958 he was sitting up in bed in New York, his leg in a cast, still troubled with regret that he had disrupted the Musica Viva season, and much relieved at Peta's generous understanding. He wrote 'I do not want to talk very much about myself *now*. I am waiting until the end of May under a heavy cast where I try to stow all my worries and anxieties.' Once out of the cast, there would be the 'painful and delicate re-education' before a return to Europe. Characteristically his thoughts were on his first concert, at Salzburg on 3 August: 'I pray God to be next to normal then.' Staying briefly at a private house (he was to return to the hospital for physiotherapy on 15 May), he had time to dwell on his greatest apprehension: whether his career would be ruined. Private emotional turmoil didn't improve matters.

> I try to be strong. I confess it is very hard. I know the world is full of immensely painful miseries and I have no right to complain. But you know... at my age and at this stage in my career, it is hard to begin again....
>
> Believe me or not. I should like to have just enough money to live in a quiet isolated place, together with a soul... a little similar to me. The rest of life, success, fame, fortune are superficial achievements....

But bee-loud glades are not for cellists and common sense returned abruptly with the modest question: 'If you want me still, what is the best period for the season next year, spring, summer, winter?'[12]

Three weeks later Fournier was acknowledging the sympathy and understanding of his friends. Practicalities had overtaken the daydreaming and he was proposing a return to Cape Town the following September. Meanwhile there would be weeks of physiotherapy, some of it in a pool. Boredom was alleviated by the arrival of the pianist Van Cliburn, in hospital for an injured finger. The two played cards at Fournier's bedside and there were visits from the conductor Igor Markevitch and his wife and from Milstein.

Convalescence at Larchmont with his sister Cécile marked the end, if not of his difficulties at least of a particularly convoluted nightmare. He would remember the two months in the cast as being 'lost at sea, with music nevertheless, as [his] guiding star.'

'Twice saved by her' he said to Gavoty, who protested 'She owes it to you!'

'No, it is *I* who owe *her* everything. You can never pay off your debt to your art.'[13]

*   *   *

Inactivity had bred thoughts of new music and in July 1958 Fournier wrote to the Swiss composer Frank Martin to ask for a cello work. 'I heard from Madeleine Lipatti' the composer answered,

> that the operation was fairly serious, more so than it appeared from your letter, and I

am very glad that you are better now and ready for work and music…. I'm busy at present on a choral work based on Huguenot psalms, for the 400th anniversary of our University of Geneva.[14] After that I'll return to a *Mystery of the Nativity* also to be done in Geneva at Christmas 1959.[15]

Martin was allowing himself a rest after the two choral works but added that he might well use the time to attend to [Fournier's] cello. 'The idea of being performed by you encourages me greatly….'[16] After a great deal of vocal music it was the instruments' turn once more.

Impatient to return to work after his treatment, Fournier appeared at the Salzburg Festival on 3 August 1958, not by way of an undemanding programme to ease himself back to the platform, but in a full-blown recital (accompanied by Franz Holetschek) – a strenuous enterprise. Lyda had tried, but failed to dissuade him, and he was, of course, not on top form.

At Salzburg he ran into Friedrich Gulda; together they were to work on a Beethoven cycle in October. He went on to Bad Gastein and played to the accompaniment of the local waterfall. (Backhaus, in the audience, was discovering the Saint-Saëns Concerto.) Fournier also went to London, more relaxed there as he always was, enjoying a prom with Sir Malcolm Sargent and 'all the excellent sound back-up of the BBC'.[17]

More apprehensive than ever about hotel, transport and platform arrangements – stairs were to be his nightmare – he was facing a dilemma: the risk of further damage to his leg, or the black dog of inactivity. His leg had improved, but the muscles were still weak. 'I waited too long' he admitted to Peta, 'but with willpower and patience I will climb a very long way *up* instead of going down irremediably.'[18]

Notes

1. A wish fulfilled: Jean Pierre won the Prix de Virtuosité. Pierre Fournier to Jean Fonda Fournier, 5 March 1957.
2. Pierre Fournier to Peta Fisher, 22 May [1957].
3. Leslie Parnas, born 1932, pupil of Piatigorsky and winner of the 1962 Tchaikovsky competition.
4. Casals had married Martita Montañez in San Juan on 3 August 1957.
5. Gabrielle Fournier was suffering from Alzheimer's disease.
6. Pierre Fournier to Peta Fisher, 6 October 1957.
7. Pierre Fournier to Jean Fonda Fournier, 7 December 1957.
8. Pierre Fournier to Peta Fisher, 30 December 1957.
9. Id. 26 January 1958.
10. Id. 7 February 1958.
11. Bernard Gavoty *Anicroches*, Paris: Buchet Chastel 1979, pp. 135–136.
12. Pierre Fournier to Peta Fisher, 23 April 1958.
13. Bernard Gavoty, op. cit., p. 136.
14. *Psaumes de Genève*. First performance under Ernest Ansermet, Geneva, 4 May 1959.
15. *Le Mystère de la Nativité*. First performance, also under Ansermet, 23 December 1959.

16. Frank Martin to Pierre Fournier, 29 July 1958.
17. Jean Fonda Fournier Archive.
18. Pierre Fournier to Peta Fisher, 3 October 1958.

22   Secret Garden

The Viennese-born pianist Friedrich Gulda was another of Fournier's duo partners. This gifted and versatile musician who played the flute and saxophone was about to turn to composition and increasingly also to improvisation and jazz. In October 1958 he and Fournier were working together in Berlin on their Beethoven cycle, something of a trial run for the Deutsche Grammophon recordings the following year. 'I trust him implicitly', Fournier wrote of Gulda, 'both as pianist and as musician. He likes playing with me and the feeling is mutual. Pity that such an effort to get things right is only to be stacked away.' Fournier hoped that all this work would be taken up by concert managers and in the end it was: Gulda and Fournier repeated the cycle in Bonn, at the Lucerne Festival, in Barcelona and in Munich.

'I'm working a lot which breaks my solitude', he continued in a letter to Jean Pierre,

> You do the same while you can. Herbert [von Karajan] arrives today. I'm curious to see Madame [Eliette von Karajan, née Mouret, the conductor's third wife]. Nikita played very well: big success but I only like this concerto [Rachmaninov's Third] with Vladimir [Horowitz] because it is a bit too feeble and basically *de la merde* when you hear it too often. Mazel [sic] is hideous to watch and to listen to.... Let him play the kind of modern music we hate but not touch the classics![1] Enjoy yourself, work even more and don't create too much scandal at Château Banquet![2]

Invited to play the Walton Concerto under the composer's baton at the opening of the 1959 Edinburgh Festival, Fournier wrote for advice. It was the first Walton had heard of the plan but he expressed delight that they were to play together. From the Casa Cirillo on Ischia he wrote:

> As regard the cello part I rather purposefully left it 'unedited', knowing from experience that every player has his idiosyncracys [sic], so you have my 'Blessing' for anything you may decide to do as regards fingerings, bowings etc.[3][4]

Besides this performance, on 23 August 1959, Fournier took part in three other concerts: Beethoven sonatas with Wilhelm Kempff, and the Dvořák Concerto with the Scottish National Orchestra and Sir Alexander Gibson (25, 27 and 30 August). In March 1960 Walton wrote again to Fournier 'delighted to hear of

[his] success with the Concerto in the Hague...'.⁵ He was hoping for a third performance at the Proms in September.

A first Soviet tour was planned for April 1959, but not under the best auspices. Lyda would not be accompanying him, and furthermore he was angered when Gosconcert announced that his carefully chosen programmes were to be altered. On whose authority? For whose convenience? He felt he was being manipulated as documentation for other cellists or to satisfy curiosity. The Lalo Concerto was substituted for the Dvořák, the Bach Suite No. 5 in C minor for No. 6 in D (his favourite), and Beethoven's C major Sonata (Op. 102/1) for the D major (Op. 102/2). Fournier's suspicions may have been well founded. He wanted none of it and decided to cancel the tour, but in January he received a letter from his friend David Oistrakh, more than likely the intermediary appealed to by Gosconcert. From the letter Oistrakh appeared not to be taking Pierre's anger too seriously, and to be confident that he would change his mind, as he applied that ever-helpful balm, a 'misunderstanding' and added that everything was arranged for his stay. The Brahms recording (the Double Concerto) continued to give him much pleasure.⁶

So the Russian tour was to go ahead after all, but meanwhile Fournier was in Cuba, writing to Jean Pierre from Havana in early February:

> Quesada [concert management] gave me your letter on arrival here and everything is very quiet and like death here, with bearded partisans armed to the teeth at every street corner!⁷
>
> I wonder if there will be any audience at the concert, the first after the *événements*! As the Caracas concert has been postponed because of the carnival, I shall return to New York on Sunday or Monday. I'll have some trouble surviving with no concerts until the 19th. I knew this tour was absurd with those long gaps, and if I didn't have to think above all of earning money with the bank debt to settle by the end of the year [due to heavy expenses on the Geneva flat and the purchase of the Goffriler cello], I should have thrown it all over, tired as I am of the chronic American bluff, with all the managers, great or small, who like the party hosts have forgotten you within the hour, having covered you with 'so wonderful', 'nice to have you here', 'hope you'll be back next year' etc, etc. We are here for money only and for nothing else but a vacuum.

In an atrabilious stream the thoughts pour out, more like grim private musings than a letter to his son. Even when addressing Jean Pierre directly there was an ominous quality:

> I hope you are working lucidly to store up all you will need for the rest of your life. If you have nothing fascinating to tell, it's the same with me... I have never felt more *ennui* everywhere.

Nothing at this moment was right. Never had he felt physically more vulnerable, nor his career more threatened by the risk of immobility. He was in an ambivalent situation and Lyda's unhappiness was a constant reproach. Their marriage was approaching a crisis, as they were both aware.

The tour had taken him to Puerto Rico. Although Fournier admired and respected Casals the artist, Casals the guru appealed less. The same letter continues:

The Pope, God, was not at P. Rico.... The musicians there have no kind words for him or the clique which follows him about... Stern, Schneider, Horszowski and Co. It appears that a fabulous amount of money has been spent on him and his festival, yet all the time his 'venerated' mother was alive he never set foot in this part of the world! Then, acting the devoted son after the wedding, he plays the *Song of the Birds* in her memory on the balcony in front of the crowd of 'pilgrims'.... I despise a world where there is nothing by courtesans and cowards....

Even the minor preoccupations tumbled out, with worries about Lyda:

I am impatient for news of Bada.[8] Embrace her tenderly for me. Think of selling my cameras and let Schultess[9] be absolutely firm with the Friedberg management for all the details of dates, concerts and fees for the autumn. This sort of tour mustn't happen again. I am flabbergasted at the minute profit, having spent so much on the journey. *Mille pensées bien tendres.* P.[10]

On 1 April, alone, Fournier left for the USSR and a total of six concerts in Moscow and Leningrad. In Riga a boy of twelve asked him for an autograph; it was the young violinist Gidon Kremer. Fournier also met a group of Franco-Armenians whose parents had settled in Riga after the First World War. They had been trying unsuccessfully to leave the Soviet Union for France. He agreed to deliver their appeal to General de Gaulle. Fifteen years were to pass before he heard from them again; they had at last obtained their exit visas.

While the struggle with fatigue and stress had become harder, Fournier continued to accept schedules as taxing as before his operation, and this conflict so permeated his letters that one would be hard pressed to sense that he was also at the peak of his powers, indeed that his artistry this year had reached beyond what even his most ardent admirers had come to expect. Celebrating 'one of the finest concerts of the season' (a Paris recital in the half-empty Champs Elysées Theatre), Claude Rostand lashed out with contempt at the 'lazy Parisians' who had not flocked to hear 'not only the first cellist in the country, but one of the greatest in the world...':

whereas they bleat in stupid and unjustified admiration at sickening mediocrities, fashionably false values and vulgar clowning... one of the most extraordinary recitals of his career... and one of the bravest... four sonatas... to an audience hungry for zapateados, elegies and other tchaikovskyisms....

And on Kodály's unaccompanied Sonata Op. 8:

What a pity that M. Pierre Fournier doesn't play contemporary music more often: with the unparalleled subtlety of his playing he would be the ideal interpreter of this complex art.[11]

*   *   *

The balance of talents and frailties which made up the singular chemistry between Pierre and Lyda was now to be gravely disturbed. In July 1959, after Milstein's recital at the Divonne Festival, Lyda returned home in advance of the others. When Pierre and Jean Pierre arrived they found her beside herself with anger, brandishing what she had found: an unmailed letter to the pianist Marie-Thérèse Fourneau which revealed that Pierre loved her.

Marie-Thérèse was by now thirty-five years old. Striking to look at with dark hair and green eyes, she possessed not only beauty and a fine talent in full bloom, but perhaps just as significantly a particular kind of sensitive and private nature which resembled his own, so that it was to a certain degree the coming together of like with like. An only child, she also had been driven to fill her time with music while never, by her own account, knowing a day's boredom in her life. At the Paris Conservatoire she had studied piano with Marguerite Long and Jean Doyen and chamber music with Joseph Calvet. She graduated with a first prize in 1942 and went on to collect awards in the Concours Marguerite Long-Jacques Thibaud and the Geneva Competition, crowning these with the Grand Prix du Disque in 1947. Combining technical brilliance with sensitivity and a sense of style, she was known not only for the classics but for her performances of Debussy, Ravel and perhaps most of all of Gabriel Fauré in which the critic Emile Vuillermoz described her as 'unequalled'.

Marie-Thérèse had her own dual purpose in life: her small daughter Marie-Caroline (of whom Pierre became very fond) and a healthy world career. This, together with an independence of spirit, enabled her to withstand philosophically the stress of an insoluble situation, for Pierre would never have abandoned Lyda, nor did Marie-Thérèse expect as much. The sensitivity with which the relationship had been allowed to develop out of friendship favoured its survival while, neither making extravagant claims on the other, it remained seriously protected, a matter for themselves and two trusted friends.

Pierre's life had a new dimension. In her shock Lyda was suddenly aware that passion had broken through the almost reassuring sequence of passing and, all in all, unthreatening infidelities. It was what she had feared: reciprocated feelings tempered with acceptance of the difficulties and, very nearly, faultless discretion. Vulnerable and very hurt, Lyda's fury (she was never slow to give as good as she got), drove her to savage retaliation through the workings of the profession, going so far as to make attempts to block her rival's engagements. She was too angry to ponder that the knowledge, previously confined to only two other people besides the lovers themselves, would now be shared with an increasing number of others. The word 'divorce' flew about ('In that case', Jean Pierre declared, 'I shall stay with *Maman*'), although the threat was little more than rhetoric. Lyda's health suffered. Her influence waned – only temporarily, it must be said. A certain peace would eventually be restored but Pierre would never voluntarily close the door on this secret garden: only distance, old age and ill-health would finally make any meeting impossible.[12]

*   *   *

Festivals filled the difficult summer of 1959: Edinburgh with Sir William Walton in his own Concerto, and with Kempff in Beethoven sonatas; Lucerne with

Karajan in *Don Quixote*, sharing the bill with the Canadian pianist Glenn Gould whose individual style in the Bach D minor Concerto bewitched Fournier. During rehearsal, in spite of the heatwave, Gould asked for the hall to be heated. He was already wearing several layers of woollens and a pair of mittens.

One of Bruno Walter's later recordings was of the Brahms Double Concerto with Fournier, Zino Francescatti and the CBS Symphony Orchestra in Los Angeles where the conductor was living. For Walter, who was suffering from severe asthma, it was a struggle, and although the initial movement was dealt with in the first session (the first cadenza had been pre-recorded), the following day the balance went wrong and Walter needed to rest. Happily the remaining movements were recorded right through without retakes.[13]

The anxious father in Fournier surfaced again in Chicago during November. The vagaries of the mail had deprived him of news of Jean Pierre who was playing in Amsterdam.

> I had written for your arrival... and cabled from Toronto on the day of your first recital – I know nothing of how it went, in spite of all my secret and so ardent wishes for your success.

Fournier had been recording with Francescatti and was touched by the interest shown in Jean Pierre by the violinist and his wife.

> Forgive me for sending you my reviews and some of the bitterness [I feel] here before a citadel I shall never conquer, having no doubt passed the age of making any sensation... I have so many unanswered questions that I feel more than ever in a desert. Ania Dorfmann sends you good wishes... also Slava [Rostropovich] whom I saw nearly all yesterday afternoon with Sacha [Brailowski] at his hotel, so spontaneous and affectionate.... I think of you tenderly, don't forget, and I'm with you at every moment. Papa.[14]

The crisis of the preceding summer appeared to have cleared the air when in February Fournier wrote to Peta, 'a sister with [her] wonderful sensibility':

> [There is] nothing to say about me except that I am happy working and playing. It is the essential part of my life, dedicated to more and more music....[15]

The spring of 1960 was dominated by the Israel tour with Jean Martinon and the French Orchestre Philharmonique. After a rehearsal, unsurprisingly, an American journalist living in Israel asked Fournier 'What about the war?'. Fournier responded by giving press conferences in Jerusalem and Haifa, fielding questions and giving a full account of his career under the Occupation, his broadcasts for Radio Paris, his visits to Germany and even his friendship with Alex Spengler. Not only did the tour proceed in peace but it turned out to be a happy one, both for him and for Lyda. Ironically, he found less antagonism in Israel than earlier in the States; his frankness had no doubt precluded the type of rumour which had found credence in America; unwittingly the journalist had smoothed his path. Lyda, sitting at the Dizenhof café in Tel Aviv with the Israel Philharmonic's delegate and first flute, Uri Toeplitz, and hearing a lot of German spoken around her, felt relaxed enough to remark that the atmosphere had something of twenties Berlin....

On Sederday, the painter Reuben Rubin invited Pierre and Lyda to celebrate the Passover with his family. Donning the *yermolka* proferred to him, Pierre played a Bach Suite.

The Franco-Algerian war was now at its height. Fournier's opinion of this was unpopular in military circles since it showed a certain sympathy for the FLN. Airing his thoughts at a Tel Aviv cocktail party given in his honour by the 'Israeli Dior' Lola Behr, he caused outrage: how could an artist of his calibre give moral support to bandits and murderers? He stuck to his point, adding that in his opinion colonialism was dead.

He had a congenial partnership with Martinon whose musicianship he admired already and whose human qualities he was now discovering. This pupil of d'Indy and Roussel had written a symphony while a prisoner of war and had found it, on his release after three escape attempts, in the Pasdeloup repertoire. He had worked in Dublin, London and Düsseldorf before heading the Israel Philharmonic. His wife Néry recalled Fournier the movie-fan shouting to their Haifa taxi driver to stop because he had caught sight of a cinema showing *Some Like It Hot*. Two hours later there was a panic-stricken rush to get dressed for the concert.

On April 2 Fournier dashed off a letter for Jean Pierre:

> All I can tell you is that the two rehearsals were warm, friendly and admiring... *La sympathie est là*. And you know how I like to feel the orchestra is with me.

The little house they were staying in was all they could wish, and in spite of the uninterrupted series of concerts – four concertos in one day (Boccherini and *Schelomo* in the afternoon, and in the evening Haydn and Schumann) – the tour was something of a holiday for Pierre who enclosed a closely-printed handbill entirely in indecipherable Hebrew for Jean Pierre's delectation; a small arrow pointed to Pierre Fournier's biographical notes.[16]

> We are off to Haifa for two days after playing here to full houses of 3000 seats which is a bit crazy, but I've managed to alter the programme by taking Schelomo out of four concerts and putting in Schumann. Now (today) they don't want a charity recital but an orchestral concert in aid of... the orchestra. Since everything changes at the last moment I am philosophical and prefer to let things happen.... We had Patin to lunch today. [He] hasn't conducted an orchestra for 25 years but believes he is the undiscovered Toscanini. He is up to his neck in compositions. Your Pnina[17] has become rather a weird shape but is still adorable. The orchestra is very kind. I had a press conference on Sunday about 1940–1945 to which I answered with an honesty which won [them] over. I know there are still some fences up. Let's hope they will have gone down before I leave.
>
> We are outside the town in a deserted spot where only a few years ago (*Patin dixit*) there were hyenas and jackals!... The little prefabricated house is very pleasant if a bit dilapidated. The town [Tiberias] is antiquated-provincial, and uninteresting. I am counting on the visit to the holy places to show me the beauties of Israel whose pretty girls are still purely in the satyr [S]'s imagination, unless harems of gorgeous creatures should suddenly open up in front of me on the road to Jerusalem.... I embrace you tenderly until my next news from the Promised Land and its chosen people. Papa.
>
> PS. Send the enclosed letter to Dr Otto Infeld, Vienna 5, Austria, Diehlgasse 27, with

the packet of strings sent to me minus the A, in other words the 3 strings of D, G and C, by registered post (sample).[18]

What might have been a difficult tour had been a triumph. Two days before leaving Fournier reported:

> …Very exhausting of course, with eleven orchestral concerts (two works each time) in 15 days, but the audience's response was worth the effort. Imagine 3000 people eleven times! I don't know of such enthusiasm anywhere else.

In Israel a young boy called Uri who had fallen under the cellist's spell, planted a tree in honour of Pierre and Lyda.

Following the Israel tour Fournier played three concertos in Munich and then returned to Paris for appearances in front of the 'ever snobbish and sophisticated audience'.[19] But in spite of the under-rehearsed OSCC orchestra, the critics laid flowers at his feet: 'In the Schumann concerto he reached the sublime.'[20] 'Among so many marvellous qualities, one which surpasses the others and encapsulates them: simplicity… Fournier is at that stage of his career when disregarding the superfluous he goes straight to the essential. He removes even the hint of effort…. A lesson in love, music and humility.'[21]

Recording *Don Quixote* in Cleveland with George Szell in October was an exhilarating experience. (They had worked at the finale together when they chanced to be staying at the Suvretta House in St Moritz.) He wrote to Jean Pierre:

> Back from a 2nd recording session, just about dead with fatigue, especially with a 2nd concert this evening! It was fairly difficult but the orchestra and Szell are so good in this work that the recording will be a fine one (at least I hope so, given the usual surprises when the cello sound is transferred to tape!). The technicians are charming and very demanding. Szell very friendly and takes all the comments with equanimity. I'm proud to have stuck it out because nobody in the world plays this better [than Szell and his orchestra].

He was impatient for news of his son's concert at Singen and of the journey with Lyda. This time a crowded schedule saved him from the spleen which habitually descended upon him when homesick for the diversity of Europe, and there were plans for a recording of the Dvořák concerto and Szell and the Berlin Philharmonic in June.

> He is one of the best conductors of the present day for the music that he loves. The beauty of *D. Quixote* in stereo is extraordinary. [After that] I'm afraid of being disappointed with ordinary equipment.
> Work well….
> I embrace you tenderly and Bada too.
> Papa.[22]

In the winter of 1960–61 Fournier recorded the Bach Suites for Deutsche Grammophon's *Archiv* label, a task he considered a huge responsibility: 'the deepest wells of German thought plumbed by this French artist.'[23]

Notes

1. This is misleading. Fournier disliked the type of avant-garde music which called for aleatory techniques such as tapping the body of the instrument; he is also on record as having referred to Berg's 'silly little pieces'. That was about the sum of his prejudice against modern and contemporary music.
2. Pierre Fournier to Jean Fonda Fournier, 16 October 1958.
3. Walton's indications are reproduced in Appendix 3.
4. Sir William Walton to Pierre Fournier, 28 August 1958.
5. Id., 7 March 1960.
6. David Oistrakh to Pierre Fournier, 19 January 1959.
7. Fidel Castro and his supporters.
8. From Jean Pierre's infant attempts to pronounce 'Lyda'.
9. Walter Schultess, MD of Konzert Gesellschaft, Zurich.
10. Pierre Fournier to Jean Fonda Fournier, 6 February 1959.
11. *Carrefour*, 8 June 1960 (Claude Rostand).
12. Marie-Thérèse Fourneau continued to enjoy a flourishing career until she contracted multiple sclerosis. She continues, however, to teach and adjudicate.
13. Fournier considered the EMI/Oistrakh/Galliera/Philharmonia version of 1956 more polished and relaxed. RCA's proposal of a recording with Heifetz never materialized.
14. Pierre Fournier to Jean Fonda Fournier, 16 November [1959].
15. Pierre Fournier to Peta Fisher, 8 February 1960.
16. Pierre Fournier to Jean Fonda Fournier, 2 April 1960.
17. Pnina Salzmann, former pupil of Magda Tagliaferro for piano, and of Fournier for chamber music, at the Ecole Normale de Musique.
18. Pierre Fournier to Jean Fonda Fournier, 6 April 1960.
19. Pierre Fournier to Peta Fisher, 17 April 1960.
20. *Carrefour*, 25 May 1960 (Claude Rostand).
21. *Le Figaro*, 7 May 1960 (Clarendon).
22. Pierre Fournier to Jean Fonda Fournier, Saturday 29 [October 1960].
23. *Basler Volksblatt*, 23 November 1962.

23 Friends and a Working Relationship

Fournier's life was not all hard labour. Letters tended to voice misgivings or record disappointments rather than pleasure (perhaps less newsworthy) or success (written about by others). Yet there was an abundance of both.

If Geneva spelt peace, St Moritz and Montreux meant summer freedom, and among the large circle of musicians and other artists visiting or living around the Lac Léman ('*la côte*'), there was, particularly in the late fifties and sixties as his son remembers, a more natural and easy-going atmosphere than that of today.

Fournier enjoyed staying at the Kulm in St Moritz where there was level terrain for his afternoon walk. Here he met the novelist John Knittel (author of the hugely successful *Via Mala*) and Knittel's grandson Roderick von Bennigsen. The talented fourteen-year-old played for Fournier on his fine Amati cello which had once belonged to David Popper. (Later Bennigsen was to invent and patent a fibreglass bow.)

Joseph Szigeti, one of the 'four spirits', and his wife Wanda left their Californian home for the canton of Vaud to be near their daughter and son-in-law Irène and Nikita Magaloff. Others to settle in the vicinity were the conductors Josef Krips, and Paul Kletzki who took over the OSR after Ansermet's retirement and who became a close friend. The Fourniers visited Sacha and Ella Brailowski, Sacha reading crime novels in his hammock while Jean Pierre was at the piano, running through sonatas with Pierre or reminiscing about his penniless Paris days as accompanist to an amateur cellist.

Oona and Charlie Chaplin gave a lunch at Vevey for Jacques Thibaud, Pierre and Lyda and the writer Paul Morand with whom Lyda was able to bathe in pre-Nazi Berlin nostalgia, Morand having served at the embassy there before the war.[1] Chaplin had heard Fournier's Dvořák recording with Kubelik and declared that he intended to write a cello concerto himself.

One evening at Roberto's restaurant in Geneva the family found Artur Rubinstein sitting alone in front of his favourite *melone con prosciutto*. Out of that meeting came the idea for the Schubert–Schumann–Brahms trio recordings with Szeryng.

On a visit to Witold Malcużyński, Richter and Jean Pierre deafened everybody with the Tchaikovsky Concerto No. 1 played on two pianos, driving Pierre frantic: 'Two pianos in this tiny studio is enough to make you loathe that music!' he protested.

Many summers were spent at the Montreux Excelsior with visits to and from the Magaloffs, Elisabeth Furtwängler, Cassadó, Gilels, Niehans, René Clair and Peter Ustinov. Like Pierre, Milstein could not be separated from his instrument. Busy all the afternoon in his hotel room, working at a cadenza of his own for a Mozart concerto, he tried out successive ideas on the telephone to Lyda's room. 'Dreadful!' was her comment, 'It sounds like... Wieniawski!' And so Milstein worked on for another half-hour. Some time later they would all walk down to the Zürcher tearoom.

Milstein disliked the Brahms Double Concerto (the cello has all the interesting entries) and when illness made Christian Ferras cancel a concert with Fournier and Paul Kletzki, he declined to step in. In the event the concert was saved, and by all accounts superbly, by the Swiss violinist Hansheinz Schneeberger. Fournier tried to persuade Milstein to record the work with him but without success. 'Why don't you transcribe it for cello? That way you cellists will have another concerto! And I could give you some good tips.'

*   *   *

In his fifties, although Fournier's powers were at their height, his handicap was beginning to weigh as much on his spirit as on his physique, and the more so since his operation. Professionally he felt he was in a vacuum, not obtaining the kind of work he desired. Even allowing for his quasi-pathological irritation with impresarios, the current incumbent had been a disappointment. This would be remedied a couple of years later by Kurt Weinhold of Columbia Artists, but in the fifties and sixties mass media coverage had not arrived: however resounding an artist's reputation, there was little to maintain a name in the public eye but concert upon concert at the right venues.

Somewhere between son, colleague and crony, Jean Pierre was the constant recipient of his father's observations, his fleeting reactions (often reversed after a little thought), and in a comical mixture of French and English the reporting of stings which might otherwise have been endured in silence and which were for the most part quickly forgotten. It was from their first professional tour together in South Africa in 1962, that Jean Pierre remembers him truly opening his heart as a father, showing all his affection and pride. In Cape Town, between his own performances of Boccherini and *Schelomo*, he played the cello solo in the orchestra accompanying Jean Pierre in Liszt's Second Concerto, declaring afterwards that his son had the greater success. On tour they often reacted in tandem, getting appalling giggles on catching sight of a nodding head in the front row during the Debussy Sonata. At the end Fournier would turn to Jean Pierre between two bows, and hiss between his teeth 'Les *imbéciles* have understood nothing!' He enjoyed spoiling his son. In restaurants he would tell the waiter to 'bring the boy a lot of sautéed potatoes, he adores them' and encouraged him to drink on concert evenings. 'With the piano your notes are already there and you have the pedal to save everything, so... *drink*!' Once in Bremen, about to perform Bach's Fourth Suite, he asked Jean Pierre to stay with him in his room:

> with a beguiling smile full of tenderness, hiding his anxiety. Afterwards he embraced me, telling me 'After all, it wasn't as bad as all that' and that I had brought him luck as my mother would have done.
>
> Sometimes in public – hotels, restaurants, bars – he would explode in anger at an article on politics or music, and I would have to soothe him like a child. He could also be diabolical, knowing exactly what would set me off in uncontrollable giggles. Once in Frankfurt I picked up a ravishing girl at the hotel bar while he was there. He wished me lots of fun, and if she was nice I was to bring her to the concert the next day, which I did. She kissed him, called him Onkel Pierre and came to dinner with us afterwards....
>
> What a lot of different facets to his character: kindness, love, anger, a hot temper, anxiety and a childlike purity, but perhaps above all a generosity of spirit. When I was nervous before a performance he would say 'Allow your real nature to express itself. Don't imitate anybody. You have a hold on your audience, just be yourself!'[1]

Fournier tended to ignore the snide remarks aroused by concerts with his son, but he was aware that while people made him ingratiating proposals of joint appearances ('We should like to help your son'), the same people were criticizing him behind his back for furthering his son's career.[3]

For Jean Pierre the collaboration with his father was a training any young musician would envy and a rewarding and unforgettable experience. 'When I saw him go on to the platform I would feel anxiety and love in equal measure, a mixture of adoration, irritation and above all respect. I was also so happy that he didn't know me only as the spoilt brat whom he saw from time to time.'[4]

Jean Pierre's choice of *nom de guerre* – Jean Fonda – was aimed, in one sense, at not trading on his father's name and in another, at avoiding confusion, his uncle being the violinist Jean Fournier. It was also something of a conspiratorial nod at the cinema after seeing *War and Peace* with Audrey Hepburn and Henry Fonda, a joke between his father and himself.

Writing to Jean Pierre from Udine in March 1961 after a concert in Rome, Fournier reported how he had teased the cellist Amedeo Baldovino over his extravagant praise for Fournier's 'Italian' cello: what a magnificent instrument, what a tone, what craftsmanship..!

> It's my Goffriler, I answered. The cello case was closed. [It was really his '*bon vieux Miremont*'.] So the illusion remains, as does the true quality of this healthy instrument which has brought me nothing but success everywhere....

He was sending one of Jean Pierre's tapes to the RAI, and then went on to mention his shock at a news item in *France-Soir*: Casals was reported to have been paid 100 000 francs for a European television broadcast sponsored by the US 'with American money, the same money which is arming his enemy Franco.' Fournier was angered by what he perceived as double standards in one whose judgmental stance had permitted him to 'pardon' the contrite Cortot.[6]

With a Turin concert ahead he wanted Lyda and Jean Pierre to listen to his broadcast of a fresh interpretation of the Lalo concerto:

> I want to know what you think of my new approach to this work, which isn't *bad* but which [needed] reworking especially after the horror I felt on hearing my faithful account of it, following all those printed indications from an age of pomposity and bad taste. *Mille choses* from Schmidt-Isserstedt seen on arrival in Rome. Apart from that, Roman society is away for the weekend. I can do without.
> *Mille tendresses.*[7]

Fournier returned to the USSR for a second tour in May 1961, but this time there was no tinkering with his choice of programmes. He gave two recitals in Moscow at the Nobles' Club, in the glorious Hall of Columns dear to Tchaikovsky and Pushkin.[8] Lyda acted as interpreter at a Conservatoire reception and enjoyed herself until a chill confined her to bed. Pierre was touched by the general warmth and by the audience's response ('enormous enthusiasm for Bach and interest in Martinů...').

Living conditions had deteriorated for most people since his previous visit, and always highly protective of Jean Pierre he warned him off thoughts of staying in Moscow to work: 'You would be completely lost. Your great Emil [Gilels] has let us down by staying away and I don't think he can be counted on to help a young hopeful like you.'

In Moscow there was intense music-making. After a recital of his own, Vladimir Ashkenazy went to Richter's flat to work with him on a concerto. Richter gave a party in honour of Pierre and Lyda, thoughtfully providing a colossal looking-glass for freshening-up operations after Pierre's recital. There was also an evening with Rostropovich and Vishnevskaya at which Richter gave an electrifying account of Prokofiev's Eighth Sonata and joined Fournier in an impromptu performance of Brahms' F major Sonata 'without a problem and with the same instinct.'[9]

> I should give a lot to play three great sonatas with him in Paris! But alas, that is a mirage: all the artists here stick together and Richter would never do anything which might hurt Slava.

He borrowed Slava's cello but found it awkward,

> going the way of Gaspar [Cassadó]'s, steel strings, Belgian bridge, Tortelier spike, making for a horrid tone... Here, as in America, the size of tone seems more important than the quality.[10]

Arriving in Kiev with Lyda, Pierre was in an absent frame of mind. The conductor Kirill Kondrashin offered to take them in his chauffeur-driven car from the airport into town. At their destination a flabbergasted Lyda watched Pierre, with an angelic smile, slide a tip into the conductor's hand, having mistaken him for the chauffeur.

In Leningrad, where seven hundred people stood at his recital in the Philharmonia Hall,[11] Lyda found her home at 7 Panteleimonovskaya Street,[12] and burst into tears. It was her first visit since emigrating as a girl in 1919. During this stay she became ill suddenly, and her feet swelled to twice their normal size. At the chief hospital she was given a Hungarian drug which cured her symptoms. However, this was to be the first sign of a grave illness developing.

*   *   *

After recording the Dvořák Concerto with Szell and the Berlin Philharmonic in three days at the beginning of June, Fournier wrote from Paris

> I'm in a fog when I think of my Dvořák. I no longer know anything, we worked so hard... so obsessed with technical performance! But I think there will be good moments, since perfection is not of this world. The orchestra will be splendid!
> I hope you're pleased with the big photograph in the Figaro![13]

There were more than a few good moments: this disc won Fournier the prize of the Académie du disque, and Nathan Milstein would later describe it as 'probably the best performance of this concerto [he had] ever heard.'[14] Szell and Fournier went on to play the concerto together at the Zurich Festwoche.

The following February (1962), Fournier appeared at the Grossenhaus in Frankfurt with Paul Hindemith conducting his own 1940 Concerto with the City Opera and Museum Orchestra. In March there was news of Poulenc. The composer was on a fortnight's Italian tour with Denise Duval, the soprano of *La Voix humaine*. '*Mon ange celliste*', he wrote from Milan,

> Thank you for your card. I also think of you and still love you but our lives are a perpetual game of hide-and-seek. I know that your last concert in Paris [a recital two days earlier] and the one with Herbert [von Karajan] and *Don Quixote* [with the Vienna Philharmonic] were sublime. I know that Karajan shed a tear at the end of *Quixote*. All that sharpened my regrets because where you are concerned admiration and affection go together. Yes, the Gloria went well but like you I am a chronic worrier.[15] Maybe that is what makes us give the best of ourselves. As for my love-life, my *gros blond* [his friend Louis], now a plumber, is very sweet to me when we are together in the Midi. He is a simple creature... a rest from the Paris intelligenzia! I'm in Milan for 3 days because Duval is giving the first performance of a little opera (for Ricordi) [*La Voix humaine*], and I've had a wonderful dinner-jacket made. You have to look after yourself as you get older.
> When you see famous conductors tell them I have a *little* talent. They don't know.
> Luckily the marvellous Georges Prêtre is fond of me. I hope the boy is working well.
> *Je t'envoie mille et mille et remille tendres baisers. Ton Francis.*
> Tell your spouse that the *gros blond* is still laughing about the quenelles à la moquette.[16]

Since 1957 Gabrielle Fournier's condition (she was suffering from Alzheimer's disease) had become so severe that she could no longer look after herself and Fournier arranged for her to move to Dr César Tauber's clinic at Muri near Bern. The Taubers' daughter, Anne-Marie, was a severe diabetic who died young. At her death Fournier played a Bach Suite beside the open coffin, and to thank him her parents presented him with her fine Bernardel cello. César and Yvonne Tauber were devoted to Gabrielle and when Fournier was playing in Bern they brought her to hear him. The first piece failed to hold her interest, but throughout the concerto her eyes never left her son, as if held there by some filament of residual memory. After the concert when she was taken to see him she said 'Oh, Monsieur, you have no idea of the pleasure you gave me!'[17]

Gabrielle Fournier died at Muri on 2 May 1962. Poulenc, who was spending May at Noizay, wrote 'very sadly and very tenderly'. As a postscript he asked 'Have the bells of Sorgues delivered the promised Suites?' The symbolic bells were to announce the arrival through the post of Fournier's Archiv recordings of the Bach Suites.[18]

In March Fournier gave the Shostakovich Concerto in New York and sent the reviews to Jean Pierre, commenting 'good for M. Schonberg' [Harold C. Schonberg of the *New York Times*]:

> The Shostako [sic] is not liked here but it sounded well in that hall [the Avery Fisher, previously the Philharmonic Hall] which is not as bad as people say but *très gloomy*, painted navy blue!! Szell has never been so emotional about me, saying marvellous things from his *own* mouth!! The orchestra adorable and so friendly....[19]

The French composer and conductor Jean Martinon was busy in the summer on his concerto for Fournier and sent the manuscript of the cello part. Fournier wrote from Lucerne:

> There appears to be *nothing to alter* from the cello point of view. But I await to see you to get a [better] idea, if you have a piano sketch, because I'm a bit lost, harmonically speaking.

The two musicians were sharing a Lucerne Festival concert with the ORTF Philharmonic Orchestra and Fournier hoped he would get enough rehearsal time. He was to play the Saint-Saëns Concerto and he had, besides, firm ideas about the Couperin pieces (*Pièces en forme de concert*):

> They are transparent, but delicate! I want them *very light*, with 3 desks of 1st violins, 3 of seconds, 2 of violas, 1 cello desk and a *single* double bass (6–6–4–2–1).
> I'm sure that once again we'll produce something fine on the platform, and I'm happy about that.[20]

Notes

1. Paul Morand (1888–1975), diplomat and novelist. Vichy's Ambassador to Switzerland, he was discharged by the Liberation government without pay, then in 1953 retired by the Council of State with a pension. He was later elected to the Académie Française.
2. Jean Fonda Fournier to the author.
3. Pierre Fournier, ORTF, 5 July 1976.
4. Jean Fonda Fournier to the author.
5. Pierre Fournier owned a great many cellos, from the 1732 Spiritus Zorzano he played in 1936 to the 'Comte Doria' Vuillaume he acquired in the 1970s: two Miremonts, a Nicolas, a Lupot, a Gagliano, two Bernardels, an earlier Vuillaume, the 1722 'Lord Gudgeon' Goffriler and others. His special treasure was his first Miremont bought in 1945, used for the Schumann, Saint-Saëns, Double Brahms and Elgar concertos, *Schelomo*, the *Rococo* Variations, Beethoven with Kempff, *Don Quixote* with

Karajan and the Stuttgart CO/Münchinger recordings of Boccherini, Vivaldi and Couperin. He liked its reliability and power with a 'blazing' A. On his Matteo Goffriler bought in 1957 he played the Bach Suites, the Schumann Concerto with Fricsay, Dvořák and Don Quixote with Szell, and with the Lucerne Festival Strings Boccherini, Vivaldi and Couperin. The A he found a touch muffled but the instrument recorded very well. For the Brahms Sonatas with Firkušny he took the Goffriler to Berlin. Then he telephoned Lyda asking her to send him the Miremont by air. She was furious.

6. H. L. Kirk *Pablo Casals*, London: Hutchinson 1974, p. 420.
7. Pierre Fournier to Jean Fonda Fournier, 21 March [1961].
8. Originally built in 1780 for Prince V. M. Dolgoruky-Krimsky, the building was redesigned as the Nobles' Club in 1784. The Hall, with its great chandeliers and 28 marble Corinthian columns, was achieved by filling in the courtyard. In 1919 it became the House of Unions and a venue for Party conferences, concerts and the lying-in-state of communist leaders. Stalin's show trials in the thirties were held in a specially built extension (Kathy Murrell).
9. Richter's playing of Liszt's B minor Sonata, on a visit to the Fourniers, was especially remembered: 'In his hands it was both poetic and diabolical, like something out of Dante'. Jean Fonda Fournier to the author, 1992.
10. Pierre Fournier to Jean Fonda Fournier, 22 May 1961. Fournier was always grateful to the composers and conductors who understood the cello's particular problem, the fear of being drowned by the orchestra or by the piano (Walton, F. Martin, Martinů, Poulenc, Boulez, Sargent, Martinon). Cassadó's 'contraption on the bridge' amplified the tone 'so that... the piano could be left open.' (Gerald Moore *Am I too Loud?*, London: H. Hamilton 1984, p. 109).
11. Confusingly, this hall where Berlioz and Wagner conducted was also in earlier days a Nobles' Club (see p. 183). Isadora Duncan danced there (Kathy Murrell).
12. This is the street-name scribbled on the back of Lyda's snapshot.
13. Pierre Fournier to Jean Fonda Fournier, undated [June 1961].
14. The late Nathan Milstein to the author, 21 January 1988.
15. Poulenc's *Gloria* had been premièred with Charles Munch at Boston in January of the preceding year. Its first European performance was on the French Radio with Georges Prêtre in February 1961.
16. Francis Poulenc to Pierre Fournier, 10 March [1962]. When Poulenc and Louis were dining with the Fourniers in Geneva, the dish holding the *quenelles de brochet* broke in two just before being served, tipping the quenelles on to the carpet (moquette). Pierre and Francis wept with laughter, the Italian maid with rage. All Paris heard about the '*quenelles à la moquette*'.
17. Cécile Niklaus to the author, 31 May 1988.
18. Francis Poulenc to Pierre Fournier, undated [May 1962].
19. Pierre Fournier to Jean Fonda Fournier, 20 March [1962].
20. Pierre Fournier to Jean Martinon, 27 August [1962].

24   'Weight and Serenity'

'The two artists [Kempff and Fournier]... have in the meantime so fashioned their style that today they are able to convey all the weight and serenity essential to great art...'

Claude Rostand, *Harmonie*, May 1966

Basle Cathedral was packed on two Sunday evenings in the autumn of 1962 to hear Fournier play the complete set of Bach Suites.[1] 'One man and four strings mesmerizing more than 2000 people... an indescribable palette of colours, or contrasts...'.[2] 'Since Casals we had not heard these suites played to such perfection...'.[3] 'The deepest wells of German thought plumbed by this French artist.... What an extraordinary demonstration of thought, of mastery, of style...'.[4] 'In the sixth Suite he was seen at his greatest...'.[5]

We know that few listeners to Fournier's Bach performances have been able to forget them; the audience before the isolated figure high on the square platform in the nave of Basle Cathedral was no exception. In the hands of this half-sceptical believer whose vocabulary was so often religious (he called the Suites 'the cellist's breviary'[6]), an epicurean whose work was ruthlessly self-disciplined, the Suites distilled Bach's humanity and his indestructible faith, the sensuality and the spirituality fused in sound.

The snakes and ladders of professional life brought this successful year to an unharmonious close with a preposterous marathon South Bank concert, conceived by Walter Legge. Three soloists, Henryk Szeryng, Hans Richter-Haaser and Fournier were delivered up to give an object lesson on how not to build a programme: the Mozart D minor Piano Concerto, K466, the Haydn D major Cello Concerto, the Brahms Double and the Beethoven Triple concertos. Fournier appeared in three of the four works.

The Times found the Haydn 'too bland', the Double Concerto 'too classical instead of richly romantic', and the Beethoven, it complained, was drowned by the orchestra.[7] 'An indigestible meal' was Martin Cooper's comment – probably the most accurate description of this value-for-money fiasco. He found the Brahms the best item of the evening, somewhat overwhelmed by 'the over-exuberance of the conductor Norman del Mar'.[8] Already irritated by the shortage of rehearsal time, Fournier was disproportionately upset by some of the reviews;

to him every concert was important, even one as ill-planned as this. This setback was compounded by the fact, intolerable to Lyda, that Marie-Thérèse Fourneau had, that same day, scored excellent notices. Some chance remark brought Lyda to boiling point during a telephone conversation with Thérèse Mayer, and she put down the receiver abruptly, regretting it immediately and writing her friend a long letter:

Ma bien chère Thérèse!

Alas, you weren't there when I called back – to ask you from the bottom of my heart to forgive me for having been what I hate most in the world – *rude* without *for a moment* wanting to aim it at you. You and Tony are in my heart and that meeting with you in London was filled with mutual affection (or at least that is how it appeared to me!). Alas it was so short and we always have so much to say to each other, but yesterday I saw Pierre really broken, denigrated and unjustly so after such an effort, and with such a true professional conscience.... Then, this like physical pain to me (as it was for Jean Pierre) and so it all exploded on the telephone whereas I wanted to share our sadness with you and also say goodbye. Then the name of X. came back to me. She had very good reviews and she is *nothing* [underlined four times] compared to Pierre.... Then I 'saw red' and I'm asking you to forgive me, you who have nothing to do with Pierre's troubles or... mine!

I must admit that I become quite helpless when I see P. in *that state*. Happily I'm not like that with him but believe me it isn't easy to encourage him to see reason when he is like that. I also want to tell you that you and Tony are a part of my life with Pierre, like a family whom one loves more than mere friends [but who] has to put up with things one would never do to friends.

As a graphologist [will you] please forgive my illegible handwriting and also, as a real Frenchwoman, my spelling mistakes. I should so like to spend a *long* moment with you next time in March when P. has a television [appearance], if you are in London.

Jean Pierre is 25 today. Twenty-five years ago he received his first cheque... from Tony M. with a sweet note. We rang him this morning. He already knew everything, having of course bought the London papers. If only you could hear his reaction and reasoning, telling us that the trouble was *that programme*, designed to put everyone in a bad temper, especially the critics who are *obliged* to go and hear everything. Also he [reminded] his father *who he is*, to console him. It was really sweet (which he *is*) and he gives us so much joy from every point of view. He told us he was giving a dinner for eight this evening and asked could he take one or two bottles of champagne out of the cellar!!!

Thérèse darling, be kind and send me a short note to say you embrace me (unless it disgusts you!!!) to prove that you have forgiven me so that I start the New Year well! To both of you I send my best wishes for New Year and may we see more of each other! If I were younger my heart would beat feverishly for Tony, who grows handsomer every day with his silver hair.

I embrace you both tenderly, and also from my two men, Your old pest, Lyda.[9]

Thérèse sent a reassuring reply, and Lyda wrote back:

Ma Thérèse *chérie*

You are a darling to me and I *am* grateful for your adorable letter but... our life has been absolute madness and you need three heads. What happened with the London press mortified [Pierre]: it was so rude and so unjust... but he'll go back, all the same, on 20 May with a recital, because they love him in London. Jean Pierre and I are encouraging him to do it and that will mean that I can see my Thérèse and my Tony again. We live too far from each other and we have so few friends.... The rest are mostly bla-bla which doesn't suit my temperament at all. Tony told us he was going through an anti-English phase. I hope it won't last, because on the whole you are happy over there? His work must be very tiring.... Excuse this screed which comes nevertheless from the heart.

I'll let you have all... interesting news.

Mille tendresses, Lyda.

PS Jean Pierre played me his programme yesterday: Schumann Fantasia and Beethoven Op. 110. I could have wept with emotion!!! He'll be playing in Paris in May!!![10]

Pierre and Lyda with their two dramatically opposed temperaments formed a couple who in their own way remained close, against all odds, to the end. United first by passion and always by an adored son, they were soldered together for 43 years by music. Lyda's lack of sentimentality about most musical matters, and her diamond-hard judgment, meant that Pierre often sought her opinion; her professional instinct also left him free to concentrate on what mattered most to him: making music.

To deduce from her outsize personality that her judgment governed all aspects of their life together would be wrong: according to their son she made the noise, he made the decisions (although there was a lot of nudging). Often he failed to listen – and to his detriment. 'I'm just a sidecar' she said to Thérèse when 'her men' were off on another tour. Few people would have agreed.[11]

* * *

Fournier liked working with Szell ('What a marvellous orchestra and how I feel at home with them!'), but one event in January was marred not only by the absence of reviews, the press being on strike, but by a painful condition in his right shoulder. Szell's doctor prescribed massage and heat treatments: 'I live on Veganin and Solucamphre' he wrote to Jean Pierre, 'with Néalgyl as an apéritif.'[12] A week later he reported a concert by a young French pianist whose hold over managements and the public mystified him: 'Chopin impossibly affected, and Beethoven superficial and so fast! *Never*', he ordered Jean Pierre, 'play the Brahms Handel [Variations] which are atrociously boring.'[13] He had just heard that Sviatoslav Richter's entire US tour had been cancelled by the Soviet authorities who had also ordered the building of his dacha to be stopped.

If there were moments when Fournier saw the American musical scene as an alien establishment dominated by committees and fundraising hostesses, one article from the 'brutal city' made him smile: Chicago's powerful Claudia Cassidy, who had savaged Rafael Kubelik after the 1949 boycott of Furtwängler, bestowed on the sceptical Frenchman her most extravagant prose, with the headline 'Pierre Fournier's Molten Dvorak Crest of the Evening.'[14]

Fournier was often careless of his health, arriving once at Frankfurt airport in light clothes when the temperature was barely above freezing; on another occasion making off to dinner at Villefranche without changing his shirt and then catching pneumonia. A strenuous concert at Chaillot in March 1965 brought on an attack of tachycardia, a reminder of Professor Delamare's warning, but this did nothing to induce him to work a little less; indeed he took the odd extra concert in his stride. With the inauguration of the new Berlin Philharmonic Hall in September 1963 (opened by Karajan with the Ninth Symphony), Fournier had appeared with Francescatti in the second concert, a Brahms programme. When Claudio Arrau cancelled a recital, the impresario Herta Adler appealed to Fournier to 'jump in'. Jean Pierre, meanwhile, was pottering on the Kurfürstendamm. Fournier waited serenely for his return to make for a Hochschule piano and go through their programme of Beethoven, Brahms and Franck, given at Bremen and Lubeck. Francescatti was so taken by their encore, Beethoven's *Bei Männern* (*Magic Flute*) Variations, that he decided he would arrange them for violin.

One of the happiest and most rewarding partnerships was with Wilhelm Kempff. Already entered upon ten years earlier and taken up again several times since then, by the end of 1963 it had gained substance. In December the two musicians appeared, unusually for a chamber concert, at the Royal Festival Hall. *The Times* noted that:

> they refused to broaden their performance to suit the hall and the result was chamber music of the utmost distinction. M. Fournier imposes some of the elegant languor of the *grand seigneur* on everything he touches.[15]

On 2 and 5 February 1965, they gave the entire Beethoven cycle, recorded live, at the Salle Pleyel. It was seen as an example of an exquisite balance of affinities: two very different artists in their maturity, able now, 'with the necessary weight and serenity'[16] to reach the essence of the music. Many listeners compared the concerts with the music-making of friends after dinner, a rest after the showing-off of virtuosos; Kempff reinforced the impression, peering at the score through his spectacles. At one moment the page-turner skipped a page; Kempff played on regardless. Fournier gently touched the pianist's arm with his bow. The audience chuckled and the concert continued happily. (Recording technology has drawn a veil over this little blip.) Kempff was rather accident prone. At the Beethoven bi-centenary in May 1970 his concert started late. He had forgotten his spectacles.

Notes

1. In the following order: Nos 1 in G, 5 in C minor and 3 in C; Nos 2 in D minor, 4 in E flat and 6 in D (28 October and 22 November 1962).
2. *Basler Nachrichten*, 29 October 1962.
3. *Basler Volksblatt*, 30 October 1962.
4. Id., 23 November 1962.
5. *Nazional-Zeitung Basel*, 23 November 1962.
6. *Harmonie*, February 1968.
7. *The Times*, 10 December 1962.

8. *The Daily Telegraph*, 10 December 1962.
9. Lyda Fournier to Thérèse Mayer, 12 December 1962.
10. Id., 14 January 1963.
11. Id., 7 November 1971.
12. Pierre Fournier to Jean Fonda Fournier, 1 February 1963.
13. Id., 7 February 1963.
14. *Chicago Tribune*, 3 April 1964.
15. *The Times*, 6 February 1963.
16. *Harmonie*, May 1966 (Claude Rostand).

25 Two Concertos

Jean Martinon's Cello Concerto Op. 52, dedicated to Fournier, had its first performance in Hamburg on 25 January 1965 with the Norddeutscher Rundfunk Orchestra under Hans Schmidt-Isserstedt. During the piano rehearsal at Düsseldorf Martinon reproached Fournier for appearing uninvolved. '*Mon vieux*', he said, 'I'd like you to be as heartrending in my work as you are in Dvořák or Schumann, less… detached.' The composer's misgivings vanished at the première. In September at the Besançon Festival Fournier was due to record the work for the French Radio with Seiji Ozawa and the Orchestre National but there was a problem: no parts – they were in America. On a telephone call from Fournier and with amazing competence, the publishers, Schott, had them copied and dispatched to Strasbourg where they were picked up at the customs and rushed to Besançon. The parts were barely dry, and the Orchestre National virtually sightread the piece.

In 1958 Fournier asked the Swiss composer Frank Martin for a concerto. Martin was at the time finishing his *Mystère de la Nativité*, and with its completion he found that the long successive immersions in choral works 'often in an archaic style' had left him unprepared for work of a very different nature. A year later, in autumn 1959, he sketched a ten-bar melody for the cello, only to find that he could think of no suitable orchestral response. He decided to set composition aside for a time. Five years later he tackled the concerto again, and after some false starts remembered the sketch which had lain half-forgotten in a drawer. The Concerto stems from this simple diatonic tune over a chromatic accompaniment. Martin was anxious about the Finale until unexpectedly in August 1965 he found the solution in a ship's lounge while on a cruise with his wife Maria off Cape North, Canada. It was the excellent band entertaining the guests every evening which inspired the jazzy passages of the last movement.[1]

'I'm beginning to believe in [the concerto]', Martin wrote in April 1965 to the conductor Paul Sacher, announcing the work for autumn 1966, 'I would rather be hanged at once than not finish it in the course of next spring.'[2] Early in 1966 Martin wrote to Fournier before sending the cello part of the third movement which had 'rather a frenzied and angry character', as he was worried about technical aspects and needed Fournier's comments. Meanwhile Ansermet was working on it for a Geneva performance.

I'm working hard at our Martin which I consider a masterpiece. Very difficult to learn, to 'hear' harmonically, but very original and perfectly shaped. I am enormously looking forward to working at it with you...[3].

The Concerto was dedicated to Fournier and to Paul Sacher who conducted it at its first performance at Basle on 26 January 1967. In Geneva it had a further hearing with the OSR under Ansermet. Martin's comparison of the two performances in a letter to Fournier throw an interesting light on a composer's reactions:

Cher Ami

By a happy chance on the airwaves last night I was able to hear your performance of our concerto quite clearly on Sottens. In spite of the unexpected accompaniments from other stations, it was a new joy for myself and my wife to hear you again singing my music, and it seemed that the audience gave you a warm and well-deserved reception.

It was very interesting for me to hear the differences between the Sacher and Ansermet versions. In spite of the contrasts between a live performance and our broadcast under precarious conditions, the orchestral texture seemed finer and richer than in Geneva. The end of the first movement and all the second were admirable. On the other hand, certain quick passages I liked better in Bâle, and especially the big saxophone solo in the middle of the first movement with its dry accompaniment. One must add that in Bâle Sacher had a saxophonist who is a real soloist. And the Finale seemed a bit slow and had no barbarity, which surprised me of Ansermet. He was probably afraid of it running away with him, which would [have been] disastrous. But he was too measured, in a word too well-behaved. I am looking forward to having the tapes of both performances so as to be able to compare them at leisure.

What remains in my head, and in my heart, is your playing, your expressiveness, your tone over the entire instrument, the delicacy of your runs and above all the singing line, exalted or melancholy or dreaming.

Thank you for having given that intense life to this concerto which gave me such joy and such trouble....

My wife joins me in telling you how grateful we are and in sending you our friendship. May Mme Fournier and your son have a big share in it.

Your old friend
Frank Martin.
The photo is on its way. I haven't forgotten it![4]

Having followed the gestation of the Martin Concerto to its birth on the concert platform, we must now return to 1965 when, after the Besançon Festival, Fournier was in Berlin to record the Brahms Sonatas with Rudolf Firkušny. This was the occasion when, having taken his Goffriler cello with him, he telephoned Lyda in Paris to send him the Miremont by air.

In September, at the Montreux Festival, he worked with Zubin Mehta for the first time, feeling an instant rapport with the young conductor. At the Montreux Palace where they were both staying, while Fournier was dressing there was a call from Mehta. Might he bring round the 'Lord Nelson' Stradivarius for him to try out? Among other valuable instruments it had been bought for the Los Angeles Symphony Orchestra at the request of Mrs Chandler, owner of the *LA Times*. Milstein joined them and Fournier tried the Strad. It was apéritif time and the concert was at 8.30 pm. Usually Fournier considered it took two or three days to get used to a new cello, but this time he said he would play it in the Schumann concerto that evening. Mehta and Milstein were horrified: 'You're not going to take that risk!' 'Oh yes I am!' He did, and all was well.

Claudio Abbado is another conductor with whom Fournier felt an affinity. On the morning of an Edinburgh Festival concert the following September 1966, they ran through the Schumann Concerto as if they had played it together countless times. Lyda wrote home declaring that this new discovery reminded her of the young Toscanini. On this occasion a critic described Fournier's statement of the opening theme as 'so lyrically poetic that it seemed more beautiful than any other melody one could readily call to mind from the entire cello repertory'.[5]

Shortly after this, illness returned in the middle of the American tour and Fournier wrote to Jean Pierre, who was in Chelsea widening his horizons and practising on Yaltah Menuhin's grand piano:

> The two concerts here were a great success in spite of something very trying which will probably force me to cancel two or three concerts. I started to feel pain in my polio foot one night, in the ankle. At the Wallensteins[6] the pain got worse and I could hardly walk. The next day, second rehearsal with orchestra the day before the concert, and in the afternoon such pain that I called Lake, the charming doctor and the only one I could reach on Armistice Day with everything closed! He examined me and immediately had me X-rayed at the hospital... X-rays normal and I was referred to a young Dr Siegal who diagnosed an infection in the joint and ankle of the foot operated on 35 years ago [1931]. Useless to tell you how the two concerts went. An announcement was made to explain my appearance on two sticks, being unable to lean on that foot since each step was unbearably painful. I played in a very relaxed way and very successfully. I have to stay without a caliper, keeping my leg warm as long as it takes for the infection to become localized, but it's very depressing. Bada is looking after me with great tenderness but I am very upset for her, ruining her stay with this immobilization which has meant calling off all my plans. If all is well I'll start again at Toledo on the 30th before Chicago and California.
>
> I think of you a lot and hope your stay in London is a very happy one in compensation for my stay here.[7]

The infection had lodged in the bad foot (*'dans une partie vulnérable de mon body'*), producing acute pain at every movement. Fournier enquired about Jean Pierre's stay 'in [his] picture-gallery' with the Countess Voronin, formerly of the Tsar's household and living in Wetherby Gardens with eight cats, a considerable collection of pictures (including a Winterhalter of herself) and, at the time, the choreographer David Lichine. Fournier continued the letter, describing a visit to [S.] who showed him his Strad, 'as wonderful as one could possibly imagine', bought from a well-established dealer four years earlier for 'next to nothing' because it was believed to be a fake; in fact it was the 'Duke of Marlborough'. 'When you think of the hands playing that instrument, you could weep.'[8]

He wrote again before leaving New York:

> I leave tomorrow for the few dates left after this stay which was spoilt, especially for your mother, by this mysterious complaint. I am better and I began to walk again three days ago, not very comfortably and with pain at every step but it's calming down and my foot is beginning to get back its normal shape. [...] Last night *gastly* [sic] dinner

with Mr and Mr Weinhold [concert managers] at the Plaza. He more and more vague and tired, with mysterious airs about plans which he never explains clearly... I have lost my illusions about a normal future in this country and I'll only come here each year for a minimum of time.

We read your letters with joy, and hope that your stay in London will produce some positive results. Here we feel we are banging our heads against a wall and that any struggle is useless. All I know is that 'everybody is playing'. Gilels giving four Philharmonic concerts, two recitals at Carnegie Hall. Gulda played four Beethoven sonatas at the Lincoln Center and jazz as an encore. Very fine reviews, they say. As for Kempff, Weinhold claims that he (W.) has put pressure on him to play with me in NY and that Kempff was *very* reticent.[9] What a disappointment this man is, passing up something which would be a success everywhere.

As an example of gratuitous meanness, he enclosed two reviews of a concert given by the respected pianist and teacher Ernest Ulmer, 'a man', Fournier wrote, 'who made a great effort and is killed off by these gentlemen'.

Barenboim came again last night before he left, and was so affectionate. Bada will tell you funny stories about him and Mehta. he is a young man well worth knowing and who is fond of us. After building up Mehta three years ago as a superman, Weinhold now runs him down in a shameful manner. Touchyness [sic] is so strong with these gentlemen that they can become worst enemies after appearing to be friends.

I'll send you the results of Chicago [in English] *how happy I'll be to see you again*. I wrote to Lesser[10] who sent me a charming letter with kind messages for you.

Ta Maman asks me to say that you haven't been forgotten in *Le Shopping*. Make the best of your last days in London and may everything go well for you.

Très tendrement, Papa.[11]

Lyda and Mehta went to hear Barenboim playing a Beethoven programme in a New York suburb. The three were standing outside the hall where the public was waiting for the doors to open, Barenboim in evening dress under a trenchcoat. Suddenly Mehta addressed the queue: 'Why are you all so keen to hear this pianist?' Barenboim grinned; Lyda looked at her feet. Outraged, a woman stepped out of the queue 'Sir, we are from Israel and you seem unaware of how popular he is!' Not a soul had recognized Barenboim in spite of his tell-tale white tie. Going back to Manhattan on the subway and still on a high, Barenboim and Mehta treated the bewildered commuters to excerpts from *Aida* in Hebrew.

Returning to Cleveland in May 1967, Fournier gave the US première of Frank Martin's Concerto with George Szell. *Don Quixote* was to end the programme and during rehearsals there was an amused complicity between Fournier and the orchestral musicians as well as a celebratory smile shared between him, the concertmaster and Szell after a difficult passage together. Backstage after the concert Fournier thanked Szell: '*C'était très, très beau*.' Mrs Szell remarked 'George almost looks pleased tonight.' Szell, with his arm around Fournier said 'We've built a cathedral out of pebbles.'[12]

Before leaving for a holiday at St Moritz in July, Fournier dealt with business and a small exercise in public relations with Peta Fisher:

If you cannot offer J. Pierre some solo appearances, I should be prepared to come *alone* with an accompanist at the conditions you propose. Needless to say, Jean Pierre would be so happy to be considered as soloist. He is engaged next season by some major orchestras (Munich with Kubelik, Zurich with Kempe, Geneva with Kletzki) and now with me at the BBC and Pallanza before making a second record with me for DGG in September....[13][14]

The disaster perhaps the most feared by a performer happened to Fournier at the Edinburgh Festival in August. During the Elgar Concerto with James Loughran and the Scottish National Orchestra he had a serious lapse of memory – the dreaded *trou*. In the same programme he had played the C P E Bach Concerto in A, a piece often played by other cellists in F on account of its difficulty in the original key. He had a sudden attack of nerves, recorded by the press as 'patches of unhappy intonation', although critics referred to the 'grave, darkly glowing beauty he brought to the slow movement'.[15]

> Thank you for understanding the state I am in as I come home. I'm very discouraged by [the critics'] stand which will give the general impression that I am no longer the same person, and no longer worthy of the past. This is the ransom of age and of the pitilessness of today which can accept no imperfection. *Iron* playing is what is wanted now, and it follows that what the heart brings is totally forgotten.
>
> Groucho Gulda rang yesterday before leaving for Pallanza. *Very* nice and friendly, wanting to form a trio with Szeryng and me!!! and saying 'Szeryng was very bad 10 years ago but now he is all right!!!' [...]
>
> Make the best of your stay and don't behave like Gunther Sachs at the Casino![17]

On a happier note he added a PS: Kempff had agreed to the hoped-for concert the following August.[18]

The miseries of this Scottish story were to be forgotten in New York where Fournier gave his first Carnegie Hall recital for three years. A cable wafted his high spirits across the Atlantic:

FINANCIALLY MORE THAN DECENT BEAUTIFULLY FILLED HALL OVERWHELMING SUCCESS YELLING PUBLIC THREE ENCORES EXCELLENT REVIEWS LETTER FOLLOWS AM HAPPY MUCH LOVE PIERRE

After Edinburgh the reversal of fortune tasted all the sweeter. The New York success also compensated for the loss of four concerts with Josef Krips in San Francisco through an orchestral strike. He wrote home full of affection and fatherly advice for Jean Pierre's thirtieth birthday, having enjoyed the 125th anniversary of the New York Philharmonic, 'a dazzling concert', the hall and reception full of the world's musical celebrities and Jackie Kennedy to boot, the Big Apple at its juiciest, 'a happy evening with friends.'[19]

Back in France in January 1968, in the amphitheatre of the Faculty of Letters at Nanterre, he gave the Dvořák concerto with the Orchestre de Paris and Jean Martinon. (This was one of a series of concerts usefully replicated at different centres.) To his habitual authority and lyricism he now added a rougher, more dramatic quality, an uncharacteristic *brusquerie* noticed by Clarendon, 'making his cello angry like a storm. The students, young insatiables, wouldn't let him go.'[20]

The prestigious Orchestre de Paris was founded in 1967 by De Gaulle's

Minister of culture, André Malraux, to replace the OSCC, and Charles Munch was appointed its first director. With Serge Baudo as his assistant, the orchestra made its first tour under Munch, then in November 1968 in Richmond, Virginia, Munch died. Herbert von Karajan was then engaged as 'musical adviser'. Inevitably there were some changes, and Fournier was irritated to hear from his agent that Karajan had switched conductors for one of the cellist's performances without consulting him. Meanwhile the *Figaro Littéraire* approached Fournier for his comments on Karajan's appointment. Lyda warned 'have nothing whatsoever to do with all that...' but Pierre was stubborn: 'I have something to say and I'll say it.' It was not one of his wisest moves. Although in this short piece he paid lip service to Karajan's prestige, he declared that the choice of programmes and soloists was the province of the orchestral committee; that authoritarianism didn't work in France; that the conductor's presence should be continuous and not sporadic; that this orchestra's very French style, established by Munch and Baudo, was not something which could be enhanced by another conductor, however great and, lastly, that the choice of Berlioz' *Symphonie fantastique* was 'a psychological error', the work having been so long associated with Munch who 'could have been commemorated in some other way'. Such words could hardly have been better designed to anger Karajan, and like so many artists who crossed the conductor, Fournier was never forgiven. He was far too honest to be talented in musical politics, and although for some time he continued to play with the Berlin Philharmonic, he never again appeared with Karajan. Eliette von Karajan told Jean Pierre some years after the *brouille* that her husband never forgot a bad turn, although Pierre was his favourite cellist and would remain so.[21]

Notes

1. Marie Martin to the author, 3 February 1997.
2. Frank Martin to Paul Sacher, 4 April 1965. Cited in Bernard Martin, *Frank Martin*, Neuchâtel: A la Baconnière, 1973, p. 155.
3. Ernest Ansermet to Pierre Fournier, 28 December 1966.
4. Frank Martin to Pierre Fournier, erroneously dated 2 February 1967; in fact March or April (Maria Martin to the author, 3 February 1997). Pierre Fournier made two concert recordings of Frank Martin's Concerto: with Ansermet and the OSR, and in April 1967 with George Szell and the Cleveland Orchestra.
5. *Daily Telegraph*, 3 September 1966 (Colin Mason).
6. Alfred Wallenstein (1898–1983), American cellist and conductor.
7. Pierre Fournier to Jean Fonda Fournier, 14 November 1966.
8. Id.
9. Having been warned in 1945 that he would be banned in the US, Kempff embarked late on an American career. Weinhold was planning appearances with Bernstein and the NYPO, and this, together with a Carnegie Hall recital, was more than Kempff could resist. Fournier was at the time of this letter unaware of these plans. Meanwhile DGG was pressing Kempff to continue recording with Fournier (Jean Fonda Fournier Archive).

10. Larry Lesser, US cellist, director of the New England Music Conservatory at Boston. Was assistant and close friend of Piatigorsky. He stayed with the Fourniers in Geneva in 1966 (Jean Fonda Fournier).
11. Pierre Fournier to Jean Fonda Fournier, 24 November [1966].
12. *The New Yorker*, 30 May 1970.
13. Schubert, Mendelssohn and Schumann pieces. The first had been a sonata record: Debussy, Martinů and Shostakovich.
14. Pierre Fournier to Peta Fisher, 24 July 1967.
15. *The Scotsman*, 25 August 1967.
16. *The Times*, 25 August 1967.
17. Millionnaire playboy and third husband of Brigitte Bardot.
18. Pierre Fournier to Jean Fonda Fournier, 30 August 1967.
19. Id., 8 December 1967.
20. *Le Figaro*, 27 January 1968.
21. Jean Fonda Fournier.

26 Partnership

Fournier's first Paris appearance with his son fell in the middle of the students' revolt of 1968, *les événements*, and might well have been cancelled: windows were broken near the Pourtalès family apartment lent for rehearsals; there were few taxis and the main thoroughfares were blocked by the CRS (riot police). At Pleyel the audience turned up nevertheless and gave the duo a good reception in spite of the tense atmosphere. *Le Figaro* welcomed the concert as one of the finest of the season '[Fournier is] too big an artist not to have taught his son to give even more respect to music than to the paternal rod of iron.' There was 'rigour as well as emotion'.[1]

After the concert the immediate problem was how to get back to Geneva for a flight to South America: there were neither planes, trains nor taxis and little petrol to be found. They were saved by a *deus ex machina*, Bernard Lefort, director of the Marseilles Opera, producing a chauffeur-driven car for their repatriation.

The previous day ('out of thoughtlessness or stupidity' as he recalled), Jean Pierre had taken a stroll down the Boulevard Saint-Germain. The well-known composer and musicologist Henri-Louis de la Grange was selling the left-wing *Nouvel Observateur* at a street corner in the midst of rioting students.

* * *

'Without flattery you are absolutely his best interpreter.' So runs a postscript to the 1968 performance of the Dvořák Concerto at the Prague Spring of that fatal year.[2] In the audience and introduced to Fournier afterwards was Dr Karel Mikysa. Director of the Dvořák Museum, Mikysa was also Secretary of the Dvořák Society and founder of a museum at the composer's birthplace, Nelahozeves on the Vltava (Moldau). For the museum Fournier contributed a short piece giving his thoughts on Dvořák and his Concerto. Besides Kubelik, Fournier worked with another distinguished Czech conductor, Karel Ančerl (1908–1973), at the Blossom (Cleveland) Music Festival. Ancerl, driven out of his country by the Soviet invasion in 1968, settled later in Toronto.

A musician who saw a lot of Fournier during the Geneva years was Claude

Viala, who as a seventeen-year-old cellist had hidden at a rehearsal in order to hear Fournier play Chopin's Introduction and Polonaise.[3] He summed up Fournier's playing in one word, 'noblesse'. Viala remembered hearing him before the war in the Brahms Double Concerto with François Capoulade, and later under Pierre Colombo in chamber concerts with Szeryng, Rubinstein and Grumiaux, at the Salle de la Réformation. This hall, with a capacity of 1600, had arguably the best acoustics in Geneva and in the twenties it had been used by the League of Nations. 'It looked austere and warm at the same time, and had lots of draughts.'[4] As well as Fournier, many other great names appeared there: Segovia, Backhaus, Gieseking, Milstein. Typical of our era was its destruction, to make way for... a bank.

The Geneva masterclasses were founded by Samuel Baud-Bovy, director of the Conservatoire, with the co-operation of some 'local' musicians: Nikita Magaloff at Clarens (Montreux), Fournier in Geneva and Henryk Szeryng who was simply fond of the place. The high point of the series was always the masters' concert and the first year this coincided with the news of the Soviet invasion of Czechoslovakia. Szeryng suggested giving his fees to help the refugees; the others agreed to do the same. At the big dinner given by the City of Geneva, the Conservatoire's chairman thanked Szeryng for his generous gift to the Czechs. There was an embarrassed silence: the others were taken aback by this unilateral gesture. The lack of tact left Magaloff resigned but Fournier angry.

Students took part in the classes for about three weeks, long enough to make some progress, but at the students' concert nerves would cause the odd performer to return to old habits. Viala recalled Fournier turning to him with 'That was not *my* doing!'[5]

Another successful partnership was formed when Kempff and Fournier were joined by the Polish-born violinist Henryk Szeryng. This fine artist, a pupil of Carl Flesch and a superb Bach player, was sensitive and adaptable in chamber music and Fournier found him easy to play with. Highly cultivated, a phenomenal linguist and once liaison officer in France with General Sikorski, Szeryng was so impressed by the welcome afforded by Mexico to Polish refugees, that he became a Mexican citizen in 1946. Nominated 'goodwill ambassador' of that country, he travelled on a diplomatic passport.

While their work together was admirable, Fournier found that collaboration with Szeryng led to some surprises. For some reason this successful artist, appreciated and honoured on and off the platform the world over, was driven by an unquenchable need to assert himself. Nothing, it seemed, was ever grand enough for him. Stories about him abound.

At the ritual concert to close the Geneva masterclasses, just before the Brahms Double Concerto, he carefully moved Fournier's chair as far back as possible and the cellist was heard mildly complaining 'I'm always put at the back of the platform!' (The orchestral manager firmly replaced the chair.) When Fournier had made a small slip in the Brahms C major Trio, Szeryng leaned across to point his bow at Fournier's score. Before a South Bank concert, when he was expected to pick up Pierre and Lyda at the Savoy following his own luncheon with the Mexican ambassador, Szeryng arrived in a hired Rolls Royce half an hour late. At the Festival Hall the orchestra had been sitting for for a considerable time and the scrupulous Fournier was beside himself. 'They can wait' replied the Olympian Szeryng. Fournier retorted 'That's amateurish!'

But all did not go Szeryng's way. In Geneva Fournier's pupil Jonathan Williams was detailed to telephone the violinist and inform him that the London *Times* considered him such an important figure that they wished to interview him in the company of a leading ambassador. Fournier passed some agreeable moments as he pictured Szeryng polishing his opening remarks. The *Times* representative was to meet him at the Conservatoire after the masterclasses. The minutes passed: half an hour, one hour; Szeryng, increasingly nervous, was pacing up and down. 'Anything wrong?' asked Fournier. Szeryng fumed 'If the *Times* wants to do this piece about me, make no mistake, they had better come soon or I shall leave!'

The sparring was taken up again at the Royal Festival Hall in the Double Concerto, when Szeryng, playing all the while, walked across the platform and obscured Fournier from the audience's view. The cellist countered with a firm little prod with his bow (*noblesse oblige*). It did the trick.

Perhaps it is because courtesy is becoming as rare as the peregrine falcon that Fournier's is remembered. One young accompanist, setting up his music on the piano, recalled Fournier insisting on being handed the cello part, although he patently didn't need it. At Aldeburgh John Owen observed him, frail as he then was, reluctant to allow a woman to carry his cello. Jonathan Williams witnessed him struggling back from Harrods with a coat for Lyda. Julian Lloyd Webber, who had sent him his own Rodrigo Concerto recording, received a carefully handwritten card in return; he also noticed that instead of running down his colleagues, Fournier habitually underlined their qualities.

*   *   *

Between 1968 and 1976 Fournier's duo partner in South Africa was Lamar Crowson. Before he had met the young pianist Fournier was cautious and sounded out Hans Kramer. 'I hear that this Mr *Crosson* plays with the lid open…?' 'Of course', Kramer replied, 'He plays at full stick, but don't worry, he adjusts his tone to the cellist.' Which he did, scrupulously.[6] Crowson's brand of humour pleased Fournier. Glancing at a page of the Honegger sonata before him, Crowson observed lugubriously 'I am overcome by this avalanche of notes.' For the Fourniers this became a stock family joke. At the first rehearsal Fournier was surprised that Crowson was doing 'all sorts of Fournierish things'. He had forgotten that Crowson's first duo partner had been Amaryllis Fleming and that they had played for him years earlier.

Crowson tells his own story:

> Rehearsing a recent Brahms series I came across Pierre's markings on my own score of the Second Sonata. He said that Brahms often wrote *diminuendo* too soon. Sometimes

1 One of the two bronzes by Léopold Morice, Fournier's grandfather, on the Pont Alexandre III, Paris

2 Gaston and Gabrielle Fournier on their wedding day, 1900. The photograph was taken in the garden at rue Erlanger

3   Gabrielle Fournier

4   Pierre Fournier, aged four

5   Pierre Fournier, aged six

6   Odette Krettly (1897–1954), Fournier's first teacher

7   Pierre Fournier, aged 10 or 11, in his grandfather's garden at Auteuil

8   Pierre and Cécile in fancy dress

9   Pierre and Cécile. Possibly in Royan 1923

10   Lyda Antik, Berlin 1920s

11   Pierre Fournier, Paris 1939

12   Tchaikovsky Cello Competition, Moscow 1966. From left to right: Gregor
Piatigorsky, his brother Shura Stagorsky, Gaspar Cassadó, Pierre Fournier, Daniil
Shafran and Mstislav Rostropovich

13   Marie-Thérèse Fourneau

14 Father and son at the Beethovenhaus in Bonn, 1974. Pierre Fournier is playing the composer's Guarnerius and Jean-Pierre his pianoforte

15 Pierre Fournier with Louis Beydts, early 1950s. Inscription reads 'To my dear partner of the pin-up boys of Besançon'

16   Pierre Fournier and Wilhelm Kempff, Japan 1954

17   Father and son, Tokyo November 1968

18   Pierre Fournier with Sir Malcolm Sargent conducting the Berlin Philharmonic in the
Dvořák concerto, 1961

19   Pierre Fournier talking to Nathan Milstein, Montreux 1954

20   Pierre Fournier and George Szell rehearsing the Frank Martin concerto in Cleveland, Autumn 1967

21 Pierre Fournier and Lamar Crowson rehearsing Beethoven at Snape, 1981

22 Pierre Fournier, Peta Fisher and Vladimir Orloff, Johannesburg

23　Pierre Fournier with Junko, his second wife, Geneva 1980

he would play it like a young man passionately in love; other times it was the older man remembering. We never discussed it but I could tell how he felt by his treatment of the *pizzicati*.

At our first concert together in Cape Town [25 September 1968], I'm so nervous, playing with the great PF. And because of his infirmity concert procedure will be different; we go on, he hangs his cane on the piano and we begin. Naturally, obviously, we won't walk off and on again. After the first piece, we bow and sit down. Then Pierre, with his left hand and with purpose, presents his bow to me. I think that he wants two hands to tune, not uncommon. I take hold of the bow carefully, but he doesn't release it. We have a friendly tug-of-war. During the interval I say 'Please excuse this stupid American.' His response is 'My dear boy, I have short arms and long sleeves.' He had put out the bow with his left hand so as to pull back the sleeve with his right! At our next concert he repeated the gesture, with more purpose. I replied 'Non, merci.'

Once during a Locatelli sonata Crowson found his page turned to reveal a naked girl from *Playboy* magazine. (Ernest Lush, a favourite target of Fournier's, was another victim of this.)

When Fournier and Crowson gave Ravel's *Kaddisch* as an encore, although Fournier played this transcription on the G string, Crowson automatically gave him the A to tune to. Then he apologized for his mistake. Fournier told him 'When I play the Paganini Variations on the A String, you can give me the G.'

> In Padua on an Italian tour, because of the long walk Pierre had a (crude) little maison built at the side of the stage. What a squeeze! Pierre, me, my page-turner and a recording engineer. We could hardly move! When Pierre went on to play solo Bach, he told me that I could now take a 'pee', 'but not through the hole facing the audience'.
>
> The modesty of this great man was beyond belief. It took him weeks to summon up the courage to ask me to record with him [*Rendezvous with Fournier*] because they were all cello pieces and not sonatas. He thought I'd be insulted! He was not well at the time and I resolved that there would be no retakes because of me. Ugh! The hardest things to accompany are such pieces where the freedoms are based on technical requirements which don't relate to the pianist. We finished a session early. Karajan's doctor, a miraculous one-armed gentleman [Dr Simon] attended Pierre and said we must stop. Luckily we did; the next morning the doctor drove us to the plane, and I mean the plane – the gangway!
>
> Without doubt, the high point of my professional career was walking on to the platform with Pierre Fournier.... Comparisons are odious: du Pré, Schiff, greats, but modern greats.... For a young musician to work with a musical aristocrat was inspiring. As a musical scholar (I hope) I was surprised, but never musically disappointed. He uplifted me, musically and personally. I was enriched by my association with Pierre Fournier.[7]

The harpsichordist André Raynaud, who played Bach sonatas with Fournier on two occasions, recalled that there was nothing of the 'authentic' baroque in his interpretations, but clearly Raynaud had the tact and good sense not to attempt to impose another style on the older man, and simply followed Fournier's indications. Inevitably this carried risks, and there were one or two near-mishaps. However Fournier's superiority remained dazzling, Raynaud stressed, especially in two areas:

> the unique tone which made the cello sound like the human voice, with none of that

rough contact between bow and string which you may like or dislike in other cellists. Also there was an extraordinary charisma which made this 'voice' seem to be the expression of this artist's soul. We know too many virtuosi who are impeccable technicians but who will never reach that standard or quality of emotion which were inherent in [Fournier's] very personality.[8]

* * *

In spring 1969 both Pierre and Lyda were unwell. Pierre was being monitored for blood sugar problems and Lyda had experienced the first pains in her hands, warnings of the polyarthritis which was to give her much suffering. Initially she was treated by a Montreux doctor, and there was some improvement. 'The morale is up a little' Pierre wrote to Peta Fisher.[9] Rapidly, however, the pain became so acute that she was soon 'unable to write a single word with her damaged hand.'[10] A weakly scrawled note survives as a postscript to a letter from Pierre to their son, sent from Monte Carlo in August. After a concert with Karl Münchinger and the Stuttgart Chamber Orchestra, they had driven to Menton with the conductor to eat at an Italian restaurant. Münchinger told Pierre that he hoped to record the two Haydn concertos with him for Decca. There had been ovations at the concert

> but friends in the audience – *none*. Nathan [Milstein] had played superbly the night before with marvellous old [Paul] Paray. We were in the Prince's box with Rainier and Grace. Afterwards there was a short reception in the private apartments. Paray very warm towards us and wants us to stay with him in Switzerland. The Tony Mayers came to see us yesterday… Nathan very funny on the subject of Maria [his daughter] and her French boyfriend who is not to Thérèse [Milstein]'s taste: she wants nothing less than an English peer of the realm. Also she is shocked at the boyfriend calling Maria '*ma petite cocotte*' all day long. They left yesterday, as warm as always and Nathan more Chaplinesque than ever.
> That is the end of the news from this artificial little world of the Côte d'Azur where you can run into Gaston Poulet,[11] the Mayers, Marcelle[12] …the Handmans,[13] all mixed up in this bizarre cocktail. […]
> *Mille grandes tendresses*, Papa.

Lyda's postscript labours, like a child's hand, painfully across the page.[14]

In the autumn Fournier wrote from Chicago. Jean Pierre was to join him in New York to hear his four concerts with Szell and he was impatient for the end of 'a very boring stay in complete solitude'.

> The weather, which is appalling, doesn't help. The orchestra has been very friendly and enthusiastic, cellists saying 'That's the *right* way to play the cello.'
> And yet, apart from the only good line in the *Chicago Tribune*, the three other papers were as *nasty* as possible, vicious and tendancious [sic]: 'indifferent form', 'tone not silky but nylon and acetate', whereas everybody loves this cello which has a magnificent tone.[15]
> I didn't hesitate, in front of the orchestra and the manager, to express my disgust at such spite. Everyone here complains of the press. *Better to forget*, but what an awful city, vulgar, brutal! [Jerzy] Semkov[16] adorable and accompanied so well.
> I shall be happy to leave, having spent my eight-day *cure de solitude* doing some great work on my Bach Suites.[17]

I am worried sick about Bada. Beg her not to get discouraged because morale has such an effect on the physical side. It is a great sadness for me, being deprived of her presence, and knowing that after [all] those trying months she had not been able to come. Tell her how near I am to her in my thoughts which are as tender as they are sad, both for her and for me. Keep me informed in time for my arrival at the Drake in New York.

J' t'embrasse si fort et je t'attends avec joie. – Papa. Make no mistake about it. If I had played as I did with a Russian name, they would have praised me to the skies. It is like that everywhere: the French are not taken seriously. *Sad! Sad!*[18]

Writing to Peta Fisher the following May (1970), Fournier reported on the coming demise of the Kempff–Szeryng–Fournier collaboration:

The recording of the trios was OK with the inevitable pompousness of the violinist... who had such a row with Kempff at the last hour of the session (for a futile reason)[19] that the last bar of the last trio marked the very final point of any co-operation... such a pity! Of course I realized, long before our last meeting, that Kempff doesn't want to play any more chamber music! On our last evening we were invited by Henry [Henryk Szeryng] (Lyda, Jean Pierre and myself) to dinner, and the whole evening he was fulminating about the 'salopard' Kempff and treating him like a real 'Boche'... so comic and sad. I suspect the *real* reason is that the DGG will be recording the violin sonatas in June in London with Kempff and... Menuhin. So the final dinner was a good occasion for Henry (whom we admire and like, as a childish Boy) to empty his heart against the whole world.... But this is a real sadness, not to play in public all together any more.

Lyda feels a little better, due to a remarkable treatment [given by] an old-fashioned and wonderful doctor in Montreux [Dr Noel Spühler]. *Pouvu que ça dure!* That is my daily prayer. I'm so grateful to you and Cyril for everything you did for me... also to dear Dr Suzman. I am *better* thanks to my strict regime[20] and the recent blood test (done in Montreux last week) proves a clear decrease in blood sugar. Bless you dearest for your affectionate care...[21]

The French television devoted its programme *l'Invité du dimanche* (The Sunday Guest) to Fournier on 10 December, and among his 'guests' was the film director René Clair whose book had just appeared.[22] Clair wrote to Fournier afterwards with the eye of the film-maker:

Mon cher Pierre
I couldn't say goodbye to you yesterday, you were the prisoner of a circle of light when I was leaving in shadow. I should have liked to tell you, and I tell you now, how touched I was by the way you spoke of my book. Thank you from the bottom of my heart. I want to tell you that everyone who has spoken to me about the programme was moved by the simplicity and the clarity with which you spoke about your art.

For me that feeling was not new.

Bronia joins me in sending our affectionate thoughts to all three. René Clair.[23]

Notes

1. *Le Figaro*, 16 May 1968.
2. Gaetano Delogu conducted the State Symphony Orchestra.
3. A pupil of Henri Buenzod, Claude Viala was leading cellist of the OSR and of the Geneva Chamber Orchestra, before becoming Director of the Geneva Conservatoire in 1970.

4. Jean Fonda Fournier to the author, 1993.
5. Claude Viala in conversation with the author.
6. Hans Kramer in conversation with the author.
7. Lamar Crowson to the author, 26 June, 9 September 1991.
8. André Raynaud to the author, 20 July 1989.
9. Pierre Fournier to Peta Fisher, 15 April 1969.
10. Id., 18 July 1969.
11. French violinist and conductor (1892–1974).
12. Fournier's much-loved Corsican stepmother.
13. Dorel Handman, Romanian-born naturalized French pianist (1906–).
14. Pierre Fournier to Jean Fonda Fournier, 9 August 1969.
15. The 'bon vieux Miremont' cello.
16. Jerzy Semkov, Polish-born conductor, born 1928. Assistant to Mravinsky, worked with Erich Kleiber and Bruno Walter.
17. J S Bach, *Six Suites*, ed. Pierre Fournier. New York: International Music Co. 1972, revised 1983.
18. Pierre Fournier to Jean Fonda Fournier, 27 October 1969.
19. Kempff wanted to work in the empty Vevey theatre used for the recording but Szeryng refused to leave the platform.
20. The 'strict régime' was supposed to be sugar-free, but was mostly in the mind: Fournier liked puddings.
21. Pierre Fournier to Peta Fisher, 8 May 1970.
22. René Clair, *Mémoires d'un montreur d'ombres. Cinéma d'hier, cinéma d'aujourd'hui*, Paris: NRF-Gallimard.
23. René Clair to Pierre Fournier, 14 December 1970.

27   Stress and Empathy

Fournier was a man of contradictions. With the hypersensitivity and the emotional dependence on a handful of intimates went a fierce need for freedom born of a physique which, although assaulted by polio, was fundamentally robust. Determined to see the Parthenon with his niece Jacqueline Peltier, he walked up without help. On a South African tour he insisted, in spite of increasing frailty, on driving Jacqueline's protesting sister Denise to the airport. (Her presence had been a pleasing coincidence: 'They will think you're my *petite amie*.') Like the métro seat in childhood, Derek Simpson's offer to move Fournier's car for him was firmly declined. A friend recalled the astonishing agility with which he swung out of a London taxi on to the wet pavement to hold the door open.

Fournier's car was a source of great pleasure and – here another nod to his cinemania – he adorned it with a mascot of Donald Duck. His astonished passenger would witness the transformation behind the wheel from gentle aristocrat into your average French driver complete with *béret basque* and impatience to match.

He enjoyed teasing, but his darker nature sometimes spread like a drop of ink into the fabric of friendship. In the summer of 1956 Szigeti was giving masterclasses at Zermatt. By chance Casals was also there. Fournier and Magaloff were rehearsing for a church concert at Sils Maria when a cable arrived for Magaloff, calling him to Zermatt to play with Casals.

At once Magaloff said 'I can't go.'

'You must', Fournier insisted, 'It's important.'

Magaloff shrugged the matter off with 'I'll say I'm busy.' Then he understood the dubious practical joke. He took it philosophically but Lyda was angry on Nikita's behalf.

Of the Right by background and education, Fournier could also voice unpopular but sincerely-held radical opinions. His Voltairean scepticism was a veneer which masked Beethovenian beliefs: 'Socrates and Jesus Christ are my models' the composer had replied when asked who were his masters, and Fournier quoted this in a short piece on Beethoven.[1] Epicurean in his taste for clothes, food and wine, five-star hotels and the company of pretty and intelligent women, he approached his art with the self-discipline of the ascetic. And as if to tease, in his seventies he would still persist, to his family's despair, in climbing a stepladder to knock a nail into the wall.

Logical he was not. He accepted work in South Africa during apartheid, and was then very deeply moved by the experience of playing to a small but fervent black audience. He broke with his old friend Cornelia Possart who had refused to invite Marian Anderson because she was black. He made eight visits to South Africa, principally to Peta Fisher's Musica Viva in Johannesburg, and to Cape Town where Hans Kramer's Concert Club attracted the world's most eminent musicians; here he found a respite from private pressures. On the other hand he felt compelled to turn down a Soviet tour in 1971 as a protest against the government's cruelty to Russian Jews. He had been angered by the trial of the number of refuseniks who had attempted to hijack an airliner to make their escape. A group of Jewish teachers in New York State wrote to thank him, expressing the touchingly optimistic hope that his stand would influence the Soviet government to cease its persecution.[2] Until then he had always gone where his cello, his talisman, had led him, for like Furtwängler he sincerely believed, naively perhaps, that the most universal of all the arts was a force which was only for good. 'He was absolutely honest: the opposite of your ambitious scheming artist.'[3] But the horrific revelations of 1945 left their mark upon him. 'One should not enclose oneself in a career' he said, towards the end of his own, 'but be aware of the suffering in the world about one, which is so much greater than the joys.'[4] There was an element of retrospection in the refusal of the Soviet tour.

Festivals were a regular feature of Fournier's life but the playing was not routine. Franz Walter of the *Journal de Genève* heard him at Montreux in the Schumann concerto:

> A cellist who has a genius for singing on an instrument which has been considered awkward.... That evening he was in a state of grace, drawing elegance out of the difficulties, appearing to invent, to improvise that music and yet submit to the orchestral context.... It was a very great moment.[5]

The arrival on the scene some years earlier of the brilliant, charismatic and enterprising Russian cellist, pianist and composer Mstislav Rostropovich had created a general stir. Twenty years younger than Fournier, he was and is temperamentally very much the reverse. The *Figaro* critic Clarendon, for one, produced a torrent of articles on the Russian cellist – at least eight in one season: it was no longer enthusiasm, it was rapture and it did nothing to curb Fournier's perpetual self-questioning. In 1971, Clarendon (Bernard Gavoty) attended a duo concert given at the Champs Elysées Theatre by Fournier and his son, after which he caught sight of the family among friends at the Relais Plaza restaurant. Gavoty came over to the table. 'I had forgotten how great you are' he said to Pierre. Pierre said nothing. '*C'est grâve*, Bernard', said Lyda, '*Tres grâve.*'

Irresistibly following his cello to the 1971 Puerto Rico festival to play two concertos, Fournier saw Casals again. His previous indignation had simmered down and was replaced by admiration at the resilience of the older man. In the course of a conversation Fournier mentioned how troubled he was by anxiety. Casals confided that he had had the same problem: put on a pedestal at a young age he had been tormented all his life by the fear of disappointing his audience. 'Don't change' he said to Fournier. 'I know from experience that you only give the best of yourself if you suffer a little beforehand and are perpetually plagued by self-doubt.'[6]

From Cordoba in the Argentine Fournier wrote to Jean Pierre:

> I am lucky with my pianists although none [of them] make me forget you. [Walter] Klien so enthusiastic about your Beethoven at the Promenade Concerts which he heard and watched on TV. He is as charming as he is unpretentious, and a perfect musician. The memory of the old, young Pau [Casals] pursues me.... What a beautiful end to a life!
>
> Embrace the *nice* people in Paris! Not the others, and may you have a big, big success. *Tendresses*, Papa.
> They like me *everywhere* – Lima, Chile etc.[7]

In September Fournier wrote again, this time from Cali, Colombia. Lyda had been ill for two years and the cost of her care was beginning to tell, as well as the cost of living; fees were not catching up with the increase. Fournier believed, erroneously as it turned out, that Lyda's severe condition disqualified her for health insurance; he continued therefore to meet all the costs himself, but with ever-increasing anxiety.

> I arrived here yesterday [and] had a painful experience with that dear conductor Olav Roots who accompanied my last recital and who nearly died of a coronary before my eyes during rehearsal. I found a tropical but pleasant temperature and shall be playing on Tuesday, leaving for San Jose Costa Rica on Wednesday after eleven hours in Panama... one of the hottest places in the universe. But they say that Costa Rica is charming and the only place in the world which *hasn't got* an army and is very peaceful. Hot memory of BA [and] great success with the orchestra (Vivaldi – Schumann at 11.15 pm after Shostakovich's 14th).
>
> As your mother said on the telephone, you are not to think I wanted to write you a pessimistic letter. I'm simply being lucid about today's world, eaten up with inflation and where everything gets more and more complicated. The days of pre-war fees, of free cheques, as it was four years ago, have gone. Everything is taxed at 25 per cent and charged from bank to bank. I'm content enough, often with great loneliness [but] very good health despite inevitable anxieties about travel. Need I say how much and how tenderly I think of you and my wishes go hourly to Bada!...
>
> The hotel is splendid and very *Americanly* comfortable![8]

Lyda's illness was becoming more severe with every passing month. Fournier moved her to the Hotel Richemond so that she should feel life going on around her when he was on tour. The financial stress became alarming. He told Etiennette Correa 'They are wonderful to me, treating me as a fully-fledged [Swiss] citizen and giving me discounts, but it is all costing the earth.'[9] He was obliged to sell his 'Comte Doria' Vuillaume cello; it was bought by a Liechtenstein collector to make up a quartet of Vuillaume instruments.

Partnering Artur Rubinstein with Szeryng for the RCA Schubert–Schumann–

Brahms trio recordings in the autumn of 1972 was both a musical and a human rediscovery. Fournier noticed the elderly pianist's uncompromising professionalism as each day, after an excellent lunch in a Geneva restaurant, he would go off to the empty Victoria Hall to work at the score in hand. Fournier remembered a recital given by 'King Artur' at the house of Winaretta de Polignac[10] in 1925, when the Krettly Quartet, of which Fournier was the youngest member, had been engaged as a stopgap in the interval. Not considered grand enough to eat with the *gratin parisien*, the quartet was fed in the pantry. 'Even after forty-seven years' said Rubinstein, 'it makes me blush with shame!'

In 1973 Fournier made his only East German tour. On the train from Erfurt to Leipzig a policeman, having bowed sycophantically over his French passport, started bullying an elderly West German woman who was, she said, visiting relations in the East: her ostmarks exceeded the official allowance. The policeman ferreted in her bag, removed letters and shouted at her. She was trembling. In English Fournier threatened to complain to his embassy in East Berlin if the letters were not immediately returned to her. Suddenly the official changed his manner and, bowing respectfully, left the compartment. 'This is not 1939!' Fournier called after him down the corridor.

Dining on the terrace of the Richemond Hotel in Geneva with Nikita and Irène Magaloff in June 1973, Fournier suddenly started shivering: he had a temperature of 40°C, a prelude to pneumonia. Having also had a gall bladder operation, he started to be more careful of his health, and from this moment he gave up smoking. Surprisingly, however, he did not take out health insurance.

*   *   *

In January 1974, father and son took part in the hugely successful after-office-hours concerts at the Théâtre de la Ville in Paris: 'an hour of paradise without an interval.'[11] An unsnobbish audience after Fournier's heart, many artists as well as commuters on their way home, and the programme repeated on five evenings. They gave a Schumann-Beethoven-Fauré-Chopin programme, and on the last two evenings people were turned away. 'A single artist divided into two performers' wrote *Le Figaro*,[12] while *Le Monde* spoke with relief of Fournier's lack of 'bow exhibitionism' which 'made certain cellists unbearable to watch.'[13]

In the late sixties and early seventies – when he was over sixty years old – Fournier had to admit to himself that his physical strength was ebbing. Bouts of anxiety alternated with lighter moments, and touring with Jean Pierre he remarked that they were more like two brothers than father and son. Although and perhaps because he persisted in stretching himself to the limits of endurance, he wondered whether his 'good' leg would carry him through. He worried about his memory, although it had rarely betrayed him. A colleague's appreciation could still overjoy him as did the ever-generous Paul Tortelier's touching letter (now lost, alas) written after a Fournier performance of the Schumann concerto.[14] He would tell Lyda and Jean Pierre that they must all return to the Mont S.

Michel, a plan which they postponed until it was too late. As with many old people his childhood memories became increasingly vivid. He remembered his grandfather Morice's garden in Auteuil, and his fond uncle, Charles Morice, who had tried to persuade him to eat a raw egg in its shell, saying it was good for developing the muscles.

By the end of 1975, Lyda could hardly move out of a chair. Masking his fears about her, Pierre lashed out at everything:

> Anyway, I haven't been murdered by the *LA Times*, and [anyway] the millions who read [the review] will only remember it for a split second! I'm off to Vancouver, driven by the dear big John Walz[15] and with the [Miremont] cello fantastically repaired by Christine Walewska's brother [a Los Angeles violin-maker], who after high precision craftsmanship over 48 hours, assures me that there'll be no more trouble and it will be stronger than ever! There must have been some weakness in the neck which didn't stand up to the dreadful manhandling at the dreadful [Johannesburg] airport, perhaps the worst in the world.... I shall try to keep it with me in the [cabin] from now on.
>
> I leave without regrets or illusions, nor am I disappointed, because I was expecting nothing here from anybody: the golden doors were not even ajar. I despise so many things here where millionaires reign....
>
> I am so saddened by your Maman's state! She must move a little as soon as possible to avoid seizing up. How much I think of her and of you!
>
> I am delivered of this concert here, thank God, the most dangerous city of the US! The parents of John Perry[16] (poor thing, he deserved better from Mr Arlen)[17] are very rich with a sumptious house in B Hills....
>
> I'll send news from Canada, happy to think I'll be busy with the three concerts 9–10–11 and the rehearsals before going on to Scottsdale (Hilton) Arizona where they await me with open arms and totally as their guest for three days.
>
> I am thinking of you and embrace you with infinite and *admiring* tenderness, never forget it!
>
> We need to ask M. Python [the local garage-owner] to put antifreeze in the car and to charge the batteries towards the end of November.
>
> Thank you for all you are doing!
>
> Papa.[18]

Fournier celebrated his seventieth birthday in June 1976 in the midst of his London galaxy of young cellists. After an Elysian summer evening at the house of Emma Ferrand and her husband the violinist Richard Deakin, there was a dinner at the Cello Club presided over by Derek Simpson and William Pleeth, and a concert the following evening at St John's Smith Square (Brahms E minor and Martinů sonatas with Jean Pierre). A sadness hung over the celebrations: the absence of one of the young professionals, Thomas Igloi. His sudden death from an unrevealed heart condition two months earlier had stunned them all and deprived the musical world of the most brilliant young soloist of his generation.[19]

On 21 September Fournier and Walter Klien played at his memorial concert in the Queen Elizabeth Hall.[20] Mrs Laszlo Igloi, the cellist's mother, recalled that in the correspondence before Tom became his pupil, Fournier addressed him as 'Dear Mr Igloi' for at least three or four letters before he relaxed into 'Dear Thomas'.[21] Igloi was more than a promising young talent: he was a highly polished cellist in whom Fournier had placed the greatest hopes; indeed, Igloi had a special place in his heart. He often visited Fournier both in Geneva, and in Germany when he was on tour.

'Papa Fournier' was popular at Aldeburgh's Snape Maltings, with his particular mixture of reserve and warmth. A girl driver dispatched to fetch him from London begged that nobody but herself be given the job the following year.

When he appeared at the inaugural concert of the Benson and Hedges Festival on 30 September 1977, it was obvious to all that he was in poor physical shape. 'The Schubert *Arpeggione* was beautiful; the Britten Sonata (added at the suggestion of John Culshaw) less happy: it seemed as if it was too physically demanding.' Lyda's illness was making him miserable. When he returned three years later he would be a different man.[22]

If there was anyone who understood Pierre's torment on the subject of Lyda's condition it was Bernard Gavoty, ill himself and undergoing dialysis in the summer of 1977.

'*Cher Pierre de mon coeur*', he wrote:

> Your letter went to the depths of my heart. You are so much more, and so much better than a friend – a brother, and what a brother. Tender and vulnerable, both [traits] being at once the cause and the result of your immense talent, the ransom of your artist's soul which craves the ideal and is by its very nature inaccessible.
>
> What touches me about this academic exercise [the dialysis] – which doesn't fool me in the least! – is the *true* affection of certain choice beings and you are among the first. Your double ordeal – both what you have undergone since birth, and what, in spite of herself, our dear Lyda is inflicting on you now – has made you even dearer to my heart since I myself am in pain, of the flesh and of the heart, saving the small amount of necessary strength to escape the pity of others, which is so often nothing more than a travesty, an easy way to salve one's conscience at the least expense!
>
> Tell our darling Lyda that Victoire and I am constantly with her and with you, reliving, through this ordeal, the happy moments of an incomparable and, I can say, unique friendship.
>
> *Nous vous embrassons tous les trois, due meilleur de notre coeur.* Bernard. My Cortot[23] is coming out on 12 September. I'll sign you a copy from my private cellar!...

It was at a time of increased travel, in 1969, that Lyda had first experienced pain in her hands. Polyarthritis was diagnosed, but fearing the known side-effects she refused the recommended gold injections and the family did not insist. As things turned out, they regretted it because, although anti-inflammatory injections gave some temporary relief and the surgeon Dr Verdan was able to insert a wrist prosthesis, the disease could not be halted: from the ribcage it spread to the spine and eventually made walking, and later any movement, difficult. In the middle of this, however, ill though she was, Lyda withstood a hip operation and was even able to enjoy a family holiday at St Moritz in 1976.

But if physically she was weakening, there was no alteration in her spirit, even less in that part of her brain relating to music: her mind remained lucid, alert and as robustly judgmental as ever as she praised or criticized from her bed. As the need came, first for stays at the Hotel Richemond while Pierre was on tour, then, as her condition worsened, for professional care round the clock, Pierre saw financial troubles mounting at the very moment when he might reasonably have hoped for security at the end of a successful career: neglecting to take out medical insurance had been a disastrous oversight. In addition, his initial handicap (the paralysis in his right leg) had generated further problems with the wearing-down of his 'good' leg and other fragilities which were the legacy of poliomyelitis. His mobility was reduced when he needed to remain active.

But he could still bewitch: of his playing of Vivaldi's *Sicilienne* Pierre-Petit wrote 'It is impossible to be more moving, more purely and simply inspired.'[24]

In early February 1978 Lyda was rushed to the Canton Hospital in Geneva, to be fed on a drip. With misgivings Pierre left for Paris and a Pleyel concert with Jean Pierre. 'The doctor says I can leave but I'm not in the right state of mind for that important programme [four sonatas]', he wrote.[25] In March he was told that the hospital needed the room and Lyda was moved, to 'convalesce' at Meyrin in the Hôpital de la Tour. Some family bitterness resulted. By May she had been in hospital for over three months 'weaker and weaker, weighing 35 kilos'. Besides, Pierre was now in serious trouble himself.

> I have increasing difficulties [in walking] in climbing the steps of [airport] buses, so I would appreciate being brought to the VIP lounge by car from the plane and being driven also by car to the Cape Town plane.[26]

In the excellent care at Meyrin Lyda had gained some weight; then suddenly in June her condition deteriorated. In handwriting which had lost its characteristic roundness and flow and become spikey like that of an old man, Pierre told Tony Mayer not to worry about the platform height at Ménerbes, adding wryly that he only hoped to prove that he was

> up to expectations, since the news of Lyda is very worrying.... Still in hospital, very weak, lucid and needing constant help. It is deeply saddening to know that there is no way back towards recovery.

He was going to Ménerbes after an August concert at Antibes, deferred by a few days 'because Sylvie Vartan [a pop star] was mobilizing all Antibes from the 1st to the 5th (5000 extra chairs which [would] no doubt be removed for the little Fourniers).'[27]

From Cape Town Pierre telephoned Lyda, and after each journey he would rush to her bedside to tell her about his tour and give her the latest gossip, performing many humble tasks for her himself. 'I married an angel' she told Emma Ferrand.[28] Until the end she refused to accept the inevitable and demanded the coming season's fashion magazines. Forty-eight hours later, on 30 July 1978, her fight was over. Lyda was buried at the Cimetière Saint-Georges in Geneva. Faced with the gaping maw of the evening, father and son decided not to cancel an earlier plan: they were relieved to be able to dine in Jacqueline Peltier's company at her house in Collonges.

Work came to the rescue: Geneva masterclasses, three Bach Suites in the church at Ménerbes, and plans with Tony Mayer for the following year: the Schubert Quintet (D 956) with Jean Mouillère and the Via Nova Quartet.

Recommending the quartet to Tony, Fournier added 'they are very good, very nice etc. I'm sure they will accept. They are *young*.' But he added the usual caveat: 'on the express condition that I play 2nd cello'. As a postscript he wrote 'Loneliness and sadness seem to increase all around each day.'[29] For the first time in his life there was no female presence at home.

Crossing the Atlantic on Concorde he wrote to Jean Pierre:

> We were a fine pair saying goodbye this morning; for me too it is a heartbreak to go off and not to be finding her on my return, even if she was only on the edge of life! Remember anyway that for me *nothing*, *nobody* can ever take her place, for she was and will always remain irreplaceable.
>
> I hope your London TV will have been a success. I embrace you tenderly while hoping for a journey without problems and with a little affection and success... one cannot comprehend the desertion of [those people who are] unconcerned, who know nothing and who bandy stupid platitudes without meaning to be unkind.[30]

Returning from Mexico in mid-October, Fournier played at the wedding of Marie-Caroline Aubert, daughter of Marie-Thérèse Fourneau. He had chosen the cello pieces himself, and the date had been especially arranged to fit in with his schedules.

After the first New Year without Lyda, Fournier returned to summer and festival preoccupations. Understandably Mouillère sought to fit in some additional concerts in the region after playing at Ménerbes, but Fournier was reluctant to commit himself: 'I'm wary of the landowners [Mouillère] says he knows and whom I would rather keep at a distance.' He hadn't the stomach for polite conversation after a concert, and a week later added:

> as for Mouillère's castles in Spain, I remain very cautious, Ménerbes being the sole object of my flying to you.... I am off for a long time, short journeys with brief returns here before Japan for one month. It is cold, and in the heart too.[31]

Despondent as he felt, he had already stumbled upon new friendships the winter before, in February 1978, when he was a dinner guest at the house of the banker Jean-Pierre Demole and his wife Alice. He had just performed the Martinů Concerto with Wolfgang Sawallisch in what was to be his last Suisse Romande concert.

Mme Demole, a woman of Pierre's generation, was very active in the musical life of Geneva and a supporter of young artists. There was much sympathy in this circle; they played bridge and celebrated New Year's Eve with a Château Banquet neighbour, Thérèse Le Roux. The warmth of these friends was inspiriting at a difficult time, companionship and shared interests taking the edge off his bewilderment after Lyda's death.

Notes

1. Pierre Fournier, *Commentaire personnel*, September 1970.
2. William Leibner and thirteen others to Pierre Fournier, 10 February 1971.

3. Gabriel Dussurget in conversation with the author.
4. Pierre Fournier, Radio Suisse Romande, 7 April 1975.
5. *Journal de Genève*, [?] September 1971 (Franz Walter).
6. Cited in ORTF *Radioscopie*, 5 July 1976.
7. Pierre Fournier to Jean Fonda Fournier, undated [1971].
8. Pierre Fournier to Jean Fonda Fournier, 14 September 1971.
9. The late Etiennette Correa in conversation with the author.
10. American-born heiress (1863–1943) to the Singer fortune, and wife of the music-lover Prince Edmond de Polignac. The couple were famously dubbed by Mme Blanche (mother of the painter Jacques-Emile Blanche) '*l'union de la lyre et la machine à coudre* (the marriage of the lyre and the sewing-machine).
11. *France-Soir*, 21 January 1974.
12. *Le Figaro*, 21 January 1974.
13. *Le Monde*, 17 January 1974.
14. With Zubin Mehta at Montreux in 1965.
15. John Walz, Los Angeles-born cellist and a Fournier student.
16. John Perry, a good musician in Fournier's eyes, played for him in California.
17. Walter Arlen of the *LA Times*.
18. Pierre Fournier to Jean Fonda Fournier, 4 November [1975].
19. Thomas Igloi (1974–1976), a cellist of immense promise and personal charm, was born in Budapest. In 1957, after the Revolution, the family came to England where Tom gained scholarships, becoming a pupil of Douglas Cameron at the RAM (where he became sub-professor in 1965), and later of Casals and Fournier. He made his début at the Wigmore Hall in 1969 and won the Gaspar Cassadó International Competition in Florence in 1971. His performances of the Bach Suites and also Kodály's Op. 8 Sonata won him great acclaim. Already embarked on a successful career, he died suddenly in April 1976, aged only twenty-nine. He had made recordings of the Fauré sonatas with Clifford Benson, and of the Walton Concerto with the BBCSO (David Strange to the author, 17 July 1993).
20. J S Bach: Recitativo from 3rd Organ Concerto, transcribed by Pierre Fournier for solo cello; Beethoven's *Judas Maccabeus* Variations; Schubert's *Arpeggione* Sonata and Brahms F major Sonata Op. 99.
21. Mrs László Igloi in conversation with the author.
22. Jacob de Vries in conversation with the author.
23. Bernard Gavoty *Alfred Cortot*, Paris: Buchet-Chastel 1977. Bernard Gavoty to Pierre Fournier, 12 August 1977.
24. *Le Figaro*, 16 February 1977 (Pierre-Petit).
25. Pierre Fournier to Peta Fisher, 7 February [1978].
26. Pierre Fournier to Peta Fisher, 19 May 1978.
27. Pierre Fournier to Tony Mayer, 15 June 1978.
28. Emma Ferrand in conversation with the author.
29. Pierre Fournier to Tony Mayer, 16 January [1979].
30. Pierre Fournier to Jean Fonda Fournier, 19 September [1978].
31. Pierre Fournier to Tony Mayer, 16 January [1979].

28   Perfect Cadence

Marked out by illness in childhood, Fournier had no experience of the clubbiness of male company, the rough-and-tumble of boarding school, sports club or regiment; the nearest he came to this was with orchestral musicians. Here he found the mutual respect of professionals but, again, being a virtuoso set him apart. Save for a few loyal friends like Tony Mayer whose introduction to Robert Krettly had set the young cellist on his path, like Nikita Magaloff, Louis Beydts and his own 'young professionals', as with many sensitive men he was generally more at ease in the company of women. And this being so, they were at ease with him. He owed them much: like a perspective of caryatids we see them staked out at crucial points in his life and career.

The pattern was set at home, with his mother Gabrielle channelling her own musicality into nurturing his, and his closest sibling, Cécile, remaining a lifelong confidante on the other side of the Atlantic. The young Odette Krettly quickly fired his passion for the cello, revealing secrets of tone and colour, of the language of music, far beyond both their ages. Lifting him out of professional drudgery, the perceptive and generous Louise Maillot gave him support and encouragement in public, and allegedly in private quite as much again. The volcanic Lyda followed, with whom from sepia his life exploded into full colour. Internationalizing his career and giving him a son, she was the inimitable consort whom he could never live constantly with nor for any length of time without. The long-lived friendship with Peta Fisher provided him with a musical and emotional haven. With Marie-Thérèse Fourneau he formed the only attachment intense and enduring enough to come anywhere near to dislocating his marriage.

Following the pattern, the end of a full and rounded life was to bring one last companion, at an age when relinquishment of love is more common than discovery. Apprehensive of age when young, perhaps excessively conscious of the passing of time, Fournier ended by showing a talent for old age, wearing his years with grace and humour. He approached the close of his life with philosophy: 'If I can no longer give of my best, I can always pass on my experience to younger artists.'[1]

Among the young prizewinners at the Geneva Conservatoire in 1971 had been a young Japanese flautist called Junko Tagushi who returned afterwards to her country. In 1976 Fournier met her in Tokyo with her husband, Hori, who was his pupil; their little son called him Uncle Pierre. In March 1979 he wrote to Jean Pierre from Japan mentioning 'I have met the adorable Junko Hori again', and over several letters he warmed in his allusions to her. After a concert with Kempff, and another in Mexico, Junko left Tokyo to join him in New York. Fournier was worried about his 'good' leg which was out of kilter after 64 years of overwork. He consulted Dr Wilson Junior (son of the surgeon of 1958) at the Hospital for Special Surgery. A further operation on his 'good leg' was unavoidable 'to save [his] last active years'. He wrote to Tony cancelling Ménerbes 'with some sinking of the heart'. He knew that he would be immobilized for four months and although he might play his cello he would have to wait three months before attempting to stand. 'With what I have on the right since the age of eight, I don't need to go into the difficulties of ... rehabilitation which will mean a hefty man around 24 hours out of 24, to help at every moment....'[2]

In May he was on tour with Jean Pierre in Mexico. 'This is the last trip I do without you', he wrote to Junko. With the operation at the Canton Hospital in Geneva now imminent, Junko took a major decision: she was going to look after Pierre, and, leaving her country, she moved to Geneva.

Junko was responding to a crisis but things did not go altogether smoothly for her. Jean Pierre's reactions were as might have been expected, given his closeness to his mother and the speed of these subsequent developments. For a while relations with his father were cool, but when they took up their work together affection and good sense restored peace, and Jean Pierre was grateful for the companionship, comfort and love which Junko showed his father in his last years.

To some, however, Fournier's setting up house with a young woman 40 years his junior only a year after his wife's death looked very much like losing his head. There were – briefly – a few raised eyebrows, some teasing too. 'Well, you're getting married, yes or no?' asked Nikita with the briskness and lack of ceremony of a very old friend. '*Mais certainement*' answered Fournier primly, closing the subject.

He remained busy in the weeks preceding the operation. On 9 June he played the Beethoven Triple Concerto at Metz with Jean Pierre and Pierre Amoyal, a musician to whom he became very attached. On 18 June he entered hospital. The operation to insert a steel shaft into his left leg, was performed by Professor Vasey on 20 June. Five days later, too impatient to wait until he could sit in a chair, he played his cello in bed, the instrument lying across his stomach. A month later he made his first attempts at walking.

'I shall be very close to you, particularly on 9 August' he wrote to Tony from hospital,

> hoping that next year we'll be able to forget this summer's defection. Give the quartet my faithful wishes for a great success. I am a third of the way through my long Patience, without being able to lean on my leg for another two months.... I shall stay as long as possible in hospital for the very lengthy rehabilitation of the muscles damaged... 25 years ago. My dear surgeon has been admirable.[3]

On 9 August Pierre and Junko became engaged and on 7 September he left hospital.

The three and a half months of rest and rehabilitation were a refined form of torture. As word went about, doubts were voiced as to whether he would ever play again. He was aware of this (which made it worse), and friends such as Claude Viala and Georges Athanasiades saw how much it troubled him. In this way the end of a long career was made more difficult through false assumptions as other stars emerged.[4]

'Why do you come to hear old Fournier?' he asked Ralph Kirshbaum. 'To hear you play one note or phrase', the young artist answered, 'means more to me than a hundred notes from other cellists'.[5]

To a certain extent repeating the return of 1958, Fournier chose, after this long break, to appear in a duo concert with Jean Pierre at Oberhausen on 8 October. He was very nervous and just before going on he whispered to Junko 'I can't play.' This was the physical legacy; 'inwardly he was perfectly sure of himself as an artist.'[6] At about this time Junko suggested that he abandon some of his heavier commitments and confine himself to chamber music. He said he was worried about money. He continued to travel, and between October 1979 and March 1980 he appeared at Coblenz, Bloomington, Denver, New York, St Louis and San Francisco, Geneva and Stockholm as well as Nice and Cannes where he gave the Beethoven Triple Concerto with Jean Pierre and Pierre Amoyal.

When Thérèse and Tony Mayer visited Pierre in Geneva early in 1980, to bring him their sympathy on the death of Lyda, they were surprised to find an altered Pierre, speaking almost lightheartedly of his forthcoming marriage to Junko. Sensing their reticence he became slightly withdrawn towards them, but, as always throughout his life, the key to all problems was music. With the Ménerbes Festival arrangements for August, the exchange of letters and finally the concerts in the little hilltop church, embarrassment was to vanish.

Pierre and Junko were married at the City Office in Geneva on 28 February 1980, with Mme Yoshiko Tsukada and the violin-maker Pierre Vidoudez as witnesses.

As though patterned on the clean lines and the space and light of a Japanese interior, Pierre's life became more ordered, the flat less cluttered, his diet lighter and his journeys well planned. He destroyed Lyda's letters and many of his professional papers. Gone were the days of pulse-quickening dashes to the airport, but if becoming more often than not a passenger in his own car was something of a relief, it was also a deprivation: driving, like photography, had been a hobby.

He could no longer hide the slowing-down process: movements and gestures were more measured, and he now had such a phobia of stairs that he became exasperated when concert organizers failed to take his disabilities into account. In Amsterdam, unable to negotiate the steps from the platform, he had to slide down. Trains posed a problem and he blessed the British carriages with their easy access. Enjoying his new domesticity he saw a little less of old friends, some of whom were surprised; conversely he and Junko noticed a sparseness of invitations. It is likely that both sides were half-expecting the other to make the first move. Of a very brief perceived coolness towards Junko, he said to Nikita '*Je suis très touchy*.'[7]

Junko cared for her husband with great devotion, an astonishing strength issuing from her slight frame, and Pierre for his part was endlessly grateful, never taking anything for granted.[8] 'He had a kindness, a gentleness and a distinction which are rare.... He seemed to have reached a perfect serenity.'[9] He was glad to have grown up when he did, among all those musicians in the twenties and thirties, and to have been part of the burgeoning of music everywhere after the Second World War, before the jet age and the preoccupation with money transformed the musical scene.[10] It seemed that his marriage to Junko had put the clock back a little way: his handwriting regained its roundness and flow, and his playing was apt to reflect his newly-won ease. This was clearly discernible in the immensely successful duo concert at Snape with his old friend Rudolf Firkušny at the 1980 Benson and Hedges Festival. They gave the Beethoven A major and Chopin sonatas, recorded like the other concerts with the co-operation of the BBC. A senior engineer commented: 'These performances can be put on disc without editing. They are stupendous.'[11]

*   *   *

A great celebrator of anniversaries, Slava Rostropovich put all his energy and enthusiasm into organizing a concert for Fournier's 75th birthday. It took place at the Tonhalle in Zurich, with Paul Sacher who had premièred the Frank Martin Concerto with Fournier and the Collegium Musicum. Characteristically ignoring baleful warnings about 'too many concerts and not enough public', Slava pushed ahead with his plan and was proved right: the concert was sold out at once.[12] Fournier played the Haydn D major Concerto, Fonda Mozart's E flat concerto K 449, Rostropovich partnered Fournier at the piano in Fauré's *Elégie*, and Magaloff and Amoyal joined him in Mendelssohn's D minor Trio. At one point there was a horrified gasp from the audience: forgetting Pierre's fragility, Slava had embraced him with an effusion which virtually brought them both to the floor. But they recovered and the concert ended happily with Davidov's *Feststück* and Klengel's *Hymnus* performed by an international ensemble of 110 cellists.

An attack of neuritis in his right shoulder obliged Fournier to cancel two engagements with Jean-Pierre Wallez and he was replaced by Tortelier's pupil, the Finnish cellist Arto Noras. During this enforced rest, and while he was dining with Junko and Jacqueline Peltier, his speech became confused. Later that night Junko called at Jean Pierre's neighbouring flat: his father was unable to speak. Dr Schlurick was called and gave him an injection. In the morning he was sitting up bed, smiling at Junko and Jean Pierre: 'I know! Last night you both thought I was going gaga....'

*   *   *

At the narrow approach to the Upper Rhone valley, in the small town of Saint-Maurice-en-Valais, stands the oldest living abbey north of the Alps, with foundations dating from Roman times. In 1942 a falling rock destroyed the nineteenth-century organ. The present instrument, a fine Kuhn, was inaugurated in 1950, the bicentenary of Bach's death. In 1982 Fournier shared a concert in the Basilica with the present organist, the composer and scholar Canon Georges Athanasiades. Fournier chose the second version of Bach's C minor Suite which he felt was particularly suited to the acoustics, and Mendelssohn's Op. 58 Sonata 'with the organ because pianists never know what to do with it'. Having persuaded the reluctant canon (who dislikes company while he is playing) to let him stay in the loft for the Mozart *Fantasia*,[13] he asked 'How do you manage to sing so, with your *feet*?'

He also made a pleasant discovery. Athanasiades had studied Fournier's own edition of Bach Chorales,[14] and had been struck by the headings. Instead of merely the customary first line, Fournier's edition gives the essence of each text (some of the chorales are from six to 23 stanzas long). In giving this emphasis to the words, Fournier had unconsciously followed Bach's wishes, 'the music being a commentary on the text which is also a prayer.'[15] The Canon quoted Johann Gotthilf Ziegler, writing in 1746 to apply for the post of organist at the Liebfrauenkirche at Halle, and describing the correct interpretation of the Chorales: 'My teacher, the Kapellmeister Bach who is still living, instructed me to bring out not only the melody but also the emotion in the words.'[16]

The concert ended with the Chorale *Herzlich tut mich verlangen* (My soul longs to depart in peace) 'which we played not like an encore, but as a prayer.'[17]

*   *   *

After a concert in Richmond, Virginia, on what was to be his last US tour, Fournier's heart trouble returned; a journey was postponed and he spent the day in bed. Occasionally at dinner with friends he would turn pale and abandon the conversation, only recovering after an hour's rest. Yet he continued to travel: to Japan and South Korea (playing to a deeply attentive audience in a huge hall in Seoul), giving masterclasses at Berlin's Charlottenburg Sommerakademie, in Finland, at Yale and at Bloomington, invited by his friend and colleague János Starker.

Between 1978 and 1983 he made four visits to the festival in the hilltop village of Ménerbes at the invitation of Tony Mayer whom he had known since Etiennette had brought him to Neuilly as a sixteen-year-old to make up a quartet. Tony recalled:

> And to think that for four or five years, once a month (or was it once a week – faltering memory!) I sat with my viola opposite this illustrious cellist, and that he came four times to this little village, into this little church, to play for people who understood nothing![18]

Fournier's letters to Tony tell their own story:

27 February 1980
Sorry about this wretched writing paper. The Vivaldi is beautiful, [if] a bit tinkered with by Vincent d'Indy. I have the part with my own markings. My apologies to the ultra purist Pincherle [musicologist and Vivaldi scholar]!.. [and] my heartfelt wishes to the ever-young septuagenarian who looks forty-eight!

10 April 1980
[The Couperin pieces were] originally for viola da gamba. Cleverly scored for quartet by Paul Bazelaire. You are right to stick up for musicians who have 'arranged' and not 'deranged' a composer's thought. Bach has given some splendid examples in transcribing many of his works for different instruments. The Vivaldi Sonata was 'collected' by Paul Bazelaire and Vincent d'Indy among a whole lot of sonatas originally for cello and not viola da gamba. You can cook up something from these meagre notes. M. Dallapiccola also got hold of Vivaldi and made a mayonnaise in very doubtful taste... you must show Bazelaire and d'Indy to advantage. [They are] completely forgotten because they were too... honest, and not in step with the present trend towards ugliness, violence and people... without talent. Upon that note *je vous baise* affectionately, and this also goes for my so very dear Junko. Pierre. No news of Mouillère.

10 June 1980
We are delighted to be your guests. No problems. The only thing is that the quartet *must* be there by the 6th to rehearse in the evening at the house, and on the 7th in the church. [The musicians had arrived late on one occasion and a string quartet had to be sightread, so Fournier's fears were understandable.] I don't promise anything if they decide to arrive on the 7th at 9 pm! [...] We'll begin with the Vivaldi, then without leaving the platform we'll continue with the Couperin. I'll also bring my own part for the Schubert [Quintet] (2nd cello)....

I'm gently steeling myself for the possibility of a concert with a rehearsal at 8 pm in the church just before the audience arrives. Anyway I'll do my best not to let down the music (poor Schubert!) [...] It will be too short but rewarding to see you both again....

16 June [1980]
[After the festival.] Your letter is infinitely touching. Thank you from the bottom of my heart for everything you say about us! Junko was so happy at our sunny meeting. She likes you both very much. As for me, I'll be delighted to play the three other Suites (2, 4, 5) to complete the cycle, if you think that this programme will go down well with the habitués of the Ménerbes Festival!

Thank you for the cheque and the return of the forgotten cane brought by the Comtesse de la Salle who arrived just after I had left the house for the first masterclass. [This class] is of a very high standard. I accepted 16 candidates out of 32! This contact with the under-thirties is very comforting!

Come and see us. You know that our two hearts remain open to you! *Je vous embrasse avec une fraternelle affection, Junko aussi.*
Pierre.

After the three Bach Suites in August 1981, Fournier wondered if the choice of fare had been a trifle too austere:

13 August 1981
Your dear letter makes me blush with genuine modesty... The main thing for me is to

know that the austere offering appeared short and not boring for that marvellous audience. Any nostalgia I have for France is directed at everything that isn't Paris. I should be delighted to return to you for a fourth visit. I don't know if you realize that the Kodály *solo* Sonata is 28 minutes long. [...] I'll think about it because I adore that work [which I came to] late in life, and I don't know if I'll have the strength to work at it again in '82!

As for France Culture [French radio station], I'm grateful for your call and letter to that gentleman, but I only believe in written and signed documents, because I'm becoming increasingly hard towards that distant city which has become so foreign to me, run by clans and even mafias in every sphere of life.

Mitterrand's government came to power in the summer of 1981:

10 January 1982.
As to what the future has in store for us, 83 will perhaps be better than 82 and M. Mitterrand, who puts up with trash on the French airwaves without complaining, will perhaps be no longer of this world.

Financial problems sent him on an awkward US tour:

28 February 1983
We are off tomorrow morning for a NY recital 7 March then three concerts next door = Vancouver, then next door to that, Richmond (Virginia) and... Geneva. I expect to bring back some cents from this stupid escapade.

At Ménerbes in August Fournier was to share a concert with the singer Maria Santava

sandwiched between 3 cello sonatas
– Sonata 1
– Aria
– Sonata 2
– More warblings
– Sonata 3

and to finish, final aria obbligato fireworks. I'll go to bed with the Diva twice at the most (given my age) and I'd like to know in advance if the cello parts are within reach of my fingers. Above all *no* [underlined four times] viola da gamba. There are too many strings.

Another thing. I adore your house but due to the increasing problems I have, alas, with my legs, we should like to be at an hotel if there is one, not far away, with bathroom, on the ground floor... I know I'm becoming impossible but I'm sure you understand.

Tony Mayer was always to remember Pierre's last concert at Ménerbes:

Disabled as he was by polio and accidents, he appeared hesitantly at the sacristy door, ready to play a last encore, then suddenly the applause stopped (cursed audience!) and slowly, sadly, he turned and disappeared. He was never to come back.[19]

* * *

On 3 February 1984 father and son gave a Brahms programme at the Queen Elizabeth Hall. Fournier had insurmountable difficulties in walking, and this could not be attempted in front of an audience; instead he appeared through a gap in the curtain upstage. Ignoring medical advice he had refused to cancel so as not to disappoint his audience although he was suffering from food poisoning, the result of a meal on the plane coming over. He was ashen-faced. It was clear that the whole enterprise was a huge struggle, and for the large number of musicians who had come to hear him it was painful to watch. This was his last London concert.

In spite of health alarms and the worsening mobility problem, he continued to play. He recorded Brahms and Grieg with Jean Pierre, and adjudicated at the Rostropovich competition in Paris. He reacted violently against the set piece by Gilbert Amy, irritated at the experimental techniques demanded of the soloist and which he equated with cruelty to cellos. Lutoslawski politely defended his colleague Amy, not wishing to be unjust towards a score which was 'not without merit'. The cellist and conductor Antonio Janigro was less appreciative: he thought its merit lay in the high number of wrong notes in print.[20]

At odd moments Jean Pierre would catch sight of his father sitting at the piano in the darkened studio, often picking out a few bars of *Tristan*. Surprised, he would turn and give his son a look of great tenderness. He seemed now as detached from events as from society. He spoke about death more than once, not in a morbid way, but simply in relation to the changing musical world, with young artists' aspirations so different now, less idealistic and more turned towards material success.[21]

Memories of Lyda returned more often, and images from childhood, like the pergola with the magnificent climbing rose which he had photographed as an adolescent in the Morice garden at Auteuil. Aware of his fragility, he said to his niece Jacqueline Peltier 'You know, I haven't much longer to live.' One evening, after giving advice to a student who wanted to photocopy one of his scores, he said 'They all want my bowing and fingering and phrasing, so that they can do what I did in the past.' Jean Pierre felt an impulse to put his arms round his father, but refrained 'out of some vague filial restraint'.[22]

Even now, Fournier still wanted to work. The fancy took him to return to a Jean Huré sonata which he had played in his youth, and he asked Jean Pierre to study it.[23] In spite of his diminishing strength his playing took on a new serenity; the reactions of critics no longer troubled him. In September 1985 at Ernen in the Valais he gave the Bach Suites for the last time. It was a performance remembered for its spirituality, and for the almost startling way that he appeared to transcend even his own deep understanding of the music.

The same month he gave masterclasses at Snape, but as Mark Lubotsky recalled 'the daily trips to the Maltings and the work with students were difficult for him.'[24] There was also a memorable concert. 'I shall enjoy very much to play [sic] with Artur Balsam' he had written to John Owen at Aldeburgh. '*One* big sonata – the Rachmaninov. I think there would be no problem with Mr Balsam.'[25] It was a neat understatement. Balsam recalled: 'We had only one short rehearsal, yet it was, I assure you, a beautiful performance.'[26] It was also Fournier's last concert appearance. There was a dinner at the Red House celebrating Peter Pears' return from a concert tour. 'Both Fournier and Pears were animated, witty and charming.'[27]

A three months' rest was planned, to be followed on 8 January by a recital in Belgrade with Jean Pierre, and then a tour of Japan. On 25 October 1985, at the concert celebrating the 150th anniversary of the Geneva Conservatoire, Fournier suddenly felt an icy grip on his right arm. 'I can't move it' he said to Junko. Bed rest and exercises had no effect on the paralysis but, determined to get back to work, he started a course of physiotherapy, gave a few lessons and insisted on having his hair cut. He enjoyed his food, and adapted to eating with his left hand. In December the family urged him to see Professor Gautier at the Canton Hospital. Before leaving he sat quietly attending to correspondence; he also gave Jean Pierre a birthday present for the following day.

Tests clearly showed a blocked vein on the left side of the head, the cause of the trouble. The possibility of an operation was mentioned and then dismissed: it would have involved half an hour's interruption of the circulation, carrying the risk, in the event of an accident, of total paralysis. Teaching was still possible, but he would never play again.

Every day, with help, he managed to walk twice the length of the hospital corridor, often talking of his plans. With Christmas approaching, Junko and Jean Pierre persuaded the consultant to allow him back to the comfort of familiar surroundings with a nurse in attendance. He was to continue physiotherapy and take a little exercise on the balcony, but co-ordination was difficult and walking now impossible.

Pierre's sister Cécile Niklaus arrived from New York; his niece Jacqueline Peltier from Collonges, Rosmarin Schultess from Zurich and other old friends. Another stroke occurred. On Christmas Eve Pierre had some friends to dinner at his bedside: Georgette Rostand (wife of the critic), Jan Grevstadt and Bettina Filipinetti. Jean Pierre cooked a *boeuf stroganoff*. On 26 December his father had a visit from the violinist Pierre Amoyal. Two days later Fournier lost the power of speech 'but his eyes remained very expressive'.[28] As life was escaping he saw the New Year in with a small slice of foie gras on toast. But it was clear that the end was very near. On 4 January Jean Pierre called Canon Athanasiades who administered the last sacraments and asked Fournier if he wished to have a mass said. Unable to speak, Fournier signalled a 'yes' with his eyes. The Canon remained with him for a time, afterwards joining Junko and Jean Pierre in the drawing room and telling them 'I said that his cello would play for us in eternity. Two tears ran down his face.'[29]

On the nights of 6 and 7 January Jean Pierre slept in the flat 'on a camp bed in the small bedroom, near the little practice piano, waking up every hour and looking through the half-open door into his father's room where a nightlight was burning'.[30] His heartbeat was now very weak, and by the time that the doctor returned on the morning of 8 January, Pierre was in a coma. At 8.45 am he died.

Fournier's coffin was placed in the chapel of the Saint-Georges cemetery. As he had agreed with Junko, he was cremated. Beside Lyda's remains is an empty grave.

Notes

1. Pierre Fournier, Radio Suisse Romande, *Entrée en question*, 7 April 1975.
2. Pierre Fournier to Tony Mayer, 17 April [1979].
3. Pierre Fournier to Tony Mayer, 23 July [1979].
4. Claude Viala and Georges Athanasiades, independently, in conversation with the author.
5. Ralph Kirshbaum in conversation with the author.
6. Junko Fournier in conversation with the author.
7. The late Nikita Magaloff in conversation with the author.
8. Junko Fournier in conversation with the author.
9. André Raynaud to the author, 20 July 1989.
10. Pierre Fournier, ORTF, *Radioscopie*, 5 July 1976.
11. Leonard Owen, *Highlights of the 1980 Festival, Snape*, September 1981.
12. The late Nikita Magaloff in conversation with the author.
13. Fantasia in F minor, K 608.
14. J S Bach, *Six Chorales*, transcribed by Pierre Fournier. New York: International Music Co. 1960.
15. Canon Georges Athanasiades in conversation with the author.
16. '*Was das Choralspielen betrifft, so bin ich von meinem annoch lebenden Lehrmeister dem Herrn Capellmeister Bach so unterrichtet worden, dass ich die Lieder nicht nur so oben hin, sondern nach dem Affect der Worte spiele.*' Johann Gotthilf Ziegler, Halle, 1 February 1746, quoted in *Bach-Dokumente* Band II, Nr 542 (*Fremdschriftliche und gedruckte Dokumente zum Lebengeschichte JSB* 1969 Bärenreiter Kassel-Basel-London-New York).
17. Canon Georges Athanasiades.
18. Tony Mayer to the author, 30 July 1993.
19. Id.
20. Jean Fonda Fournier to the author, 1993.
21. Id.
22. Id.
23. Jean Huré (1877–1930), composer, organist, pianist and teacher. This Sonata, written in 1907, was the first of three, and was dedicated to Diran Alexanian.
24. Mark Lubotsky to the author, 5 April 1991.
25. Pierre Fournier to John Owen, 22 February 1985.
26. Artur Balsam to the author, 20 December 1988.
27. Mark Lubotsky to the author, id.
28. Jean Fonda Fournier to the author, 1992.
29. Canon Georges Athanasiades in conversation with the author.
30. Jean Fonda Fournier to the author, 1992.

Appendix 1   A Bach Chorale

At the funeral mass in Geneva's Basilica of Notre Dame the organist Richard Jeandin played a Chorale particularly associated with Pierre Fournier, *Herzlich tut mich verlangen*. In his address Canon Athanasiades drew a parallel between the history of this melody and Fournier's life.

The original secular poem about a young lover's turmoil, *Mein G'müt ist mir verwirret*, was set to music in 1601 by Hans Leo Hassler who later gave it the sacred words. Half a century passed and the poet Paul Gerhardt added two new sets of words, *Befiehl du deine Wege* and, with a slight alteration of rhythm, the Passion stanzas *O Haupt voll Blut und Wunden* based on St Bernard of Clairvaux' Meditations on the Cross. The melody appears twice in the Christmas Oratorio, at the end as the joyful *Nun seid Ihr wohl gerochen*.

Conceived as the setting of a secular poem and then transformed from profane to sacred, the melody moved through the dramatic treatment of the Passion to end as a triumphant hymn. Like a journeying soul it has passed from human love through suffering to ultimate joy.

Appendix 2 Fournier's Exercise in Bow Control

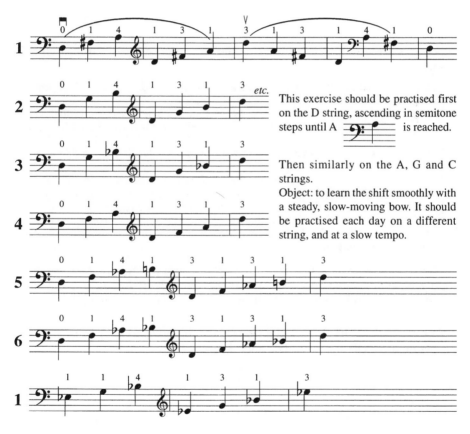

This exercise should be practised first on the D string, ascending in semitone steps until A is reached.

Then similarly on the A, G and C strings.

Object: to learn the shift smoothly with a steady, slow-moving bow. It should be practised each day on a different string, and at a slow tempo.

Appendix 3 Walton Concerto: Composer's Indications

Indications given to Pierre Fournier by the composer in a letter from Ischia, 27 August 1958.

> The metronomic tempi are mine & are more or less correct. Perhaps the opening is marked a little too fast & ♩ = 63 is a better tempo.
>
> You may use the "ossie" or the original as you think fit. The former are probably more effective and playable. The only places where I incline to the original are Mov. II three bars after 14 (if they are indeed practicable) & the end of the cadenza, before 19. But I have no strong feelings about them & I leave it entirely to you to decide what you prefer.
>
> Mov. III – not too slow 6 before 6 nor the 2 before 7. It is necessary to make the first solo improvisation very strong & forceful – it has to wake up the movement! 6th before 8 could be "Pizz" throughout the bar & "arco" in the following one.
>
> One thing I can assure you about is that you are never in danger of being overwhelmed by the orchestra except for the passage in Mov. II before 3 & 5, but even there it is only a question of keeping the orchestra down & the cello being slightly aggressive.

Fournier made some emendations to the second movement which the composer approved, inviting him to make 'any others [he might] feel inclined... which would clarify the cello part' (Sir William Walton to Pierre Fournier, 7 November 1958).

At three bars before 8, Fournier delayed the *diminuendo* to *poco ritenuto* one bar before 8 – a characteristic Fournier device.

Témoignages / Musicians on Pierre Fournier

Sage et seigneurial, précédé par sa canne...

André Tubeuf, *In Memoriam Pierre Fournier*, DGG

My favourite cellist. The most musical interpreter on his instrument.

Wolfgang Stresemann, former Intendant, Berlin Philharmonic, to the author,
21 August 1991

The ability to create a feeling of intimacy with the audience is what constitutes the genius of Pierre Fournier.

Bernard Gavoty, *Anicroches*, Paris: Buchet-Chastel 1979

I admired and loved Pierre not only as an artist but also for his human qualities and his dedication to his art. Our collaboration belongs to my most cherished memories and I miss him greatly.

Rudolf Firkušny to the author, 2 January 1989

He was a very great artist, a very fine musician and a wonderful cellist. His performance of the Dvořák Concerto with George Szell is probably the best performance I ever heard.

Nathan Milstein to the author, 21 January 1988

He was not yet the great international artist he was to become, but he was already a magnificent artist and he brought great joy to my youth.

Vlado Perlemuter, speaking of their youthful collaboration in the 1920s
when Fournier was 19, in conversation with the author

I considered him a giant of a cellist, a great artist and musician and one of the most decent human beings I ever met. His place in the history of cello playing is secure. I miss him.

János Starker to the author, 14 December 1992

Pierre Fournier was a very great artist and a first-rate cellist. I shall never forget him.

Artur Balsam to the author, 20 December 1988

I admired him tremendously as an artist.... He deserves to be honoured.

Josef Gingold to the author, 28 November 1988

Today's students cannot imagine the impact of Fournier on a musically and particularly cellistically-starved scene. We went anywhere to hear him.

Amaryllis Fleming, Pierre Fournier Celebratory Concert, RCM 16 February 1987

He had such a love of music and such a gift of communication that one felt in touch with the composer through him.

Emma Ferrand in conversation with the author

My abiding memory is of Fournier's musicality, which is, after all, what it is all about.

Sir Charles Groves in conversation with the author

Pierre Fournier – A Discography

Pierre Fournier's recording career extended from the 1930s to the 1980s and this is the first attempt at a comprehensive list, with as much detailed information as available at the time of going to press. The advent of digital remastering means that by its very nature a discography is more than ever an unfinished exercise. As I write, new Fournier CDs are being issued, many of them composed of recordings made on widely differing dates over more than forty years, including live performances.

The 78 rpm and LP recordings are listed first in chronological order. For works later issued on compact disc an asterisk refers the reader to the CD section and label. The CDs themselves are in a separate section under each relevant label, giving the years of the component recordings and thus enabling the reader to turn back to the original details in the 78 and LP sections. LPs are limited to first issues.

I have to thank a number of specialists for their valuable help in the compilation: Ken Jagger of EMI Classics; Malcolm Walker; Alan Newcombe of DGG in Hamburg; Rémi Jacobs of EMI France; and in the USA Gene Gaudette of BMG Classics, Michael Wilcox and Michael Gray (former Editor, ARSC Journal); Jonathan Summers of the British Library National Sound Archive; Raymond McGill of CBS Sony Classics; E de Bourgknecht of Cascavelle.

Others who have kindly supplied information are Elizabeth Lawrence of Decca, Callum Ross of Priory Records, Linn Miles of Pavilion, Albert Spano of Ermitage. To all I extend my thanks.

In such a profusion of recordings it is possible, in spite of all care, that an error may have slipped through the net. In this case the author and publishers would be glad to be notified so that it may be corrected in a subsequent edition.

A.H.

Discography

Recording date Location Other details	Composers, works, contributing artists	matrix	catalogue (78 rpm)
	L'ANTHOLOGIE SONORE, PARIS		
Recording dates unknown. Producer: Curt Sachs			
Catalogues			
1937–8	J.C. Bach. Quintet No. 6 for fl, ob, strings G.Grunelle, fl/L.Gromer, ob/J.Fournier, vlc/ P.Villain, vla/P.Fournier, vlc	AS 115 AS 116	Disque 50
1937–8	Haydn. Trio No. 5 in E flat J.Fournier, vln/P.Fournier, vlo/ J.Février, p	AS 144-1 AS 145-1	Disque 55
	Finale of Haydn Trio (3rd side)	AS 146-1	
	F.X.Richter. Larghetto in F sharp minor (extract from Trio in A). Same artists. (4th side)	AS 147-1	Disque 56

Recording date Location Other details	Composers, works, contributing artists	matrix	catalogue	LP
1946	Boccherini. Sonata No. 2 in C for vlc and continuo P.Fournier, vlc/R. Gerlin, p	AS 150-1 } AS 151-1	Disque 66	
1946	Stamitz. Quartet for vla.da gamba, vln, vla and vlc E.Heinitz, vla da gamba/J.Fournier, vln/ G.Figueroa, vla/P.Fournier, vlc	AS 186 } AS 187	Disque 85	

1937–1943 LA VOIX DE SON MAITRE (HMV FRANCE)

Recording date Location Other details	Composers, works, contributing artists	matrix	catalogue	LP
4.5, 27.9.'37 Paris Studio Pelouze E: Walter Ruhlmann	Schubert. Arpeggione Sonata, D 821 with Jean Hubeau, p	2LA 1777–80	VSM L1037–38 HMV 1057–8	See CDs PEARL and EMI France Les Introuvables
10.5.'40 Paris Pathé Studios	Fauré. Piano Quartet No. 2 in G minor, Op. 45 with Jacques Thibaud, vln/Maurice Vieux, vla Marguerite Long,p		DB 5103–6	COLC 76 Columbia Masterworks
[?] '41	Couperin, arr. Bazelaire. Pièces en concert with Loewenguth Quartet			
10.6.'41 Paris Studio Albert E: Eugène Ravenet	Tchaikovsky. Variations on a Rococo Theme, Op. 33 Lamoureux Orch./Eugène Bigot	2LA 3570-73	DB 5152–3	See CDs PEARL and EMI France Les Introuvables
30.10.'42 Paris Studio Pelouze E: Walter Ruhlmann	Schumann. Abendlied, Op. 85/12 Brahms, arr. Fournier. Feldeinsamkeit, Op. 86/2* with Mme Pellas-Lemon, p	OLA 3861 OLA 3862	DA 4958 DA 4955	*See CDs EMI France Les Introuvables

Recording date / Location / Other details	Composers, works, contributing artists	matrix	catalogue	LP
20.9.'43 Paris Studio Pelouze E: Walter Ruhlmann	Fauré. Papillon, Op. 77 Nocturne de Shylock.* Leclair. Sarabande, Tambourin from Sonata in D, Op. 2/4 arr. Kreisler. With Tasso Janopoulo, p	OLA 4155	DA 4957 DA 4958	*Id.
24.9.'43 Paris Studio Pelouze E: Walter Ruhlmann	Weber. Polacca from Violin Sonata No. 6 in C, arr. Casals/Piatigorsky Stravinsky. Chanson russe (Mavra) arr. the composer* with Tasso Janopoulo, p	OLA 4164	DA 4955 DA 4956	*Id.
c. 1943 [?] Details unknown.	Haydn. Minuet and Variations in C Debussy. Prélude à l'Enfant prodigue. Pianist unknown			

1946–1953 HIS MASTER'S VOICE (UK)

Recording date / Location / Other details	Composers, works, contributing artists	matrix	catalogue	LP
13.9.'46 (1947) London Abbey Road Studio 3 P: unknown E: unknown	Recital with Gerald Moore, p Schubert, arr. Cassadó. Allegretto grazioso Wagner, arr. Goltermann. Prize Song (Meistersinger) Saint-Säens. Le Cygne*† Rubinstein, arr Popper. Melody, Op. 3/1 J S Bach, arr. Fournier. Three Chorales O Mensch bewein' dein Sünde gross' BWV622 Das alte Jahr vergangen ist BWV 614 Wenn wir in höchsten Nöten sind BWV 641	OEA 11208-2 OEA 11211-1 OEA 11209-1 OEA 11210-1 } 2EA 11212-1 2EA 11213-1 }	DA 1867 10" Victor Brazil DA 1868 10" DB 6372 12"	*RCA Victor LHMV 1043 †See CDs EMI France Les Introuvables
24.9.'46 Paris Studio Pelouze E: Walter Ruhlmann	Schumann. Fantasiestücke, Op. 73* with Babeth Léonet, p Fauré. Romance in A, Op. 69 (4th side) with Tasso Janopoulo, p	2LA 4696-98 2LA 4699	DB 11143-4	*See CDs EMI France Les Introuvables

Recording date / Location / Other details	Composers, works, contributing artists	matrix	catalogue	LP/CD
6–7.6.'47 (1947) London Abbey Road Studio 3 P: Walter Legge E: Douglas Larter	Beethoven. Sonata in A, Op. 69 with Artur Schnabel, p*			
	(i) Allegro ma non tanto	2EA 12099-2	DB 6464 12"	RCA Victor LCT 1124
	(i) continued	2EA 12101-1	RCA Victor 1231m	LP 01383
	(i) concluded	2EA 12102-1		with D major Sonata Op. 102/2
	(ii) Scherzo (Allegro molto)	2EA 12103-1	DB 6465 12"	*All Beethoven
	(iii) Adagio cantabile	2EA 12108-1		Sonatas with
	(iii) concluded	2EA 12109-1	DB 6466 12"	Schnabel on CD: EMI France Les Introuvables
			AC: DB 9123/9125	
10.12.6.'47 (1948) London Abbey Road Studio 3 P: Walter Legge E: Douglas Larter	Beethoven, Sonata in C, Op. 102/1 with Artur Schnabel, p			
	(i) Andante – Allegro vivace	2EA 12111-2	DB 6500 12"	RCA Victor
	(i) concluded	2EA 12112-4	RAC Victor 1370m	LCT 1124
	(ii) Adagio – Tempo d'andante	2EA 12113-1		LP 01382
	(iii) Allegro vivace		DB 6501 12"	with F major &
	(iii) concluded	2EA 12114-3		G minor Sonatas
29–30.9.'47 (1948) London Abbey Road Studio 1 P: Walter Legge E: Robert Beckett	Saint-Saëns. Concerto No. 1 in A minor, Op. 33* Philharmonia Orch/Walter Susskind			*See CD TESTAMENT
	(i) Allegro non troppo	2EA 12263-1	DB 6602 12"	
	(i) contd (ii) Allegretto con moto	2EA 12264-1		
	(ii) contd (iii) Allegro non troppo	2EA 12339-2	DB 6603 12"	
	(iii) concluded	2EA 12340-1		
30.8.'47 Edinburgh Usher Hall	Brahms. Piano Trio No. 1 in B, Op. 8	Not issued on record. A recording exists in the Swedish Radio Archive.		

The BBC Central Hall Westminster series of 1947 being a special case and not officially recorded, I have listed the complete series for the interest of the dedicated discophile and concertgoer, just in case anything further is discovered about the unofficial recordings. (If any concerts merited being preserved on record, it was these.)

BBC Chamber Music Series. Joseph Szigeti, vln/William Primrose, vla/Pierre Fournier, vlc/ Artur Schnabel, p

22.9.'47
London
Central Hall
Westminster
BBC Third Programme

Brahms. Piano Quartet No. 3 in C minor, Op. 60
Violin Sonata No. 1 in G, Op. 78
Schubert. Piano Trio No. 2 in E flat, D 929

24.9.'47
Id.
BBC Home Service

Brahms. Piano Trio No. 3 in C, Op. 101
Cello Sonata No. 2 in F, Op. 99
Piano Quartet No. 2 in A, Op. 26

26.9.'47
Id.
BBC Third Programme

Brahms. Violin Sonata No. 2 in A, Op. 100
Mendelssohn. Piano Trio No. 1 in D minor, Op. 49
Brahms. Piano Quintet in F minor, Op. 34 (with Ernest Element, vln)

29.9.'47
Id.
BBC Third Programme

Brahms. Piano Trio No. 1 in B, Op.8*
Violin Sonata No. 3 in D minor, Op. 108
Schubert. Piano Quintet in A, D 667 ('Trout')

1.10.'47
Id.
BBC Home Service
& Third Programme

Brahms. Piano Trio No. 2 in C, Op.87
Schubert. Piano Trio No. 1 in B flat, D 898†
Violin Sonata in A, D 574

3.10.'47
Id.
BBC Third Programme

Brahms. Cello Sonata No. 1 in E minor, Op. 38
Schubert. Fantasia in C for Violin and Piano, D 934
Brahms. Piano Quartet No. 1 in G minor, Op. 25

*Recorded off the air in 1947 by a former Paris resident, in whose collection the discs still reside. Source: Journal of the Association of Recorded Sound Collections.† David Bloesch: Schnabel Discography.
†LP: Discocorp RR-488 '94

†Vol.18, Nos. 1–3, 1986
Issued Nov. 1987

Recording date Location Other details	Composers, works, contributing artists	matrix	catalogue	LP
	Beethoven. Sonata in D, Op. 102/2, with Artur Schnabel, p			
21–22.6.'48 London Abbey Road Studio 3 P: Peter Albu E: Harold Davidson	(i) Allegro con brio (i) concluded	2EA 13167-1 2EA 13168-1 }	DB 6829 12"	RCA Victor LCT 1124
	(ii) Adagio con molto sentimento d'affetto (ii) continued	2EA 13169-1 2EA 13176-1 }	DB 6830 12"	
	(ii) concluded (iii) Allegro fugato (iii) concluded	2EA 13177-2 2EA 13178-1 }	DB 6831 12" AC: DB 9438/9440	LP 01383 with A major Sonata Op. 69
	Beethoven. Sonata in F, Op. 5/1, with Artur Schnabel, p			
23.6.'48 London Abbey Road Studio 3 P: Peter Albu E: Harold Davidson	(i) Adagio sostenuto (ii) Allegro	2EA 13179-1 2EA 13180-2 }	DB 6836 12"	LP 01382 with C major and G minor Sonatas
	(ii) continued (ii) concluded	2EA 13181-2 2EA 13182-2 }	DB 6837 12"	No release on 78 rpm 2XEA 209 Reserve (LP matrix)
	(iii) Allegro vivace (iii) concluded	2EA 13183-2 2EA 13184-1 }	DB 6838 12"	
	Beethoven. Sonata in G minor, Op. 5/2 with Artur Schnabel, p†			
24.6.'48 (1972) London Abbey Road Studio 3 P: Peter Albu E: Harold Davidson	(i) Adagio sostenuto ed espressivo (i) concluded	2EA 13185-1 2EA 13186-1 }	DB 6833 12"	†No release on 78 rpm
	(ii) Allegro molto più tosto presto (ii) concluded	2EA 13187-1 2EA 13188-1 }	DB 6834 12"	2XEA 210 Reserve (LP matrix)
	(iii) Rondo (Allegro) (iii) concluded	2EA 13189-1 2EA 13190-1 }	DB 6835 12"	

Recording date / Location / Other details	Composers, works, contributing artists	matrix	catalogue	LP
18–19.10.'48 (1949)	Dvořák. Concerto in B minor, Op. 104			*See CD
London	Philharmonia Orch./Rafael Kubelik*			TESTAMENT
Abbey Road	(i) Allegro	2EA 13347-1	DB 6887 12"	
Studio 1	(i) continued	2EA 13348-1		
P. Lawrance Collingwood	(i) continued	2EA 13349-1	DB 6888 12"	
E: Robert Beckett	(i) concluded	2EA 13350-2		
	(ii) Adagio ma non troppo	2EA 13351-1	DB 6889 12"	
	(ii) continued	2EA 13352-1		
	(ii) concluded	2EA 13353-2	DB 6890 12"	
	(iii) Allegro moderato	2EA 13354-1		
	(iii) continued	2EA 13355-1	DB 6891 12"	
	(iii) concluded	2EA 13356-1	AC: DB 9337/9401	
?: 1949	Dvořák. Concerto in B minor, Op. 104			*See CD PEARL
Berlin	Berlin Philharmonic Orch./S. Celibidache*			
Titania Palast				
P: unknown				
E: unknown				
26–27.5.'51 (1952)	Haydn, arr. Gevaert. Concerto No. 2 in D, Hob VIIb/2			*See CD EMI FRANCE
London	Cadenza by Fournier. Philharmonia Orch./Rafael Kubelik*			Les Introuvables
Abbey Road	(i) Allegro moderato	2EA 15650-2		
Studio 1	(i) continued	2EA 15651-3	DB 21448 12"	
P: Walter Legge	(i) concluded. Cadenza – Tempo 1	2EA 15652-3A		
E Douglas Larter	(ii) Adagio	2EA 15653-2	DB 21449 12"	
	(ii) concluded (iii) Allegro	2EA 15654-7		
	(iii) concluded	2EA 15655-5	DB 21450 12"	RCA Victor
			AC: DB 9743/9745	LHMV1043

Recording date Location Other details	Composers, works, contributing artists	matrix	catalogue	LP
3.6.'51 (1952) London Abbey Road	Fauré. Elégie, Op. 24 with Ernest Lush, p*	2EA 15669-3 2EA 15678-2	DB 21333 12"	RCA Victor LHMV1043 Coupled with Saint-Saëns: Le Cygne, with Gerald Moore, p
Studio 3 P: Walter Legge E: Harold Davidson				
6.6.'51 (1952) Id.	Ravel. Pièce en forme de habañera* Lili Boulanger. Nocturne	OEA 15686-2 OEA 15688-3	DA 2005 10"	USA LHMV1043
	Fauré. Berceuse, Op. 16* Debussy, arr. Fournier. Rêverie* with Ernest Lush, p	OEA 15679-2 OEA 15687-2	DA 2028 10"	*See CD TESTAMENT

1952–1956 DECCA (LONDON) – LONG-PLAYING

Recording date Location Other details	Composers, works, contributing artists	catalogue
2.10.'52 (1953) Decca Studios Broadhurst Gdns. P: John Culshaw E: Gill Went/ Cyril H. Baker	Recital with Ernest Lush, p J S Bach, arr. Fournier. Chorale Herzlich tut mich verlangen, BWV 727. Sonata in G, BWV 1027* Bloch. Nigun Kreisler.Chanson Louis XIII et Pavane Debussy, arr. Heifetz. Beau Soir Fauré. Fileuse, Op. 80/2 Gershwin, arr. Fournier. Prelude J. Nin. Granadina	LXT 2766 US LL700 *See CD DECCA, coupled with Brahms Sonatas/W. Backhaus
6.1.'53 Ludwigsburg P: V. Olof E: G. Went/ C.H. Baker	Boccherini, arr. Grützmacher with Stuttgart CO/Karl Münchinger Vivaldi, arr. d'Indy. Concerto in E minor, RV 40 Couperin. Pièces en concert } LW 5196	LXT 2765 US LL687
27.8.'53 (1953) Vienna Grossersaal, Musikverein P: Viktor Olof E: Cyril Windebank	R. Strauss. Don Quixote, Op. 35* with Ernst Moraweg, vla/Vienna PO/Clemens Krauss	LXT 2842 US LL855 s ECS 609 *See CD DECCA
7.4.'54 (1954) Geneva Victoria Hall P: V.Olof E: G.Went	Haydn. Concerto in D, Hob VIIb/2 Stuttgart CO/Karl Münchinger (coupled with Boccherini Concerto, 1952 recording: see above)	LXT 2968 US LL1036 s ECS 548

Recording date Location Other details	Composers, works, contributing artists	LP	CD
26.6.'54 (1955) Vienna Grossersaal Musikverein P: V.Olof E: C.Windebank	Dvořák. Concerto in B minor, Op. 104 with Vienna PO/R. Kubelik	LXT 2999 s ECS 512 US LL 1106	
1–3.5.'55 (1955) Geneva Victoria Hall P: V.Olof E: G.Went/C.H. Baker	Brahms. Sonata in E minor, Op. 38 Sonata in F, Op. 99 with Wilhelm Backhaus, p*	LXT 5077 s ECS 785 US 11 1264	*See CD DECCA coupled with J S Bach Sonata in G BWV 1027

Recording date Location Other details	Composers, works, contributing artists	LP	CD
	1956–1959 COLUMBIA		
29.2/3.3.'56 London Kingsway Hall P: Walter Legge E: D. Larter	Brahms. Double Concerto in A minor, Op. 102*† with David Oistrakh, vln/Philharmonia Orch/ Alceo Galliera Coupled with Brahms: Tragic Overture, Op. 81	33CX 1487 SAX 2264 SXLP 30185, 35353 (Angel) *Also coupled with Beethoven Triple Concerto Oistrakh/Philharmonia/Galliera EMX 2035	†See CD EMI Classics (UK)
15–16.3.'56 (1957) London Kingsway Hall P: Alan Melville E: D. Larter	Schumann. Concerto in A minor, Op. 129 Tchaikovsky. Variations on a Rococo Theme, Op. 33 with Philharmonia Orch./Sir Malcolm Sargent	33CX 1407 SAX 2282	
28, 29, 30.9.'57/ 1.10.'57 (1958) London Abbey Road Studio 3 P: Walter Jellinek E: Arthur Clarke	Two Recitals with Gerald Moore, p* J S Bach after Vivaldi, arr. Fournier. Recitative from Organ Concerto No. 3 Haydn, arr. Piatti. Menuetto Schumann. Abendlied, Op. 85/12 Weber, arr. Piatigorsky. Rondo from Violin Sonata, Op. 10 Mendelssohn. Song without Words, Op. 109 Chopin, arr. Fournier. Introduction and Polonaise, Op. 3 Rimsky-Korsakov, arr. Kreisler. Hymn to the Sun (*The Golden Cockerel*). Flight of the Bumble Bee (*Tsar Saltan*) arr. Shrimer Saint-Saëns. Le Cygne (*Le Carnaval des Animaux*) Fauré. Berceuse, Op. 16 Granados, arr. Fournier. La maja dolorosa (*Collección de tonadillas*). Intermezzo (*Goyescas*) arr. Cassado. Kreisler, arr. Fournier. La Gitana	33CX 1606	*See CD EMI France Les Introuvables

Recording date Location Other details	Composers, works, contributing artists	catalogue	CD
	COLUMBIA contd		
	Two Recitals with Gerald Moore, p (contd)*		
1.10.'57 (1959) London Abbey Road Studio 3 P: W. Jellinek E: A. Clarke	II Boccherini, arr. Piatti. Adagio and Allegro in A from Sonata No. 6 J S Bach. Chorales arr. Fournier Nun komm' der Heiden Heiland, BWV 599 Ich ruf' zu dir, Herr Jesu Christ BWV 639 Herzlich tut mich verlangen, BWV 727 O Mensch, bewein dein' Sünde gross', BWV 622 Ravel. Kaddisch (No. 1 of *Deux mélodies hebraïques*) arr. Garban. Pièce en forme de habañera, arr. Bazelaire Debussy, arr. Rogues. Prélude (*L'Enfant prodigue*) Fauré. Sicilienne, Op. 78. Papillon, Op. 77 Elégie, Op. 24	33CX 1644	*See CD EMI France Les Introuvables

Recording date / Location / Other details	Composers, works, contributing artists	LP	CD
	1959–1971 DEUTSCHE GRAMMOPHON		
Vienna, Brahmssaal, Musikverein P: Karl-Heinz Schneider E: Heinz Wildhagen	Beethoven Cycle with Friedrich Gulda, p		
20–21.6.'59 (1959) 21, 22, 28.6.59	Sonata in F, Op. 5/1 Sonata in G minor, Op. 5/2 }	138081	See CD section: DG
23–24, 28.6.'59 24–26.6.'59 19.6.'59	Sonata in A, Op. 69 Sonata in C, Op. 102/1 Seven Variations on *Bei Männern* (Mozart: *Die Zauberflöte*), WoO 46 }	138082	Id.
26–28.6.'59 18–19, 28.6.'59 17–18.6.'59	Sonata in D, Op. 102/2 Twelve Variations on a theme from Handel's *Judas Maccabeus*, WoO 45 Twelve Variations on *Ein Mädchen oder Weibchen* (Mozart: *Die Zauberflöte*), Op. 66 }	138083	Id.
24–26.5.'60 (1960) Paris, Salle de la Mutualité. P: Hans Ritter E: Harold Baudis	Lalo. Concerto in D minor Saint-Saëns. Concerto in A minor, Op. 33 Bruch. Kol Nidrei, Op. 47 with Lamoureux Orch./Jean Martinon }	138669	See CD section: DG

Recording date Location Other details	Composers, works, contributing artists	LP	CD

1959–1971 DEUTSCHE GRAMMOPHON contd

Recording date / Location / Other details	Composers, works, contributing artists	LP	CD
27.5–1.6.'60 (1961) Berlin Jesus Christus Kirche P: Otto Gerdes E: Werner Wolf/Günter Hermanns	Beethoven. Triple Concerto in C, Op. 56 with Wolfgang Schneiderhan, vln/Géza Anda, p/ Berlin Radio SO/Ferenc Fricsay. Grand Prix du Disque 1962, Académie Charles Cros, Paris	136236	See CD section: DG
	J S Bach. The Six Suites		
20.12.'60 (1961) 25.2.'61	Suite No. 1 in G, BWV 1007	Archiv 198356–8 s 419 369–1	See CD section: DG
20–21.12.'60 25.2.'61	Suite No. 2 in D minor, BWV 1008		
21.12.'60 25–26.2.'61	Suite No. 3 in C, BWV 1009		
22.12.'60	Suite No. 4 in E flat, BWV 1010 Suite No. 5 in C minor, BWV 1011		
28–29.12.'60, 27.2.'61	Suite No. 6 in D, BWV 1012		

Hannover, Beethovensaal
P: Dr Hans Hickman/Karl Heinz Schneider
E: Heinz Wildhagen

Recording date Location Other details	Composers, works, contributing artists	LP	CD
	1959–1971 DEUTSCHE GRAMMOPHON contd		
1–3.6.'61 (1962) Berlin, Jesus Christus Kirche P: Hans Weber E: Günter Hermanns	Dvořák. Concerto in B minor, Op. 104 Berlin PO/George Szell. Grand Prix du Disque 1962, Académie Charles Cros Paris. Academy Award 1964 Tokyo	138755	See CD section: DG
10–14.10.'61 (1962) Zürich, Gemeindesaal der Neumünsterkirche P: Hans Ritter E: Heinz Wildhagen	Boccherini, arr. Grützmacher. Concerto in B flat. Cadenzas by Grützmacher CPE Bach. Concerto in A, Wq 172 Festival Strings Lucerne/Rudolf Baumgartner	138816	See CD section: DG
20–21.12.'63 (1964) Zürich, Gemeindesaal der Neumünsterkirche P: Dr Manfred Richter E: Harald Baudis	Vivaldi, arr. d'Indy/Bazelaire. Concerto in E minor RV 40* Couperin, arr. Bazelaire. Pièces en concert with Festival Strings Lucerne/Rudolf Baumgartner	138986	*See CD section: DG
17–19.12.'64 (1968) Zürich, Gemeindesaal der Neumünsterkirche P: Dr Manfred Richter E: Harald Baudis	Haydn. Concerto in D, Hob VIIb/2 with Festival Strings Lucerne/Rudolf Baumgartner* [See also 12–13.5.'67 same artists]	139358	*See CD section: DG

Recording date Location Other details	Composers, works, contributing artists	LP	CD
	1959–1971 DEUTSCHE GRAMMOPHON contd		
1–7.2.'65 (1965) Paris: Salle Pleyel P: Karl Faust E: Heinz Wildhagen	Beethoven Cycle with Wilhelm Kempff, p Sonata in F, Op.5/1 Sonata in G minor, Op. 5/2 Sonata in A, Op. 69 Sonata in C, Op. 102/1 Seven Variations on *Bei Männern* (Mozart's *Die Zauberflöte*) Wo0 46 Sonata in D, Op. 102/2 Twelve Variations on *Ein Mädchen oder Weibchen* (*Die Zauberflöte*) Op. 66 Twelve Variations on a theme from Handel's *Judas Maccabeus*, Wo0 45	138993–5	See CD section: DG
12–14.4'65 (1965) Hannover, Beethovensaal P: Karl Faust E: Klaus Scheibe	Stravinsky. Suite italienne Chanson russe with Ernest Lush, p	138986	
16–20.9.'65 (1965) Berlin, UFA Studios P: Hans Weger E: Klaus Scheibe	Brahms with Rudolf Firkušny, p Sonata No. 1 in E minor, Op. 38 Sonata No. 2 in F, Op. 99	139119	

1959–1971 DEUTSCHE GRAMMOPHON contd

Recording date Location Other details	Composers, works, contributing artists	LP	CD
27–30.12.'65 (1966) Berlin, Jesus Christ Kirche P: Hans Weber E: Günter Hermanns	Richard Strauss. Don Quixote, Op. 35 with Giusto Cappone, vla Berlin PO/Herbert von Karajan	139009	See CD section: DG
20–23.10.'66 (1966) Berlin, UFA Studios P: Wolfgang Lohse E: Klaus Scheibe	Elgar. Concerto in E minor, Op. 85 Bloch. Schelomo Berlin PO/Alfred Wallenstein	139128	See CD section: DG
12–13.5.'67 (1968) Lucerne, Verkehrhaus P: Dr Manfred Richter E: Harald Baudis/ Günter Hermanns	Haydn. Concerto in C, Hob VIIb/1 coupled with Concerto in D, Hob VIIb/2 (recorded Zürich 17–19.12.'64, see above) with Festival Strings Lucerne/Rudolf Baumgartner	139358	
25–28.9.'67 (1968) Berlin, UFA Studios P: Rainer Brock E: Hans-Peter Schweigmann	Schubert. Arpeggione Sonata in A minor, D 821 Mendelssohn. Variations concertantes, Op. 17 Schumann. Fantasiestücke, Op. 73 Fünf Stücke im Volkston, Op. 102 with Jean Fonda, p	139368	See CD section: DG

1959–1971 DEUTSCHE GRAMMOPHON contd

Recording date Location Other details	Composers, works, contributing artists	LP	CD
8–10.1.'69 München, Plenarsaal der Akademie der Wissenschaften P: Hansjoachim Reiser E: Heinz Wildhagen	Rendezvous musical with Lamar Crowson, p* Francoeur, arr. Trowell. Adagio cantabile and Allegro vivo from Sonata in E Haydn, arr. Piatti. Minuet from Sonata in C Weber, arr. Kreisler. Larghetto. Rondo (presto) arr. Piatigorsky from Violin Sonata No. 3 Chopin, arr. Fournier. Nocturne, Op. 9/2 Rimsky-Korzakov, arr. Kreisler. Hymn to the Sun (*The Golden Cockerel*). The Flight of the Bumble Bee (*Tsar Saltan*), arr. Shtrimer Schumann, arr. Grützmacher. Adagio and Allegro, Op. 70 Bach-Gounod. Ave Maria (Meditation) Tchaikovsky. Valse sentimentale, Op. 51/6 Brahms, arr. Fournier. Feldeinsamkeit, Op. 86/2 Popper. Elfentanz Dvořák. Rondo, Op. 94 Saint-Saëns. Le Cygne (*Carnaval des animaux*) Paganini, arr. Silva. Variations on a theme from Rossini's *Mosé*	135132	*See CD section: DG

1959–1971 DEUTSCHE GRAMMOPHON contd

Recording date Location Other details	Composers, works, contributing artists	LP	CD
	Beethoven Trios and Variations with Henryk Szeryng, vln/Wilhelm Kempff, p For Op. 11, Karl Leister, cl	643 656–660 set 2720 016	See CD section: DG
20–26 8.'69, 28–30.4.'70 Vevey Theatre in co-operation with Beethoven Archive, Bonn P: Dr Wilfried Daenicke RS: Dr Manfred Richter E: Heinz Wildhagen	Piano Trio No. 1 in E flat, Op. 1/1 Piano Trio No. 2 in G, Op. 1/2 Piano Trio No. 3 in C minor, Op. 1/3 Trio in B flat for clarinet, cello and piano, Op. 11 Piano Trio No. 4 in D ('Ghost'), Op. 70/1 Variations on *Ich bin der Schneider Kakadu*, Op. 121a Fourteen Variations, Op. 44 Piano Trio in E flat, Wo0 38 Piano Trio in B in one movement, Wo0 39 Piano Trio No. 6 in B flat ('Archduke'), Op. 97		
12–15.1.'71 München Residenz Plenarsaal der Akademie des Wissenschaften P: Karl Faust RS: Werner Mayer E: Klaus Scheibe	Chopin. Sonata in G minor, Op. 65 Franck. Sonata in A. arr. Fournier from Violin Sonata, with Jean Fonda	2530 141	See CD section: DG

Recording date Location Other details	Composers, works, contributing artists	LP

Miscellaneous: Recordings 1959–1981 on LP **CBA MASTERWORKS USA (Sony)**

20.11.'59 (1960) Hollywood, American Legion Hall P: John McClure E: Harold Chapman	Brahms. Double Concerto in A minor, Op. 102 with Zino Francescatti, vln/Columbia SO/ Bruno Walter	ML 5493 MS 6158
28/29.11.'59 (1961) Cleveland Severance Hall P: Howard H Scott E: Buddy Graham	R. Strauss. Don Quixote, Op. 35 Cleveland Orch./George Szell	LC 3786 BC 1135

MELODIYA (Moscow)

1961	Recital with Naum Walter, p Fauré. Elégie, Op. 24 Ravel. Pièce en forme de habañera Debussy, arr. Heifetz. Prélude à *l'Enfant prodigue* Stravinsky. Chanson russe Bloch. Nigun Francoeur. Largo and Allegro J S Bach, arr. Fournier. Chorale O Mensch bewein' dein Sünde gross' BWV 622 Haydn. Minuet Weber. Polonaise in C, Op. 24 Nin. Granadina Chopin. Introduction and Polonaise brillante, Op. 3	08330 (TY 35) 12558/63

Recording date Location Other details	Composers, works, contributing artists	LP	CD
	Miscellaneous: Recordings 1959–1981 on LP (contd)		
	PEARL		
1963 (1981)	Mendelssohn. Variations concertantes, Op. 17 Schumann. Fantasiestücke, Op. 73. Fünf Stücke im Volkston, Op. 102 Schubert. Arpeggione Sonata, D 821 with Dorel Handman, p	s SHE 562	
	CBS LONDON		
?.2.'67	Debussy. Sonata Martinů. Sonata No. 1 (dedicated to Fournier) Shostakovich. Sonata in D minor with Jean Fonda, p	s 72613	
	EMI ELECTROLA		
See 1947, 1950 1974 Paris, Salle Wagram	Beethoven. The Five Sonatas with Artur Schnabel, p Poulenc. Sonata (dedicated to Fournier) with Jacques Février, p (in Poulenc Chamber Music series)	c 147–01382–83	See CD section: EMI

Recording date Location Other details	Composers, works, contributing artists	LP	CD
	RCA VICTOR RED SEAL		
	Miscellaneous: Recordings 1959–1981 on LP (contd)		
	Trios with Henryk Szeryng, vln/Artur Rubinstein, p		See CD section: RCA
4–10.9.'72 Geneva, Victoria Hall P: Max Wilcox E: Richard Gardner	Brahms. Trio in B, Op. 8 Trio in C, Op. 87 Trio in C minor, Op. 101 Schumann. Trio in D minor, Op. 63	ARL 3–0138	
13–19.4.'74 Geneva, Victoria Hall P: Max Wilcox E: Hellmuth Kolbe/ Paul Goodman	Schubert. Trio in B flat, Op. 99 Trio in B flat, Op. 100	ARL 2–0731	
	National Academy of Recording Arts and Science (US) Best Chamber Music Performance 1975 and 1976		
	PHILIPS (Japan)		
9–10.12.'76 27–29.4.'77 4/5.5.'77 Geneva St Boniface Church	J S Bach The Six Suites for Unaccompanied Cello	25 PC 166–8	

Recording date Location Other details	Composers, works, contributing artists	LP	CD

Miscellaneous: Recordings 1959–1981 on LP (contd)

VOX – TURNABOUT

1977 Monte Carlo Salle Garnier (Opera)	Saint-Saëns. Concerto in A minor, Op. 33 Lalo. Concerto in D minor Monte Carlo Opera Orch./Josif Conta	TV 34731 US 5842–43	

CBS SONY MASTERWORKS (Japan)

1,2,5.4.'81 Tokyo, Ishibashi Memorial Hall P: Mobuaki Arai E: Ken-ichi Handa	Perre Fournier 75th Birthday Celebration with Michio Kobayashi, p Martinu. Sonata No. 1 Debussy. Sonata Schubert. Arpeggione Sonata, D 821 Schumann. Adagio and Allegro, Op. 70	28–AC–1296	See CD section SONY Japan

PAN RECORDS

16–17.6.'81 Vienna Baumgartner Casino	Joseph Flury. Concerto in A minor (dedicated to Fournier). Wiener Volksopern Orch./the Composer	130036	See CD section PAN

Recording date Location Other details	Composers, works, contributing artists	CD

Pierre Fournier on CD

DEUTSCHE GRAMMOPHON

Recording date / Location / Other details	Composers, works, contributing artists	CD
	The Art of Pierre Fournier. 18 CDs: concertos, sonatas, famous pieces, the six Bach solo Suites, Beethoven trios and variations	DG Japan POCG–9711–28 447 665–2
1961	Homage to Pierre Fournier. Two CDs: Dvořák. Concerto in B minor, Op. 104 Berlin PO/George Szell	
1966 1960	Bloch. Schelomo. Berlin PO/Alfred Wallenstein Bruch. Kol Nidrei, Op. 47. Lamoureux Orch./ Jean Martinon.	447 349–2 GDB
1969 1967	Recital with Lamar Crowson, p: 13 pieces Schubert. Arpeggione Sonata, D 821 with Jean Fonda, p	453 667–2 GFS
1963 1964 1961	Vivaldi, arr. d'Indy. Concerto in E minor, RV 40 Haydn. Concerto in D, Hob VIIb/2 Boccherini, arr. Grützmacher. Concerto in B flat with Festival Strings Lucerne/Rudolf Baumgartner	445 028–2 GR
1960	Beethoven. Triple Concerto in C, Op. 56 with Wolfgang Schneiderhan, vln/Géza Anda, p/ Berlin Radio SO/Ferenc Fricsay. (Coupled with Brahms Double Concerto: W. Schneiderhan, vln/János Starker, vlc)	CD ADD 429 934–2 GDO 449 847–2 GCL 449 847–4 GCL (MC)

Recording date Location Other details	Composers, works, contributing artists	CD

DEUTSCHE GRAMMOPHON (contd)

Recording date	Composers, works, contributing artists	CD
1961	Dvořák. Concerto in B minor, Op. 104. Berlin PO/ George Szell	CD ADD 423 881–2 GGA
1966	Elgar. Concerto in E minor, Op. 85. Berlin PO/ Alfred Wallenstein	
1965	R. Strauss. Don Quixote, Op. 85 (coupled with *Tod und Verklärung*). Berlin PO/Herbert von Karajan	CD ADD 429–184–2 GGA Galleria dr
1966	Elgar. Concerto in E minor, Op. 85. LSO/Eugen Jochum Coupled with Enigma Variations, Op. 36 Coupled with Dvořák Concerto/Cleveland/G. Szell	s 445013–2 GR Resonance CD ADD 423 881–2 dr
1961	J S Bach. The Six Cello suites on two CDs	CD ADD 449 711–1 GOR 2 'The Originals'
1959	Beethoven. Sonatas and Variations with Friedrich Gulda, p	CD ADD 437 352–2 GDO 2 Dokumente
1965	Beethoven. Sonatas and Variations with Wilhelm Kempff, p	CD ADD 453 013–2 GTA 2
1969–70	Beethoven. Five Piano Trios with Henryk Szeryng, vln/Wilhelm Kempff, p, on 3 CDs Beethoven. Two Piano Trios with same artists: Op. 70/1 ('Ghost'), Op. 97 ('Archduke')	CD ADD 415 879–2 GCM 3 CD ADD 429 712–2 GGA

Recording date Location Other details	Composers, works, contributing artists	CD
Pierre Fournier on CD (contd)		
	DECCA	
1955	Brahms. The two Sonatas with Wilhelm Backhaus	Historic 425973–2DM CBA 924 TDC 251
1953	R. Strauss. Don Quixote, Op. 35 Vienna PO/Clemens Krauss	425 974–2 DM
	RCA	
1972	In the Rubinstein Collection Brahms. Trio on B, Op. 8 Trio in C, Op. 87	6260–2–RC
	Schumann. Trio in D minor, Op. 63 Trio in B flat, Op. 99 with Henryk Szeryng, vln/Artur Rubinstein, p	6262–2–RG
	EMI Classics (UK)	
1957	Brahms. Double Concerto in A minor, Op. 102 with David Oistrakh, vln/Philharmonia Orch./ Alceo Galliera Coupled with Beethoven Triple Concerto. Oistrakh Trio/Philharmonia Orch./Sir Malcolm Sargent	EMI CZS 762854–2
1956	Tchaikovsky. The Concertos. 2 CDs Variations on a Rococo Theme, Op. 33 Philharmonia Orch./Sir Malcolm Sargent	0777 767822 2 5

Recording date Location Other details	Composers, works, contributing artists	CD

Pierre Fournier on CD (contd)

SONY CLASSICS (Japan)

Recording date Location Other details	Composers, works, contributing artists	CD
1960	R. Strauss. Don Quixote, Op. 35 with Cleveland Orch/George Szell Coupled with Hindemith: Symphonic Metamorphosis on Themes by Weber	32 DC 490 dr
1959	Bruno Walter Edition: Brahms. Double Concerto in A minor, Op. 102 with Zino Francescatti, vln/Columbia SO/Bruno Walter Coupled with Beethoven Triple Concerto, Op. 56 J. Corigliano, vln/L. Rose, vlc/NYPO/Bruno Walter	SMK 64479
1981	Pierre Fournier 75th Birthday Celebration with Michio Kobayashi, p Martinů. Sonata No. 1 Debussy. Sonata Schubert. Arpeggione Sonata, D 821 Schumann. Adagio and Allegro, Op. 70	38 DC 24 dr

Recording date Location Other details	Composers, works, contributing artists	CD
	Pierre Fournier on CD (contd)	
	TESTAMENT (under EMI UK licence)	

1948	Dvořák. Concerto in B minor, Op. 104
	  Philharmonia Orch./Rafael Kubelik
	Saint-Saëns. Concerto in A minor, Op. 33
	  Philharmonia Orch./Walter Susskind
	Pieces with Ernest Lush, p:
	  Fauré. Elégie, Berceuse
	  Ravel. Habañera
	  Debussy. Rêverie
	and with Gerald Moore, p:
	  Saint-Saëns. Le Cygne
		SBT 1016

	CASCAVELLE	
1.2.'67 Geneva, Victoria Hall Live E: Radio SR, Espace 2	Mémoires Collection, Orchestre de la Suisse Romande First Series Frank Martin. Concerto (also Petite Symphonie concertante, fragments from *La Tempête* with D. Fischer-Dieskau, b, and *Ballade* for flute with André Pépin, fl) OSR/Ernest Ansermet/ Frank Martin	VEL 2001

Recording date Location Other details	Composers, works, contributing artists	CD
Pierre Fournier on CD (contd)	**CASCAVELLE** (contd)	
6.2.'57 15.3.'78 19.12.'62 Geneva, Victoria Hall Live E: Radio SR, Espace 2	Second Series Schumann. Concerto in A minor, Op. 129 Martinů. Concerto Shostakovich. Concerto No. 1 OSR/Ferenc Fricsay/Wolfgang Sawallisch/ Jascha Horenstein	VEL 2009
	TAHRA	
25.4.'62 Lugano Festival Live E: Dr Ermanno Briner	Dvořák. Concerto in B minor, Op. 104 Orchestra della Radio della Svizzera Italiana/ Hermann Scherchen (with Brahms. Symphony No. 3, Op. 90)	TAH 116 E: dr Jean-Pierre Bouquet
13–16.11.'43 14.11.'43 Berlin Live	From Homage to Furtwängler: 4 CDs Schumann. Finale from Concerto in A minor, Op. 129 Berlin PO/Wilhelm Furtwängler	TAH 1008–1011

Recording date Location Other details	Composers, works, contributing artists	CD

Pierre Fournier on CD (contd)

ARKADIA

Recording date Location Other details	Composers, works, contributing artists	CD

18.12.'72 Crissier: European Broadcasting Union Live	Schubert. Trio in B flat, Op. 99
	  Trio in E flat, Op. 100
	Mendelssohn. Trio in D minor, Op. 49
	  Trio in C minor, Op. 66
	  with Arthur Grumiaux, vln/Nikita Magaloff, p
		CD HP 598–1
		CD HP 606–1

MEMORIES (US)

28.10.'67 Cleveland Live	Frank Martin. Concerto (dedicated to Fournier) R. Strauss. Don Quixote, Op. 35 with Cleveland Orch/George Szell	HR 4136

STRADIVARIUS

4.'84 Zürich, Boswil Church	Brahms. Sonata in E minor, Op. 38 Grieg. Sonata in A minor, Op. 36 with Jean Fonda, p	STR33320 ADD

ERMITAGE

21.8.'64 Ascona Settimane musicale Live	Beethoven. Sonata in G minor, Op. 5/2 12 Variations on a theme from Handel's *Judas Maccabeus*, WoO 157 12 Variations on *Ein Mädchen oder Weibchen* from Mozart's *Die Zauberflöte*, Op. 66 Sonata in A, Op. 69 with Jean Fonda	ERM 111 AD

Recording date Location Other details	Composers, works, contributing artists	CD

Pierre Fournier on CD (contd)

Recording date Location Other details	Composers, works, contributing artists	CD
25.2.'62 Lugano Festival Live	Dvořák. Concerto in B minor, Op. 104 Orch. Radio Svizzera Italiana/Hermann Scherchen (with Brahms: Symphony No. 3, Op. 90)	ERM 1702
11.9.'70 Locarno San Francisco Church Live	Vivaldi. Concerto in E minor, RV 40 with Festival Strings Lucerne/Rudolf Baumgartner (coupled with Bach: Piano Concerto in G minor, M. Horszowsky, p)	ERM 1662
10.10.'75 Ascona, Settimane Musicale, Live E: Lucienne Rosset	Miscellaneous Pieces, incl. Fauré: Elégie with Jean Fonda, p	ERM 1525–2 dr Jochen Gottschall

PAN RECORDS

| 16–17.6.'81 Vienna Baumgartner Casino | Joseph Flury. Concerto in A minor (dedicated to Fournier) Wiener Volksopern Orch./the Composer | PAN 130036 |

Recording date Location Other details	Composers, works, contributing artists	CD

Pierre Fournier on CD (contd)

PEARL

1937	Schubert. Arpeggione Sonata, D 821 with Jean Hubeau, p	GEMM 9198 ce Roger Beardsley The Schubert Sonata also included on GEMM CDs 9984–6 The Recorded Cello, Vol. II
1941	Tchaikovsky. Rococo Variations, Op. 33 Lamoureux Orch./Eugène Bigot	
1949 Titania Palast Live	Dvořák. Concerto in B minor, Op. 104 Berlin PO/S. Celibidache	

PRAGA

?.5.'59 Prague May Festival Live	Kodály. Sonata for unaccompanied cello, Op. 8 from Fournier recital. (With miscellaneous Kodály chamber works by other artists.)	PR 250 065

ARLECCHINO

The Art of Pierre Fournier: Public Performances Vol. 1

?.5.'59 Prague May Festival Live	Dvořák. Concerto in B minor, Op. 104 Czech PO/ Georges Sebastian	ARL 169 ADD
6.11.'49 New York Carnegie Hall Live	Schumann. Concerto in A minor, Op. 129 NYPO/ Stokowski	

Recording date Location Other details	Composers, works, contributing artists	CD

Pierre Fournier on CD (contd)

ARLECCHINO (contd)

	Vol. 2	
1952, 1961 Moscow Live	Virtuoso Pieces and Encores, with E. Lush, p/ N. Walter, p	ARL 193
	Vol. 3	
1959 Live	Elgar. Concerto in E minor, Op. 85 Munich PO/ P. Kletzski	} ARLA 66
12.8.'59 Opening concert Edinburgh Festival Usher Hall Live	Walton. Concerto. Royal Philharmonic Orch./ the Composer	

EMI FRANCE

	Les Introuvables de Pierre Fournier: 4 CDs Compact Disc 1	7243 5 69708 2 3
1951	Haydn, arr. Gevaert. Concerto in D, Hob VIIb/2 Philharmonia Orch./Rafael Kubelik	
1956	Schumann. Concerto in A minor, Op. 129 Philharmonia Orch./Sir Malcolm Sargent	
1946	Fantasiestücke, Op. 73 with Babeth Léonet, p	
1941	Tchaikovsky. Rococo Variations, Op. 33 Lamoureux Orch./Eugène Bigot	

Recording date Location Other details	Composers, works, contributing artists	CD

Pierre Fournier on CD (contd)

EMI FRANCE (contd)

Les Introuvables de Pierre Fournier (cont)
Compact Disc 2
Beethoven Sonatas with Artur Schnabel, p

1948	No. 1 in F, Op. 5/1
1947	No. 2 in G minor, Op. 5/2
	No. 3 in A, Op. 69

Compact Disc 3
Beethoven Sonatas with Artur Schnabel, p (contd)

1948	No. 4 in C, Op. 102/1
	No. 5 in D, Op. 102/2
1937	Schubert. Arpeggione Sonata in A minor, D 821, with Jean Hubeau, p

| 1942 | Schumann. Abendlied, Op. 85/12 |
| | Brahms. Feldeinsamkeit, Op. 86/2, with
Mme Pallas-Lemon, p |

1946	Fauré. Romance in A, Op. 69
1943	Nocturne de Shylock
	Stravinsky. Chanson russe (*Mavra*), with Tasso Janopoulo, p

| 1951 | Lili Boulanger. Nocturne. With Ernest Lush, p |
| 1946 | A. Rubinstein, arr: Popper-Moore. Melody in F, Op. 3/1
with Gerald Moore, p |

Recording date Location Other details	Composers, works, contributing artists	CD

Pierre Fournier on CD (contd)

EMI FRANCE (contd)

Les Introuvables de Pierre Fournier (contd)
Compact Disc 4

1957, 1959 — Short Pieces with Gerald Moore, p
Chopin. Introduction and polonaise brillante, Op. 3
Mendelssohn. Romance sans paroles, Op. 109
Rimsky-Korsakov. Hymne au soleil (*Le Coq d'or*)
Le vol du bourdon (*Tsar Saltan*)
Saint-Saëns. Le Cygne (*Le Carnaval des Animaux*)
Fauré. Berceuse, Op. 16
Grandos. La maja dolorosa, arr. Fournier (*Colleción de tonadillas*)
Intermezzo (*Goyescas*)
Kreisler, arr. Fournier. La Gitana
Fauré. Papillon, Op. 77. Sicilienne, Op. 78
Debussy, arr. Rogues. L'Enfant prodigue, prélude
Ravel, arr. Bazelaire. Pièce en forme de habañera
Kaddisch (*Mélodie hébraïque* No. 1, arr. Garban)
J S Bach, arr. Fournier. Chorales
O Mensch bewein' dein' Sünde gross', BWV 622
Herzlich tut mich verlangen, BWV 727
Ich ruf' zu dir, Herr Jesu Christ, BWV 639
Nun komm der Heiden Heiland, BWV 599
Boccherini, arr. Piatti. Adagio & Allegro (Sonate No. 6)

1974
Paris
Salle Wagram — Poulenc. Sonata for cello and piano
with Jacques Février, p
In Poulenc Chamber Music Series

CZS 7-62736-2

Select Bibliography

History and Social Background

Azéma, Jean-Pierre *From Munich to the Liberation 1938–1944*, (Cambridge History of Modern France), Editions de la Maison des Sciences de l'Homme and Cambridge University Press 1984.

Bernard, Philippe and Dubief, Henri *The Decline of the Third Republic 1914–1938*, (CHMF) EMSH and CUP 1985.

Cossart, Micheal de *The Food of Love, Princesse Edmond de Polignac (1865–1943) and her Salon*, London: Hamish Hamilton 1978.

Craig, Gordon W. *Germany 1866–1945* (Oxford History of Modern Europe), OUP 1978.

Cronin, Vincent *Paris on the Eve*, London: Collins 1989.

Ehrenburg, Ilya *Men, Years, Life,* London: Macgibbon and Kee 1963.

Everett, Susanne *Lost Berlin*, London: Hamlyn 1979.

Friedrich, Otto *Before the Deluge*, London: Michael Joseph 1974.

Gold, Arthur and Fizdale, Robert *Misia, the Life of Misia Sert*, New York: Knopf 1980.

Goldman, Emma *My Disillusionment with Russia*, London 1925.

Kolb, Eberhard *The Weimar Republic*, London: Unwin Hyman 1988.

Lottman, Herbert *The People's Anger*, London: Century Hutchinson 1986.

Mayeur, Jean-Marie and Rebérioux, Madeleine *The Third Republic from its Origins to the Great War 1871–19* (CHMF), EMSH and CUP 1984.

Nabokov, Vladimir *Speak, Memory*, London: Penguin Books 1969. (First published as *Conclusive Evidence*, Weidenfeld and Nicolson 1967.)

Rioux, Jean-Pierre *The Fourth Republic 1944–1958*, (CHMF) EMSH and CUP 1987.

Shirer, William *The Rise and Fall of the Third Reich*, New York: Simon and Schuster 1960.

Sinclair, Andrew *War like a Wasp*, London: Hamish Hamilton 1989.

Vassiltchikov, Marie ('Missie') *Berlin Diaries*, London: Chatto and Windus 1985.

Willet, John *The Weimar Years, a Culture Cut Short*, London: Thames and Hudson 1989.

Musical Biography, Letters etc.

Baldock, Robert *Casals*, London: Gollancz 1992.
Campbell, Margaret *The Great Cellists*, London: Gollancz 1988.
Collaer, Paul *Darius Milhaud*, Paris: Editions Slatkine 1982.
Fauré, Gabriel. Correspondance. Textes réunis, présentés et annotés par Jean-Michel Nectoux, Paris: Flammarion 1980.
Gavoty, Bernard *Pierre Fournier*, Geneva: Kister 1956.
———— *Alfred Cortot*, Paris: Buchet-Chastel 1977.
———— *Anicroches*, Paris: Buchet-Chastel 1979.
Geissmar, Berta *The Baton and the Jackboot*, London: Hamish Hamilton 1944.
Gillis, Daniel *Furtwängler in America*, Palo Alto, Ca.: Rampart Press 1970.
Goubault, Christian *Jacques Thibaud (1880–1953), violoniste français*, Paris: Champion, 1988.
Hell, Henri *Francis Poulenc, musicien français*, Paris: Fayard 1978.
Hoeree, Arthur *Albert Roussel*, Paris: Editions Rieder 1937.
Kirk, H. L. *Pablo Casals*, London: Hutchinson 1974.
Long, Marguerite *Au Piano avec Gabriel Fauré*, Paris: Julliard 1963.
Marnat, Marcel *Maurice Ravel*, Paris: Fayard 1986.
Martin, Bernard *Frank Martin*, Neuchâtel: A la Baconnière 1973.
Menuhin, Yehudi *Unfinished Journey*, London: Macdonald and Jane's 1977.
Meylan, Pierre *Honegger, son oeuvre et son message*, Lausanne: l'Age d'Homme 1982.
Mihule, Jaroslav *Bohuslav Martinů*, Prague: Orbis 1979.
Milek, Joseph *Hermann Hesse*, Fredericton, N B 1984.
Nabokov, Nicolas *Old Friends and New Music*, London: Hamish Hamilton 1951.
Orledge, Robert *Gabriel Fauré*, London: Eulenburg 1979.
Piatigorsky, Gregor *Cellist*, New York: Doubleday 1965.
Poulenc, Francis. Correspondance 1915–1963, réunie par Hélène de Wendel, Paris: Editions du Seuil 1967.
———— *'Echo and Source' Selected Correspondence 1915–1963*, translated and edited by Sidney Buckland, London: Gollancz 1991.
———— *Moi et mes amis*, Geneva: La Palatine 1963.
———— *Entretiens avec Claude Rostand*, Paris: Julliard 1954.
Reid, Charles *Malcolm Sargent*, London: Hamish Hamilton 1968.
Saerchinger, Cesar *Artur Schnabel*, London: Cassell 1957.
Schönzeler, H. H. *Furtwängler*, London: Duckworth 1990.
Szigeti, Joseph *With Strings Attached*, New York: Knopf 1947.

Poliomyelitis

Halstead, L. S. and Wiechers, D. O. *Research and Clinical Aspects of the Late Effects of Poliomyelitis*, 1986 Conference Proceedings paper, Warm Springs, Ga., White Plains, NY 1987.

Paul, John R. *A History of Poliomyelitis*, New Haven: Yale University Press 1971.

Paul, J. R., Debré, R., Thieffry, S. and Ritchie Russell, W. *Poliomyelitis*, WHO Monograph Series No. 26, Geneva 1955.

Peabody, Draper and Dochez *A Clinical Study of Poliomyelitis*, Rockefeller Institute Medical Research Monograph No. 4, New York 1912.

Ripley, H. S., Bohnengel, C. and Milhorat, A. T. 'Personality Factors in Patients with Muscular Disability', *American Journal of Psychiatry*, Vol. 99, No. 6, Baltimore, May 1943.

Seidenfeld, Morton A. *The Psychological Sequelae. The Nervous Child*, Vol. 7, New York 1948.

Index